The Mistress Of Langdale Hall: A Romance Of The West Riding

Rosa Mackenzie Kettle

THE

MISTRESS OF LANGDALE HALL:

A Romance of the West Riding.

BY

ROSA MACKENZIE KETTLE.

"Red and white roses on terrace and wall,
Stars of white jasmine illumine our Hall;
Old checker'd woodwork, cream white and dark brown;
Moonlight o'erflooding the clough and the down,
Lights sparkling out on the hillside and crest;
Fountains at play, and all nature at rest."

LONDON:

SAMUEL TINSLEY, 34, SOUTHAMPTON ST., STRAND.

1872.

"LANGDALE HALL,"

From a drawing by   CLARA MACKENZIE KETTLE.

PART THE FIRST.

THE HALL AND THE GRANGE.

WHERE are the ancient halls and towers
  That used to stand in pride,
Girt round by streams,—pranked out with flowers—
  On many a green hill side?
Halls of the old West Riding!
  This cannot be your fate!
You dare not say yon mouldering pile
  Was once a Tower of State!

The beck flows swiftly from the moor,
  Dashed with dull russet stains;
The sunlight flickers on the floor,
  Through stained and storied panes;
Under the eaves the swallow builds,
  Where, deep cut in the stone,
The eyes of God's good Providence
  On the old house look down.

R. M. K.

MISTRESS OF LANGDALE HALL.

CHAPTER I.

N that part of the West-Riding of Yorkshire border-ing upon the wild hills which separate the county from Lancashire, about the middle of the present century, an old house, which had been unoccupied for several years, was suddenly filled, from basement to garret, by a large family. Godley Grange, so the place was called, derived its name, some people said, from having been at one time the residence of the Puritan Oliver Heywood; but more learned authorities pronounced that Cromwell's fanatical follower had, in reality, dwelt in a neighbouring mansion, and that the appellation was bestowed in honour of the good lea, or meadow, watered by a sparkling stream, which surrounded the ancient mansion.

"The name of this property," says an unpublished manu-script, " is evidently derived from the *yode lea* (good meadow), lying low in the vale and bordering on the rivu-let. Yet a wide-spread mistake has attributed it to the sanctifying influence of the Puritan Nonconformist, Oliver Heywood, who resided at an adjoining house, and so Godley, as I have been told, won its name from its supposed relation to this really earnest good man. The ring of a word often

1—2

in the mouths of that party to which Heywood belonged, and one that irresistibly strikes the ear with a puritanical jingle, may, perhaps, explain the source of this false etymological inference.

"The name had become a dead letter; its primitive and expressive notion lost; but a time came when the current word, defaced and worn to such a degree that no vestige of its original stamp could be detected, was, as it were, melted down and coined afresh, and shortly in circulation, tamped with the bold and life-like image of the godly Oliver Heywood, and, possessing the true ring of his currency.

"It was well, perhaps, that it should be linked even with this erroneous signification—better than to remain lifeless —but we must remember that it is our fault when names become so. We should study them as we do antique pictures and statues, endeavouring, if possible, to throw ourselves entirely into their meaning. As we cannot understand the full import of the lesson the artist would teach us without the same requisite, or the book of Nature—as the yellow primrose will only be a yellow primrose to the unreflecting—so, and even more emphatically so, are names always on the tongue certain to become utterly meaningless to those who merely give them utterance. To such persons the substitution of an insignificant epithet for a fine old name, fraught with a sentiment embalmed in it ten or twelve centuries ago, would be no matter for regret, except on the score of sound.

"The name of our own valley—the Sheep Deane, or Valley of Sheep—sweeps us back centuries, to an ante-enclosure period, when the woolly flocks were grazing, after their manner, on our hills and leas, and a few shepherd families were the sole representatives of the well-peopled Shibden Vale of our day."*

* Manuscript found in the library at Shibden Hall, near Halifax.

The old Yorkshire mansion, approached by stony cause-ways, with precipitous embankments of the same hard material, lay deep down in the dale, overhung by lofty trees, close at hand, and darkened still more by the shadow of a wooded hill which shut out from view a large manufac-turing town. Two tall chimneys, recently erected, were just visible, serving as a warning of what might be hereafter, should the land fall into the hands of persons less careful of its wonderful beauty than its present proprietor. From the narrow casement windows of The Grange nothing could be seen but its own immediate grounds, which were not exten-sive. The architecture was very picturesque—beautiful ancient windows, set deep within stone mullions, and filled up with stained glass of rare antiquity, were garlanded with jessamine and honeysuckle. Great stacks of carved, twisted, chimneys peeped out of masses of shrouding ivy, which an antiquarian would have torn away. Over the door was inscribed a motto in Latin, bidding those within to Rest Secure; and to those who came from without, Welcome!

There was a great deal of bustle and confusion before the new-comers settled down into their respective places. The children swarmed like bees "up stairs and down stairs," and everywhere excepting "in my lady's chamber." They ran, helter-skelter, through the large stables, offices, fruit and flower gardens; planning all sorts of impossibilities, for money was less abundant than olive branches in that house-hold. They played at hide and seek among the empty bins and wine casks in the great echoing cellars.

The cawing of the rooks in the tall elm-trees delighted these children. It was an unaccustomed sound, for they had not been brought up in England. Often in their de-lighted wonder they spoke to each other in German. "Ach,

wie schön !" came more naturally to their lips than " Oh,
how beautiful !"

Only one room in that house was kept sacred from hurrying footsteps. A great calmness seemed at once to settle
down upon it, and the quick tread and laughter of the children were stayed and softened as they passed the door, or
entered. The invalid wife and mother, sorely fatigued, was
resting there after her long journey.

She was not, however, left entirely alone. Whatever
might be their respective occupations or amusements, one
or other of the large family always waited upon and cheered
their suffering mother. It was necessary, in her enfeebled
state, that some attentive companion should be always
close at hand.

In contrast with his patient wife the new master of the
Grange was never still. He was nervously, irritably active,
as if to make up for her infirmity. In the early years of
their marriage, he and the children's little mother, as he
called her, had been inseparable ; now, though from long
habit he sometimes called her, " Abra" could not come.

He had never entirely reconciled himself to the decree
which stayed that light elastic tread. Though he was a
religious, good man, and a kind father, as well as a most
tender husband, something had been taken from him which
he missed so sorely, that he strove in vain to imitate the
meek submission of the principal sufferer. He went on
hoping for improvement ; struggling and chafing against the
conviction that, so far as complete recovery was concerned,
her case was hopeless.

Each change of season and of place was regarded as possibly bringing relief. Even shocks of sorrow were welcomed
if they might restring nerves and faculties once vigorously
and harmoniously attuned ; but as yet no important altera-

tion had occurred. With more or less of suffering, days, weeks, and months, and years, wore on.

The eldest daughter, though only just seventeen, was the active head, in all feminine matters, of the establishment. In her the best qualities of both parents were combined. For hours the young, beautiful girl would sit unwearied, unoccupied, at times when any movement jarred her mother's quivering nerves. On other occasions the light-heartedness and industry of the Haus-Fräulein were equally remarkable. Steady as a woman, serene as an angel, playful as a child, Gertrude Lang was like a semblance of summer, or a soft stream of moonlight in her home.

Mr. Lang's eldest child and only son was at present absent from home. Truthful, impetuous, and quick-witted, Fritz, as his companions called him, in the German university where he had been educated, won almost every prize for which he took the trouble to contend; and he was now striving manfully to obtain the crowning honour of his scholastic career. In the midst of every burst of youthful joy over the wonders of the new house—in the mother's low-voiced ejaculations of thankfulness at having safely arrived at her haven of rest—in the father's active superintendence of the settling in the old mansion—in the loving prayers of Gertrude, his favourite sister, as she knelt for the first time beside the strange bed in her English home—the name of Fritz—suggestions for his accommodation and comfort, as well as the wish that he might speedily join them, were uttered fervently.

Mr. Lang did not waste many days in idleness. He had accepted employment in the great house of business for which he had been agent in Prussia, and he at once applied himself to what were to be henceforth his daily labours. His knowledge of the German language and of the habits of a country with which, commercially, England and the great trading cities and towns of Yorkshire are so closely connected, made him a valuable assistant to the firm, and he was well known in the county. The house he lived in was his own, and he was heir presumptive to a much larger property.

Perhaps it was from false humility, which is the same as secret pride, that Mr. Lang chose to drop one-half of his patronymic. A name of one syllable, he said, was enough for a clerk in a house of trade. No one was permitted to call him Langdale, though he was so like his cousin, the present mistress of Langdale Hall, the representative of the Langdales of Langdale, that it was impossible to forget the relationship.

The settlement at Godley Grange, he said, saved house-rent. The place was so overshadowed by the Langdale woods, and the Langdale prerogatives, that no one else could, or would, live in it. The dwelling was spacious, well adapted for an invalid, and for the accommodation of his family. There was coal under the soil, and plenty of stone in the quarries. He meant to make what he could of his slice of the family property—sink a shaft, if necessary and likely to be profitable, without fear or favour.

As is the case in German households, the habits of the young people were extremely simple. Their hours were primitively early, and they were all as busy as bees long before the breakfast-bell at the Hall rang out over the dale. The children soon knew its tones well. They served them as a clock, punctually summoning the little girls to their tasks, after the hour allowed for working in their gardens and feeding their pets had expired; and they were accustomed to say, "Now their majesties are going to sit in state at their banquet." They had read of the royalties of France being served on bended knee at their lévées and repasts. In their plays the children often pretended to be the ladies at the Hall, and were more arrogant than any crowned heads, princes, princesses, or potentates.

Over the tops of the high walls could be seen the tall trees in the park of Langdale Hall; and, from the garden of the Grange, a glimpse might be caught of the lake, set like a brilliant jewel amid emeralds in the bosom of the smooth sward, and' changing its hue as light and shadow swept over its surface. There was a boat on the water, and a couple of swans sailing proudly, ruffling up their white feathers, as though vain of their own reflected beauty. The children at Godley peeped through the trees at the silvery sail and stately birds, gleaming in the sunlight, but they never went near its banks when the Langdale ladies were taking their pleasure on the waters of the lake. They knew that their father would not approve of idle curiosity.

It was not in human nature, however, shut in and circumscribed as they were, for those young creatures not to let their thoughts wander within the jealously-guarded adjacent enclosure, more especially as they had a particular reason for taking an interest in the place.

Over and over again, in that far-off German home, to which, in its perfect freedom, the children often looked back with fond regard; they had heard their father say, when stung by some fresh mark of unkindness on the part of their English relative—

"My cousin Maud may act as she pleases now, but, whether she likes it or not, she cannot prevent Fritz being one day, if he lives long enough, the Master of Langdale Hall."

CHAPTER II.

On one of the few holidays which the summer afforded to
the busy managing clerk, Mr. Lang's children persuaded
him to accompany them to Hazeldon Crags, a place where
the finest and rarest ferns might be found. The twins,
Annie and May, were making a collection, and Frances was
anxious to sketch the rocks overhanging the river.

The foreign-looking girls, with their simple but well-cut
blouses, with leather belts girding their slender waists,
broad hats, and rush baskets, clustered fondly round the
grave, care-encumbered man. Little Flo, the youngest of
the party, as usual kept them waiting, and came down at
last with two left-hand gloves ; but she was the spoilt pet
and darling of her much older sisters, who ran hither and
thither to supply all her deficiencies. Fully equipped, at
last, and with a wicker basket for wild flowers, lent by her
mother, in her hand, Florence was the prettiest of the group,
as they set forth from the antique portal of the Grange.
Although she was the image of her father, Florence was
not his favourite. Mr. Lang loved better his fair-haired
German girls, who resembled their mother. "The little
one," as she was called in the family, at whose birth so dire
a calamity had fallen upon his previously active, helpful
wife—a cloud which, strive as he might to drive it away by
toil, always lowered over his altered home—reminded him
too keenly of his bitter woe ever to seem to him like the
sunny-faced darlings who had flitted after their girlish-look-
ing mother in the terraced garden of the old *Schloss* where
they first drew breath.

The great delicacy of Mrs. Lang's health, previous to her last confinement, had induced her husband to winter in Italy, after he had vainly endeavoured to secure a pleasant reception for her in the neighbourhood of his English relatives. There were times when the man who had, since the birth of her youngest child, lost the sweet companionship in which his soul delighted, could not bear to look upon the infant named after the fair Tuscan capital. This feeling of repulsion softened gradually, but it never entirely left him. The black-eyed, straight-browed, regular-featured girl, who resembled the Langdales, was not so dear to Frank Lang as his other children.

The thought, how all these young creatures were to be brought up and set forward in the world, was a heavy care to their father, which he kept locked up in his breast. His children were not to him what his wife had been, though he loved them tenderly ; and in losing her active co-operation, he often felt as if he had lost all. On her he suffered no care to intrude that could by possibility be kept from her. He bore his own burden silently, but its pressure never lightened.

Frances, the eldest of the party—Gertrude having remained at home with her mother—walked demurely beside her father, glancing from side to side for the best points of view for sketching. The twins were running about looking for specimens of beech and oak ferns, and calling fearlessly to their father for assistance in plucking them from crannies in the rocks high above their heads. "The little one" wandered on alone, gathering wild flowers, which she sometimes collected in her basket, or put into the band round her hat, or the girdle at her waist. At last, with her hands full of freshly-gathered ferns, and foxgloves with long, unmanageable stalks, she sat down on a stone by the river-side, to arrange her treasures. Frances could scarcely have found a prettier foreground for her picture than the little maiden, hat in hand, with her long, dark, silky curls falling below her waist; sitting among the feathery fern and grass and great dock leaves, on the bank, with her head bent seriously over the flowers in her basket and the garland she was weaving.

A lady, on horseback, drew in her rein sharply, and stopped just in front of the child, who looked up at her shyly. It was not usual for any person to enter these woods —which were the property of a nobleman who did not reside in the neighbourhood—without permission ; and, at a certain spot, carriages and horses were dismissed, or kept waiting. There was not even a regular foot-path.

Mr. Lang had gone farther on, past an intervening barrier of rock, and was now assisting Frances to cross the stream. He intended to come back for the little one, and to carry her over the water, which in this part was shallow, rippling joyously among stones and pebbles.

" Shall I take you across the river ?" said the lady. "Why are you all alone ?"

Florence was delighted with the proposition. Though she looked bashful, the child loved change and new faces. She started up, twisting the end of her unfinished wreath into the ribband of her hat, and letting the rest of her flowers fall among the grass.

Light as a bird, with the aid of the lady's strong, firm clasp of her hand, Flo sprang up into the saddle, nestling down in front of her new friend. She felt herself to be very securely held, and was not in the least frightened, though she had never in her life been on horseback.

The little one was perfectly at her ease, and chattered away freely, longing to overtake her father and sisters. She was proud of the notice taken of her, and rather unwilling to descend from her elevated station. She wished them all to see how carefully the beautiful lady, on the tall black mare, was holding her fast in the saddle.

The words of a German ballad, in which the sound of a steed tramping through water and stones was imitated, came into the child's recollection, and she murmured them softly.

"Are you a foreigner, little maid?" said the lady; "your accent is very good."

"No ; I am English. Papa and mamma are both English, and my sisters and brother, but we were all born abroad in Germany and Italy. I think Frances is on the other side of that great rock sketching. Annie and May are not far off. How surprised they will be to see me !"

She stretched her slender neck in vain at present, the great boulder hid the whole party from sight. There was no level ground on either bank ; the lady was riding in the shallow bed of the river. Steep rocks, garlanded with creepers, their crevices set thick with fern and moss, rose on either hand ; but there was ample space for the sure-footed, high-mettled steed to pick its way over the shining pebbles. The rein hung loose on its neck.

"We are all English girls," continued the little one, proudly; "and we live in our English house. Won't you come and see us ? There is nice grass in our large meadow, and such great coach-houses and stables, but no horses in them."

"Take care, take care," said the lady, as the little girl bent down to stroke the glossy neck, which arched itself at her caress; "Christobel is as lively as she is gentle. You have a brave spirit. Are your sisters like you ?"

"No; I am not at all like my sisters. They are all fair. I am like my father's family," the child said, haughtily. "The Langdales are dark, and my nurse says that I might have walked out of one of the old picture-frames at Langdale Hall."

The arm that had held her so firmly suddenly relaxed in its pressure, and Florence nearly fell into the water; but the lady, though less tenderly, kept her hold, just preventing her from slipping down. "Why do you not take more care?" she said, severely; "I told you to keep still. Now, I shall set you down. Your friends are on the other side of this rock; I hear their voices, and I do not wish to meet them. See, there is a narrow strip of turf at its base; you can easily creep round dry-shod."

Edging the tall steed close to the bank, the lady assisted the little girl to descend. Flo was afraid to speak, she looked so stern and grand; and tears rose to her eyes, but she was too proud to let them fall. "Thank you," she managed to say, when she was safely deposited on the ground; but she did not venture again to ask her new friend to come and see her.

There was a slight opening in the trees and the bank was lower at the place where the lady had stopped. Setting her teeth, and without another glance at the child, she struck a small spur, which was concealed by her long riding-habit, into the mare's glossy flank, and, tapping her sharply with the whip on the shoulder, whilst she gathered up the reins tightly, Christobel reared, and sprang into the thicket, forcing a path through the bending boughs.

The thorns of the underwood caught the lady's skirt and the boughs brushed against her face, but she pushed through them, recklessly, until she reached a narrow path along which she rode with a frowning brow. After a time the track was lost as she came out upon wild, barren moors, which overhung the clough through which the river flowed.

When the lady found herself upon the turf she once more pricked her willing steed, and rode at a swift gallop on her homeward way. All the time she seemed to hear the child's voice repeating the refrain of the wild German song, and to feel the little warm clasping hands pressed close to her heart.

CHAPTER III.

MR. LANG was just turning away from the spot chosen by Frances for her sketch, intending to go back for his little daughter, when Florence emerged slowly from behind the great grey boulder of rock. She was quite crestfallen, and she said very little about the adventure, which would have furnished conversation for the whole afternoon if its termination had been as pleasant as its commencement. Something in the lady's way of setting her down and parting from her had hurt the child's sensitive feelings, and Florence could not endure ridicule. She was reserved to a fault, and afraid of her father's slighting, sarcastic tone; which she more than others provoked him to use, by indications of vanity.

The twins clambered about, searching for ferns, and Frances sat still on the bank sketching, while her little sister watched her progress thoughtfully. Mr. Lang fancied that the rough walk had tired "the little one." He was very kind to her on the way home, carrying her over the stones, but, even while her head rested on his shoulder, Florence was thinking regretfully of the proud lady with the jewelled riding whip, and the long, fine, cloth habit, mounted on the beautiful black mare which had borne her also so deftly over the rough stones in the channel of the stream, and left her, sad and solitary, at the base of the grey lichen-covered rock !

Mr. Lang took the little girl straight up to her mother's room. Although his manner was often cold and abstracted, his heart was very tender, and he feared that Flo had been frightened at finding herself alone on the bank of the river ; a longer time than he intended having passed away in the discussion of the best points of view.

"Marina, the little one is tired," he said, after greeting the invalid tenderly, "Keep her with you. She has not spoken six words all the way home. I am afraid the walk was too long for her."

Mrs. Lang looked anxiously at the child. If not her father's favourite, Flo was her mother's darling. Maternal instinct taught her that the child was more vexed than weary, but she asked no questions. Florence shared her mother's tea, while Gertrude went down to hear the adventures and misadventures of the day, to admire Frances' pretty sketch, and to help to plant the beech and oak ferns among the stones of the rockery.

"Where are my wild flowers, Flora?" said Mrs. Lang. "Have you not even brought me a tuft of heath ? I never knew my little goddess to be forgetful of me before. I hope you have not lost my pretty German basket ?"

Florence coloured over neck and brow. It occurred to her now, for the first time, that she had dropped the basket at the place where she had been sitting weaving her garland of wild flowers.

"Oh, mamma, I am so sorry, I thought of nothing but the lady and the horse. I must have left your basket behind me on the bank."

"You should have told your father. He would have gone back for my basket, it is one that I value extremely.

Tell me, Flora, what you were thinking about all the way home when your father says you were so sad and silent. What had the lady and the horse to do with your losing my ·basket ?"

Flora hid her face in her mother's dress to conceal her tears.

"I was so tired," she faltered out. "I wanted to ride home. I was vexed, too, with the lady. I wonder why she was angry with me, and put me down all alone after being so kind.

Mrs. Lang drew the little girl fondly towards her, and soothed her. When Florence ceased crying, she said softly, "I should like to hear all that happened to you, my pet. Perhaps I may be able to explain what puzzles and grieves you."

"A lady on a very tall black horse came past me while I was gathering flowers," said Flo, very gravely, with her eyes fixed not on her mother's face, but on a dark spot in the carpet, and with the air of a child repeating a difficult lesson. "No, I had left off gathering flowers. I was making them into a garland for my hat. She said, 'Jump up, little one,' and up I got. I felt quite safe, and I could look up and see the blue sky through the trees, and down on the tops of the rocks. I longed to stop and gather the ferns and moss, but I would not trouble the lady. I was not a bit frightened or troublesome. I was quite happy."

The little girl stopped abruptly. Her rising tears impeded speech.

"I am glad you enjoyed it, dear," said her mother, with interest ; "I was very fond of riding myself, formerly," she added with a sigh.

"I was thinking about the river and the pretty coloured stones," continued Florence. "We rode in the bed of the

2

stream, with the water splashing up all round us. It seemed such a strange thing to do, and·I fancied how surprised papa and my sisters would be when I came up to them.. All of a sudden the lady's arm seemed to slip. She had been holding me quite tightly before—so tight that it hurt me a little, but I did not complain. I almost fell off, but she gripped me fast, and saved me. 'You should keep still,' she said, crossly, and then she set me down all at once on a green patch of turf, and struck the beautiful mare with a whip till it reared and sprang right away through the bushes. They were gone in a moment. And now I have lost your pretty basket. Oh, how I wish I had never gone near those nasty crags !"

Mrs. Lang kissed and comforted the little girl, who was now crying bitterly. " It is of no consequence, love. Most likely the basket is where you left it, hidden among the long grass. Some one shall be sent to look for it to-morrow. Never mind about my basket. It is not worth so many tears. I do not quite understand what vexes you so sorely. The lady certainly might have been more considerate., Perhaps she has no little ones of her own, and does not know as well as I do how easily their hearts are wounded."

" I want to ride the pretty mare again !" said Flo, brushing away her tears, and looking straight at her mother, with a passionate gleam in her dark eyes. "Riding is much nicer than walking. It did not tire me a bit. Why have we no horses? What is the use of those great stables and yards, and the nice grass in the meadow, if we have nothing to put there ? I think the lady despised me when I said we had no horses of our own."

"It is for your father to decide, Flora, whether it is right and proper for us to keep horses," said her mother, reprovingly. " You are much too young to have an opinion on the subject. Ah, if you knew, my child, what I would give to walk by your father's side, as you did to-day, to wander about with you and your sisters, gathering the flowers with which God's beautiful earth is set so thickly at this season, you would care less for luxuries. But I am not angry with you," she said, checking herself. "I do not wonder that you were vexed and frightened. How glad you must have been to get back to your father and sisters."

Again she soothed and caressed the child, but Florence was not easily comforted. All night she dreamed that she was mounted before the lady on the tall mare, or that she was slipping off, or set down, ignominiously.

The first thing that met Flo's eyes when she came down the next morning, was her basket on the stand in the hall. It was filled with choice fruits, and rare hot-house flowers, with a few very delicate fern leaves laid on the top. The person who brought it said that there was no message, and did not wait a minute.

Florence distributed her fruit with lavish generosity, but she kept the flowers to herself. There were none like them, she said, in the garden or in the fields. The little girl was never weary of questioning her mother about these precious exotics. She treasured them till they faded, and then the relics were put carefully away.

The ferns Annie and May had planted, Flo said, were so insignificant compared to the waving, feathery hot-house beauties in her aristocratic bouquet. It was true that the more hardy tufts grew and flourished, long after the child's costly bouquet had withered. Even her hopes, rekindled by her anonymous present, faded. No further notice was taken of her ; she saw nothing of the lady or of Christobel, though she looked out for them furtively every day, as she searched for wild flowers in the wooded lanes.

2—2

CHAPTER IV.

HER haughty head slightly bent—her searching eyes fixed with a strange eager glance on the face of her young half-sister—Maud Langdale stood on the terrace of the old Hall in the West-Riding, which owned her as its mistress. You may see exactly the same attitude, the same expression, in the portrait which hangs over the door, between the drawing-room, and what was then generally termed the house-body, at Langdale Hall.

It is not altogether a pleasant countenance which looks down upon you from the oak panel, although strangely beautiful and suggestive. The eager glance seems to follow your slightest movement. You cannot help looking at that picture of a lady in a riding-habit, with short dark hair, curling like a boy's, round her bright, animated face; one large, white, well-shaped hand clasping a gold-mounted, jewelled whip; the head bent forward; her red lips, half smiling, yet with a proud, firm, settled purpose in their clearly marked curve and close pressure. You would never expect a jest from those lips.

In the courtyard on the opposite side of the old black and white-timbered mansion, in front of the jasmine-covered porch, a tall black mare was pawing the ground impatiently, and a hound, by its noisy baying, resented the unwonted delay on the part of one whose movements were usually punctual and rapid. As the great clock over the stables clanged forth the hour, a groom began to lead his mistress's horse up and down the walled enclosure.

"Yes or No! How can you hesitate, Ellinor?" said Miss

Langdale, imperatively addressing her much younger half-sister, who trembled under the conviction that much of the colouring of her future life depended on the answer she might give to the question. " Is there a man on the face of the earth whose love is worth what lies before your eyes? Yonder great Carr, wooded from base to summit—those green slopes dotted with sheep—the cattle in the rich meadow grass—this dear old place—our ancient name! Choose, Ellinor! Will you go to your grave, as I intend to do, unmarried, or must I find another mistress, after I am dead, for Langdale Hall?"

"Give me time, Maud. Let me think it over. Remember I am not like you, firm of purpose. If I decide hastily, I may repent hereafter."

" You have had the whole night for deliberation, Ellinor, and you are not one bit forwarder. You ought to know your own mind by this time."

" No, I am farther off than ever from a conclusion, Maud. It seems wrong to pledge myself as you desire."

" Nonsense!" said the elder woman, tapping the balustrade on which Ellinor was leaning, with her whip. " Lands or Love! You cannot have both. You may have neither."

"Leave me in peace, Maud!" said the girl, passionately. " I will not give you an answer now. Hark, there is Christobel pawing up the gravel. Do not keep her waiting."

The mistress of Langdale Hall read in her sister's countenance a resolution as determined, for the moment, at least, as her own, and turned away. Stooping her head, though it was not absolutely necessary, Maud passed through the deep porch, fringed with jasmine, and along a wide, low passage, which divided the old house into two portions, each fronting north and south.

Round the courtyard were lofty walls and peaked gables

clothed with ivy, belonging to stables and offices. Under a
lofty archway fell a flood of light on golden sheaves waiting
to be unloaded. Pigeons cooed on the steeply-pitched roofs;
a peacock spread his tail on the top of a low wall; half-a-
dozen silver-haired terriers ran forward yelping and barking
at sight of their mistress, but fell back obediently at a sign
from her whip.

The old house had not survived so many generations of
occupants, without bearing traces of their different tastes.
Whatever may be thought of mine, I confess there is a
charm for me in such tokens which brick and mortar, stone
and stucco, do not, simply on their own account, possess.

The lofty arch of the gateway, the battlemented walls,
blackened by coal-smoke from the not far-distant furnaces,
frowning over the valley, might be, as judges in such matters
affirmed, quite out of character with the chequer-work of
black and white timber, and the ancient gables—set, like
precious jewels, between the Norman tower, added by one
proprietor, and the new drawing-room fronted by a conser-
vatory, supplemented by another—but these luxurious ap-
pendages added greatly to the size and comfort of the house,
and were veiled from sight by clinging creepers, choice
flowers, and shrubs. The lofty walls shut in the beautiful
valley of the Lang from the busy, noisy traffic ceaselessly
carried on outside the barrier, along the dusty highway
leading to the neighbouring town.

Maud turned off the thoroughfare by a steep stone-paved
track which wound up to the top of the highest acclivity in
that hilly district. Perhaps she wished to see the dale from
end to end, with the rivulet winding like a silver thread
through emerald turf, for she pulled in her rein sharply, and
sat still, contemplating the prospect. Her rich red lips
were tightly, scornfully, compressed as she marvelled whether

her young half-sister would make up her mind to relinquish the prospect of succession to all that goodly heritage, or consent to remain unwedded till the day of her death.

At the head of the valley, far above the turn of the winding road where Miss Langdale had stopped to look down upon the river and its wooded banks, stood one of those clusters of habitations for mill-hands, or farm labourers, and their families, into which many of the old halls of the West Riding have degenerated. The arms of an ancient and once influential family, a date carrying back the imagination to a time when those verdant heights were redolent of the song of birds instead of echoing the screech and whistle of the railway—a boastful Latin motto proclaiming that for so long as it would take a tortoise to travel round the world, and for an ant to drink up the waters of the sea, the land should belong to the race by whose name the place was still known—were nearly all the traces left of the sway of its old masters at Noel Hall. A child bearing a pitcher, her clustering curls pressed down by a bright coloured handkerchief, is coming to draw water from the well in the courtyard—a pretty dark haired girl looks out from a narrow stone-mullioned window—two aged crones are gossiping under the stately portal—all alike unmindful of the boastful inscription falsified in the lifetime of the son of the proud man who set it on high.

Inside of the old walls, several poor families, in this instance, agricultural labourers, are located ; no mill spans the beck, its bright waters are not reddened by cloth-die. It flows, dancing down over stone and peat from the moor, as freely and gladly as when the first stone was laid of the now ancient mansion.

These people, rude as they look, feel some pride in the

tokens of antiquity around them, when an opportunity arises for pointing them out to strangers. There are panes still left in the richly stained windows, emblazoned with quaint devices and armorial bearings. It is true that, necessity having no law, and the wind blowing from the Yorkshire moor no mercy, sheets of brown paper or canvas have been nailed across some of the panes ; and, over the richly carved balustrade of the gallery above the central hall, whence formerly highly-born beautiful ladies may have looked down, a row of dilapidated family garments is hanging to dry.

Round the large open fireplace in the hall are congregated some children in tattered garments ; two or three half-starved curs, a fierce-looking cat bristling up her fur in anger at their intrusion ; and her mistress, who is regarded by the neighbourhood as an arrant witch, as mischievous as ever haunted Pendle Forest.

" Did ye say it was Maud Langdale as gev' ye the shilling, lad ?" she said, addressing her grandchild, a curly haired boy who had just handed up the coin for inspection. " Ye must have done her a good turn. She's none so fond of parting with her money."

" I picked a stone out of the black mare's hoof," said the urchin ; " she might have stumbled on the causeway. The lady rides down and up the hill as fast, and faster than Meg yonder can clamber."

The cat purred in acknowledgment of the compliment, but, when the boy offered to stroke her, she scratched him violently, and then flew off to avoid the blow he aimed at her.

" Let Meg bide. Ye'll come off the worst if ye meddle with her," said his grandmother. " But, good lack ! who is coming across the court ? I'll engage it's the lady herself."

An elderly man, who was sunning his gray hairs at the

window, looked up sharply as Miss Langdale, in her usual costume, a dark cloth riding habit and high black beaver hat, holding the long skirt up with one hand, and carrying her whip in the other, entered the hall.

The dogs barked in chorus and flew at her, but a few strokes of the gold-mounted whip sent .them back cowering to the chimney corner.

" Who keeps these yelping curs ?" she said, uncourteously, without acknowledging the old dame's obsequious salutation. "No wonder my keepers complain ! That great cat looks like a terrible poacher. I have heard tales of her prowess."

The dame dared not tell the lady to let Meg alone; but the cat's grey-green, eyes glared defiance at her through the banisters.

"Come, sit ye down, Miss Langdale. Draw in the settle. Yer wont harm our Meg, I know. The curs' bark is worse than their bite, as is the case with yourself, I fancy. The cat's the only beast that owns me: the curs belong to the neighbours. Drive them out, Ned."

The boy, who had been enlisted as the lady's retainer by the gift of the shilling, laid about him vigorously, dispersing the clamorous terriers from the vicinity of the hearth.

Miss Langdale sat down in the high-carved oak settle with her back to the door. In this position she faced the man who was still sitting in the window. He had not risen on her entrance, or made any obeisance. Cold and firm as Maud Langdale usually was, a sort of instinctive fear crept over her, and her cheek flushed hotly as she looked at him.

"Who is that person sitting in the window out yonder?" she said, in a low tone. "He is a stranger to me."

The woman turned herself round and stared. "Oh, you be there, be you?" she said, unceremoniously; "the place is like a rabbit-warren. Yes, Madam, that be the last comer;

The General, the folk here and the children call him, because he's been in the wars, beyond seas, in South Ameri-
kay. They read about it in the papers. You can say what
you like, without troubling yourself about him—he's mortal
hard of hearing. He just likes to bide in the sunshine."

Miss Langdale asked no further question for the moment
about the intruder, but questioned the old woman about the
state of repair of the forlorn old building which, at the request of her steward, she had ridden over to inspect. She
had bought the property when it was brought to the hammer, after the death of the last of the old race in poverty
and exile. Most of its occupants worked on her land. Ned's
father had been thrown from the top of a waggon and lost
his life, two years before, in the harvest-field. Miss Langdale allowed his grandmother and the boy shelter, rent free,
at the old Hall.

"The water comes in at all points, and the floors are that
rotten some of us expect to fall through. The boy ketched
his foot the other day in a crack, and well-nigh sprained his
ancle. I'm almost afeard to sleep in my bed for the rats;
but for Meg they'd have the child out of his'n. The birds
build in the big chimley, and make the fires smoke fit to
choke ye, and the slates rattle off in the wind. The place
be scarce fit for Christian folk to bide in. Good enough for
such as he as comes from among the Blackamoors, and has
roughed it with all sorts of customers. He says he don't mind
it, and somehow he manages to keep things comfortable about
him. He's picked up some sense in his journeyings, as well
as that queer old cloak that helps to make the young folk
think that he looks like an officer."

The old woman jerked out her thumb in the direction of
the window. As she ceased speaking the man rose, shrouding himself in the dark blue roquelaure to which she had

alluded, and which had dropped off him as he sat in the warm sunshine. He was above six feet high, and his frame was still erect and powerful. Without in any manner saluting the lady, he stalked past the hearth and out of the hall.

Miss Langdale's countenance darkened. "I do not at all like that person's appearance and manners," she said, angrily. "I wonder that Mr. Haywarden allows such vagrants to squat here. He looks more like a bushranger than an officer, or even an old soldier. Does he lead an entirely idle life? He seems active and vigorous."

"He does a stroke of work sometimes. For that matter, he's not unneighbourly," said the old dame, who had her own reasons for not wishing to rouse Miss Langdale's fiery temper against one who had done her many a good turn, in reward for the use of the seat he liked in the hall-window. "He says he's got a fancy for the place yonder, and, poor body, he does no harm. When the fits are not on him he's quiet enough, and, when he's bad with them, he shuts himself up, and wants nought but a jug of water set at his door. Any of the lads and lassies will draw it for him; and, when one is empty, he just sets it outside and fetches in another. No one sees him till he's better. I wouldn't wish to harm him, and few people would lodge where he puts up. It's the oldest part of the building, and, one of these windy nights, 'twill be a mercy if it does not all come rattling down a-top of him. I fancy he pays his rent regular. Your ladyship will scarce get a better tenant if you shift him."

"Well, if the poor creature has fits, and is contented with his lodging, I should be sorry to disturb him," said Maud, more kindly, as she rose and gathered up her long skirt. "I will tell Mr. Haywarden he had better ride round and see what can be done for you. If I were to put this place into complete repair, the first thing I should do would be to eject you all; so, if you wish to remain, the fewer complaints I hear the better."

The old dame stood up, and went on curtseying as long as Miss Langdale remained in the hall. Meg, more sincere than her mistress, arched her back and put out her claws, sputtering with wrath, and prepared to spring down from the staircase; but a glance from the dame quieted her.

With scant leave-taking, and no token of generosity, Maud left the old house, followed by no good wishes. In the corner of the courtyard the veteran, draped in his military cloak, was sitting in the sunshine. For a moment Maud hesitated whether to address her new tenant, but the man looked so stolid that she could not make up her mind to speak to him.

He watched her tall figure, as she crossed the courtyard and went out at the gateway in front of which Christobel was standing. The boy was rather in hopes of a second benefaction, as he took the rein of the mare and led her towards the lady; but Miss Langdale was no prodigal. She vaulted into the saddle unassisted, and pursued her haughty, careless way, followed by the hound, without even troubling herself to say "Thank you" or "Good day" to the lad, whose blue eyes would have gleamed joyfully if the lady had vouchsafed him a single kind word.

CHAPTER V.

ELLINOR LANGDALE remained on the terrace long after the sharp sound of the horse's hoofs on the gravel died away. Her thoughts strayed involuntarily; now following the white curls of smoke from rural homes, well-known to her from childhood, as they floated over the valley; now blending with the rush and roar of the railway trains, as they swept round a curve on the opposite hill before plunging into the dark aperture of a tunnel. Her senses seemed preternaturally active; and she strove in vain to reflect calmly. She was distracted by watching some little girls in white frocks, working in a garden on the other side of the lake, and the labourers in the fields by the beck.

Yonder, amid the trees, glowed the tranquil waters of the lake—nearer at hand splashed the foamy cataracts of the fountains, casting showers of spray on the glistening pebbles of the walks. Ellinor's eyes filled with tears as she gazed at the old house; especially at the long low window of what had been her own mother's room and was now occupied by herself. The girl loved every stone of the old house, which had been in the possession of her family for centuries. She had as yet never thought seriously of leaving home. Love and marriage had small place in her thoughts; and the question whether the property would become her own, had never, until the night before, been brought under her consideration. Maud had told her then; and not for the first time, that she never intended to marry; no man should ever lord it over her in Langdale. Would Ellinor make the same compact? Engage to live and die unmarried?—If so, she would at once exert the power which she possessed, in common with other female owners of property, of leaving a life interest in the estate to Ellinor.

Eventually Maud continued with bitter emphasis, 'The land must all belong to their cousin, Frank Langdale, the heir-at-law, and descend to his children—the white-frocked crew by the lake—but as long as she lived, and it was in Ellinor's power to extend the exemption much longer, no coal should be dug, no stone quarried, no more railways be made in the dale. The one line, which passed over the upper end of the lake and under the hill, had been carried through the estate, against Maud's wish, in her father's lifetime.

This question was what the girl must answer before nightfall. How could she reflect upon it calmly while her thoughts vibrated with the soft gushes of the summer wind, the notes of the birds, and the plash of the fountains.

Just as the sun sank below the hill, casting a golden gleam over the valley, Ellinor arrived at a conclusion.

Better to be poor—to lose everything—to be an exile from this dear home—than to barter her freedom, her womanly feelings and judgment for lands and gold. Her resolution was taken, and with a firm step—without venturing to cast another glance round her—Ellinor passed beneath the jasmine-covered porch and entered the house. She then sat down quietly in the old oak-panelled hall, after making some slight alteration in her dress, and awaited her sister's return.

Hour after hour went by, and still no chorus of barking in the yard announced Maud's approach. Ellinor grew cold and impatient as she watched the moon rising above the clough, whilst the sounds of rural life died away and silence settled down upon the valley. Through the small panes of the mullioned casements the rays glinted fitfully, now catching the salient angles of the dark oak furniture, now lying in a long line, like water, on the polished floor. Ellinor changed her place in the room to avoid the eyes of the picture, which seemed again to ask the question she had mentally solved. At last, solitude becoming unbearable indoors, she went out again on the terrace.

A fiery eye seemed again to be watching her; but it was only the signal-light of the railway trains—now one colour, now another—according to the direction in which they were moving. Although it increased the value of the property, great opposition had been made to this line—Maud would never have allowed it to be brought through the Dale ; but, in reality, the passing trains, viewed at a distance from the terrace of the old Hall, were not unpicturesque. Especially at night, Ellinor liked to watch them as they flashed to and fro ; and to see the light in front of the long trains of carriages plunge into, or emerge from, the tunnel under the great hill.

Beautiful as Langdale Hall was at all times, it was most lovely by moonlight. The wide terrace walks, with trees and statues on either hand ; the bright borders of flowers ; the glittering fountains ; the white-starred jasmine mantling the deep-set casements, with the silvery rays sparkling on the diamond-panes, or, here and there, a light shining from within, casting a redder gleam on the chequered timber work of the old gables, imparted to the mansion magical loveliness.

Ellinor stood at some distance, gazing at the home of her infancy and youth ; wondering to whom, if she spurned the gifts, Maud would bequeath it. Not to Frank Langdale, the heir presumptive ; for he and, still more, his wife, were the objects of her intense dislike. As far as her half-sister knew, the mistress of Langdale Hall had no personal friends, no favourites of any description. Her tastes were all for seclusion and solitude ; and acquaintances were kept at a distance by her cold manner. Maud was kind to the poor, and to dumb animals ; but any one who exercised independence enough to dispute her will, soon ceased to be in favour with her. Even her sister, just attaining womanhood, after being as a child Miss Langdale's pet and plaything, must learn this bitter truth.

Ellinor went round the outside of the old house to the courtyard, when she heard Christobel's hoofs on the gravel, and all the dogs barking. Maud rode very slowly up the avenue, and, after dismounting unaided, threw the reins to a groom, and entered the house silently.

She did not speak to her sister, but rang the bell sharply for lights, ordering the servant to close the heavy shutters of the hall and drawing-room. Ellinor regretted the exclusion of the moonlight, but she said nothing; and, sitting down at the table, occupied herself with her needlework.

Miss Langdale pushed back her hat with an unwonted expression of lassitude, and, finally, took it off, passing her hand over and through her short curls, and shaking them into order, much in the same manner that a water-spaniel might do after emerging from a stream or a pond. Winter and summer she spent most of her time out of doors, returning home at irregular hours, and attending to few of the forms and habits of domestic feminine life. A plunge in an ice-cold bath, night and morning, a rapid toilette, neat but plain, and scarcely altered by the change of season or fashion, satisfied the strong-minded woman, who, though still young, cared little for appearance. Ellinor's habitual attention to the conventionalities of life was a subject for ridicule with her sister.

Miss Langdale drank off hastily the large goblet of water, the only beverage she patronised, which was placed in readiness for her; whilst Ellinor made tea for herself, in the little old-fashioned set of china, which would have delighted a cognoscente in such matters—egg-shell cups, almost transparent, and filigree silver spoons and sugar-tongs.

"How tired you look, Maud," she said affectionately. "Did you ride far?"

"Right over the hill, past Noel Hall, where I stopped to

see what repairs are wanted—then to the Crags, and home over Hazel Down. I had to go back, too, for something that a little girl whom I carried over the river had dropped on the bank. I thought she would be sorry to lose it, and I remembered seeing it fall from her arm after I had gone some way over the Down—it was a pretty, foreign-looking basket. The child would have missed it, later, and might have been scolded for carelessness. Ellinor," she said, gravely, after a pause, "was it not strange? this child, who attracted me wonderfully, a beautiful, brave little creature, proved to be a daughter of Langdale of the Grange, the youngest of his children. There he was, with the whole kit of them, within twenty yards of me. I found it out just in time to avoid meeting him."

"I wish you had seen each other," said her sister: "old prejudices die out in time. I dare say he is very much altered. We have certainly heard nothing which is not to his credit respecting his present mode of life."

"How dare you say so?" said Maud, flushing to her temples. "Is it creditable that our cousin, the heir of Langdale, should be managing clerk in a house of trade at Hazeldon? If his tastes were so grovelling, he might have had the decency to take himself, and his pauper brood and infirm wife, to Leeds or Manchester, instead of parading his German radicalism at my very gates. Little as I care for long life, I hope I may be an old woman ere I die, to spite the Langdales."

"I hope you may live long enough to survive these uncharitable feelings," said Ellinor gently. "But tell me more about the little girl whom you liked so much."

"She is a thorough little lady!" said Maud enthusiastically; "not a bit like her mother, but dark and distinguished-looking, as her father was before he married and went into

3

business. No doubt that has roughened him—there is no other word for it. The little girl reminded me of the lady of whom the country people in the south tell a fable, in which she was changed into a mole, or wont, as they phrase it, because, when her friends urged her to set her delicate foot to the ground, she said, 'I won't.' Her delicate little hands, or fore feet, still remain the portion of the mole or wont! The slender, dark-haired child looked inclined to cry when I set her down on God's earth—just like the proud lady in the legend. Frank Langdale's penniless girls will have to foot it over rough paths!"

"Little ones are as easily vexed as flattered," said Ellinor compassionately. "Perhaps you put her down suddenly, and frightened her."

"It was lucky I did not drop her into the river, when I found out whom I had in the saddle before me," said Maud. "You need not look so shocked, Ellinor, I set the little lassie down all right, high and dry, on the bank. At first I did think that Christobel had an imp on her neck, an evil sprite, but the child clung so lovingly to me, that I was not likely to harm her. I am glad I gave her a sharp lesson; but I took some trouble to fetch the little creature's basket, and you have my leave to fill it with the choicest fruits you can gather, and send it back to her. Only, remember, it must be left at the Grange, with no card or message. If Frank Langdale expected to be noticed by his family, he should not have married a pauper—a waif and stray cast ashore in a storm, and left upon the beach like a coil of sea-weed!"

CHAPTER VI.

"Mother," said Florence Lang, lifting her dark curls from their resting-place on her invalid parent's knee, and looking up in her face; "why does not Miss Langdale call upon us?"

Mrs. Lang was silent for a moment; the fair, sweet face clouded over; then she said,

"What made you ask that question, Flo?"

"Because Miss Langdale is the lady who rides Christobel, the tall, beautiful black mare," said the little girl impetuously. "I saw her pass our gate, yesterday, and turn up the road to the Hall. Meredith says it is a shame that she takes no notice of us, as she is my father's first cousin."

"Meredith ought to know better than to express an opinion on a subject she does not understand; especially to a little girl like yourself," said Mrs. Lang, colouring with vexation. "But you were quite right to tell me, and I expected that some day you would ask this question. I am quite willing to answer it now."

"Did you guess that the lady who took me up before her in the saddle, was Miss Langdale?" said Flo, her eyes opening wide with admiration. "Mother, you sit up here so quietly, and yet you know everything."

"Not quite, my darling," said Mrs. Lang, smiling; "but I did guess that the lady who was so kind at first, and so stern afterwards, was Miss Langdale. Your father knew it also. He is not on friendly terms with the lady at the Hall, though they are near relations. It is not in the least likely that Miss Langdale will call upon us."

Flo's eye filled with tears.

3—2

"Then I am not to see that nice lady again," she said. "I thought it was wrong to go on being angry. If she has been naughty, should not my father forgive her?"

"It is not exactly a question of forgiveness," said Mrs. Lang, gravely. "People, older than you are, often disagree without either party being naughty. I hope this alienation may not last for ever; but, just at present, I cannot advise your father to take any steps towards a reconciliation. I am sure, if our rich neighbour came forward, he would meet her with an outstretched hand."

The little girl looked dissatisfied.

"There is a boat on the lake, and the beautiful mare to ride, and numbers of pretty walks, that we are never allowed to take, near the Hall. Did you tell Meredith that we were not to go through the little gate into the Park opposite to the church? Numbers of people go that way on Sundays. It seems open to everybody."

"Your father and I do not wish you to go that way," said her mother. "The gate is open by favour on Sundays, to those who live in out-lying cottages belonging to Miss Langdale. It would not shorten your walk."

"I want to go through," said Flo passionately. "Last Sunday a little common child ran in, and shut the gate in my face. I was not going into the park, but I wanted to look at the river winding under the old bridge. Frances says what a pretty sketch it would make, and the palings are too high to see over. It seems so hard that Meredith should call us back, when every other child in the parish may pass through."

"I am glad Meredith obeys my orders. Florence you are very wilful," said Mrs. Lang, with displeasure. "Your sisters never dispute their father's will and mine; they are content to be ruled by it without asking for as much explanation as I have given you. They are older and wiser than my little spoilt pet."

"I am sure I saw Christobel grazing under the trees, and there were so many little dogs running about," said Flo, scarcely attending to her mother. "I dare say Miss Langdale would let me play with them, and be ever so kind, if I told her that I did not mean to make her angry."

"In this matter, Flo, you must be ruled by me," said her mother, kindly but firmly. "Set your heart at rest. You did nothing to make the lady angry; and, therefore, there is no reason why she should be asked to forgive you. It was because she recognised that you were her little cousin Florence Langdale,—for that you all know is your name, though it suits your father to alter it slightly—that she put you down so hastily. Surely you do not wish to intrude upon her, if she does not wish to see more of you, or to know me and your father, brother, and sisters? There are occasions on which it is right even for a little girl like yourself to keep up her dignity and self-respect. Even if Miss Langdale were to offer to take you up before her, or invite you into her park, you must not profit by the indulgence. I am not blaming you, love, for what you did in ignorance, but, now that you know our wishes, it must not occur again."

A whole host of dazzling visions faded away. The child's imagination had been actively at work. Florence had ridden Christobel fearlessly, had played with the blue and grey silver-haired terriers for hours—had been invited to enter the park, and to sail on the blue waters of the lake, time after time, in fancy. She could not bear to hear that she was not to respond to the lady's advances.

"Some day she will say she was sorry to have vexed me," said Flo, struggling with her tears. "What am I to do then?"

"My love, I do not think Miss Langdale will ever condescend so far," said Mrs. Lang. " Be as grateful as you like for her involuntary kindness ; forget the mortification that followed as soon as you can ; but remember, that it is not my wish or your father's that you should accept any favours from the Lady of Langdale Hall. Do not say another word."

Florence was silent, but she remained wholly unconvinced and very dissatisfied. Her disposition was entirely different to the sunny confiding natures of her sisters. Mrs. Lang's ill-health had at one time caused her education to be neglected. During this period of anxiety the child had been left greatly to the care of an affectionate but injudicious nurse. Like many old-fashioned faithful domestics, Meredith had as many prejudices as good qualities. Florence was her favourite, and the pet and darling of her elder sisters. She had not escaped unscathed from the fiery furnace of over-indulgence.

Maud Langdale had not reverted to the question which had caused her half-sister so much pain. An unwonted softness had crept into her heart, betraying itself involuntarily in voice and manner.

Over the arid soil, swept bare in her passionate youth, Miss Langdale had, with her own strong will and firm hand, guided the ploughshare which was to root up every tiny blade, every flower that sprang up unbidden. While still quivering with regret for the loss of all that makes life worth having, she had scotched the snake ; tearing out and rooting up every flattering illusion, and leaving the present as blank and desolate as the past and future. Since the destruction of her first dreams of happiness, Maud had suffered no fresh human affections to spring up in her heart.

Her affection for her young half-sister was not a softening characteristic At the smallest assertion on her part of independence, Maud tightened the rein which at other times hung loose. In her eyes Ellinor was still a child, and would continue to be so, till some ebullition of womanly feeling broke the bond woven by the habits of companionship.

Quite another feeling had sprung up in the breast which had for so many years been cold, for the beautiful daughter of Frank Langdale. Never, since, had Maud vaulted into her saddle, without fancying that the child's tenderly clasping fingers rested on the arm that encircled her slender waist. The musical voice of the little maiden sounded close to her ear during Miss Langdale's long, solitary rides. She heard it in the murmur of the beck, and the cooing of the wood-pigeons.

When the boughs closed over her head, making a soft green twilight, Maud remembered the clear dark eyes of the child, looking up at the net-work of foliage overhanging the crags and the river. If Christobel arched her neck for a caress after stepping daintily over the ford of the river, Miss Langdale seemed to see again, nay even herself to feel the pressure of the small white hand laid timidly upon the flowing black mane. The wild flowers, scarcely noticed usually, recalled the beautiful vision which had first attracted her attention, of the dark-haired girl, half hidden among the large fern-leaves and rushes, weaving her garland on the brink of the river.

Child and woman, alike wilful, suffered their imaginations to run wild. There was no kindly feeling towards the parents of Florence in their kinswoman's suddenly evoked partiality. Maud bitterly envied them the possession of their pet lamb. She would have robbed them of their darling without the slightest compunction. Had the woman lived in earlier times she would without scruple have armed her retainers, and carried off the pearl she coveted. Frank Langdale had wounded her pride, and she longed for retaliation.

Little did her parents dream, in spite of all their precautions, how constantly Florence's glance turned towards the stately lady who stood or sat, with the crimson curtains parted back, in full view of the congregation during the morning service in Langdale Church. In winter a large fire was kept up in the great warm comfortable pew half the size of the chancel. Above her head gorgeous entablatures and escutcheons, memorials of her family,—about her still handsome person, every sign of worldly prosperity.

Florence knew every one of her costly rings ; for she always took off her gloves, and the child loved to see the flash of the diamonds. She watched, enviously, the lady moving slowly through the curtseying crowd about the church door, distributing a word or two right and left, as she waited for the handsome equipage from the Hall, to draw up at the gate. The little girl never bestowed a glance on the fair, simply dressed, graceful girl, who came up in haste from the side aisle to join her sister.

Neither the jewelled fingers, nor the stately bearing of the lady of the Hall, attracted the attention of the handsome chestnut-haired student who had recently returned from the German University, where he had won the coveted prize, and received from his comrades every possible token of good will. After their simple fashion, a festival in the green wood had been given to the fortunate English youth who had distanced all competitors, and he went on his way rejoicing.

The young man was delighted at first with the old family mansion, overhung with ivy, and picturesquely situated. For a few days he wandered about with his sisters, in a state of perfect contentment ; but, when a fortnight had passed away, he was less satisfied with his position. It was true that the stream, meandering through the meadow, was full of trout, but he could not pursue its course after it flowed under the stone bridge at the entrance of Langdale Park. The game was strictly preserved, and although the keepers were disposed to treat civilly the aristocratic-looking youth, whose prospective heirship was well known, Fritz knew his father's proud reluctance to accept any favour from their haughty kinswoman, too well to profit by their courtesy. Even his rambles with his sisters were circumscribed by the high walls and park-palings. Before he had been a month at Godley Grange, Fritz heartily wished that his father had not pitched his tent under the Langdale beech trees.

Annoyed by these restrictions on his freedom, the young man heartily disliked their proud neighbour, who had not deigned to notice his mother and sisters, and had inflicted numberless annoyances on his father. On the first Sunday after his return, he had left the family pew without waiting for his father and sisters, in order to avoid the crowd. A lady, to him perfectly unknown, was passing down the middle aisle, and, with instinctive courtesy, the young man stood aside for her to pass. Their glances met for one moment, as, without the smallest recognition of his civility, Miss Langdale swept past.

A very different form and face had riveted Fritz's attention during the singing. A sweet, clear voice, true and harmonious, had satisfied the ear accustomed to German music. It was a keen disappointment, when he rejoined his sisters, and ascertained that the fair girl in blue, who sang so well, was another Miss Langdale. He felt inclined to ask whether the Lady of the Manor had a right to monopolise every good thing in her vicinity.

More than one of the rural congregation, as the young
man stood bareheaded in the church, remarked how like he
was to Miss Ellinor. They were cousins on the father's
side, it was true, but Fritz had his mother's sunny brow
and sweet expression, bright brown hair and azure eyes.
There was no relationship between Marina Lang, the waif
and stray picked up on the coast after a storm, and the
Langdales of Langdale.

As Fritz walked, staff in hand, with his favourite sister,
Gertrude, one Sunday evening, up the steep Roman road
from the Grange, he inquired why she and Frances did not
help in the singing, like the young lady in blue ; and whether
they taught in the school, and made themselves useful.

"It would not do for us to put ourselves forward in this
parish," said Gertrude. "Miss Langdale manages everything, and is most generous in her charities and benefac-
tions. She gave that fine organ to the church last year."

"She preserves strictly in all senses of the word," said
Fritz, bitterly. "No one may do good, or carry a gun on
these lands, or cast a line in these waters. So long as you
keep to the foot pathway the gates are open, but if you step
to the right or left you are sure to stumble upon a placard
announcing vengeance against trespassers ! I cannot understand my father's bringing us to live in a place where we
are so completely overshadowed by this arrogant woman."

"My father is universally respected," said Gertrude.
"There was an opening for him here, which might not have
offered elsewhere ; and it is a great consideration to have a
large house rent-free."

"I would rather live in a nutshell than under Miss Langdale's park wall," said Fritz impetuously. "Gertrude, this
was an ill-advised removal. How happy we all were in
Germany ! Count Max gave me the run of his woods in

the vacations ; and you and the little girls used to bring us our luncheon, and warble as sweetly as nightingales. Here we are caged like convicts !"

A bright blush mounted up to the roots of his sister's fair hair, as Fritz's words recalled past pleasures in the life they had led among the Thuringian forests.

"If your friend comes to see us at Godley, we will not shut him up in prison," she said, softly. "You shall ramble about over the hills together, and we will bring you your luncheon and sing to you, if you like, as of yore."

Fritz looked at his sister inquiringly.

"Shall I write and tell Max to come, Gerty ? He will not need much pressing ; only, I am afraid he will want to take away what we may not like to lose."

"Then do not invite him," said Gertrude, looking stead-fastly away from her brother. "My father and mother have nothing to spare. They cannot in this time of trial be generous to strangers."

"Well, he must bide his time. To tell the truth, I was a little jealous of Max, last summer. We will not disturb him in his political considerations now that he is a member of the Reichs-Rath. I doubt whether I shall stay long in England, myself. My father wants me to choose a profession, but he can give me a helping hand in nothing but commerce, and I have no fancy for dangling my legs on a stool behind a counter. It is hard to pass one's best days in drudgery, with the prospect of such a glorious inheritance, when one is too old to enjoy it. That woman looks as if she would live for ever !"

The brother and sister walked on, talking of various matters, and did not again revert to the Langdales. The moonlight was silvering the waters of the lake in the woods, as they wound their way home.

CHAPTER VII.

MISS LANGDALE had not lost the disagreeable recollection of "the General's" contemptuous neglect of the obsequious civility usually shown to her by her dependents, when she rode over to the neighbouring town to consult her friend and land agent, Mr. Haywarden, respecting the repairs to be effected at Noel Hall.

The country lawyer was steward and agent for many of the county families, and was highly respected ; very straightforward, indeed rather blunt in manner, yet possessed of considerable tact, well connected and gentleman-like, Mr. Haywarden was a person of consequence in the neighbourhood. No one had half so much influence with Miss Langdale. He alone could laugh her out of a prejudice, or persuade her to desist from some proceeding more eccentric, than usual.

His cool reception of Maud's passionate reproaches for allowing vagrants to roost in the old Hall, staggered her at the first burst. The man was a stranger, certainly, Mr. Haywarden admitted, but, in the present state of the place, distinguished occupants were not to be expected.

"To tell you the truth," he added, " the old fellow rather won me over. He is quite a character, and has, I am sure, known better days. He fought with Garibaldi in Central America. I have no doubt he is a democrat, and I dare say would not take off his cap to the queen. His rent was paid beforehand, and he offered to give more than I should have thought of asking for a nook in the Gateway Tower of the old hall."

"I do not care what he offered," said Miss Langdale,

angrily; "pay him off and get rid of him. I believe he is
an escaped convict, and may prove an incendiary, or at best
a lunatic. I will not harbour him on my premises a week
longer."

Mr. Haywarden looked annoyed. "Pardon, me, Miss
Langdale," he said, gravely. "It is not quite so easy as
you imagine to dislodge a tenant who pays a fair rent regularly, and who brought me unexceptionable references. If
this be indeed your wish, I must give the man proper legal
notice."

"The sooner it is done the better," replied Miss Langdale.
"Who recommended him to you?"

"Oh, he is known to one or two people in Hazeldon,"
said the lawyer, carelessly, conscious that to acknowledge it
was her cousin, Frank Lang, his own oldest and dearest
friend, who had asked him to allow the old soldier to take
rooms at Noel Hall, would be to seal his sentence of dismissal. "I am very sorry that you dislike the General, upon
my word I believe him to be a capital fellow. He must have
some property, for he has fitted up the two rooms he occu-
pies with some degree of taste. Let me advise you not to be
hasty. His infirmity, perhaps, made him quite unconscious
that he was in the presence of the Lady of the Manor. It
would be an act of cruelty foreign to your nature, to dislodge him for what might, after all, be an unintentional discourtesy.

"The people complain bitterly of the state of the buildings," said Miss Langdale, changing her tone when she
perceived that Mr. Haywarden was not inclined to yield the
point, and was on the brink of being seriously offended.
"I do not want the old house to be flooded, or the women
and children crippled with rheumatism; but farther than is
absolutely necessary I will not go. I will not lay out an addi-

tional shilling. As for your favourite—the General," she added, with a propitiatory smile, "I suppose I must give him brevet rank to please you ; what on earth makes him wish to lodge at the old Hall ? I sometimes wish I had never bought it !"

"The land was not a bad bargain," said the lawyer. "As for the Hall, as you chose to purchase it, against my advice and warning that I did not approve of the title, and that the house and offices were falling into ruin, you ought to have laid out money in necessary repairs twenty years ago, instead of allowing its present tenants to occupy separate portions. If you wish to get rid of the place it is by no means impossible that the old family may wish to buy it back again. That property of the Noels in the North Riding is improving, and might pay even Cuthbert Noel's debts over again."

Miss Langdale rose abruptly. "That is more than any man can affirm," she said, sternly. "Men may search the bottom of the sea, but there has never yet been found a line long enough to reach the bottom of a selfish, unprincipled spendthrift's extravagance."

She shook hands with Mr. Haywarden, and left his office without another word. Apparently she had relinquished her vengeful purpose, and Mr. Haywarden was not inclined to remind her of it.

Maud rode swiftly along the stony high road to the gates of her own mansion, which were set open at the sound of Christobel's approach. As she pursued the beautiful winding drive, overlooking the valley, her mind was full of thoughts partly suggested by the objects which came successively into view.

Above her frowned the blackened towers which, though comparatively recent additions to the old Manor House— owing to the polluted state of the atmosphere near Hazeldon

—looked grim and sepulchral. Below wound the rivulet, a tributary of the Lang, and on the opposite bank, set among trees, were farms and cottages, of which she was the owner.

Maud paused, and, turning in her saddle at a spot where a wider view opened, looked along the wider valley of the Lang, into which the brook entered. Many a time in her impetuous girlhood, wilful as now, had she so turned and looked back ; but it was years since she had literally or metaphorically stayed her course. The action was involuntary now, but she did not check it. Why must she to-day, willingly or unwillingly, sit silently gazing past croft and spinny, at the hill which shut in the valley ; seeing, instead of the ruinous abode she had recently visited, a noble mansion, full of tokens of luxury and extravagance—all that her soul revolted from now, but which, in her girlish folly, was most prized ?

Maud's grip of the rein tightened as the past, of which she never spoke, and seldom thought, rolled back into her memory :—the mad rides, taken in defiance of parental authority, sometimes alone, sometimes attentively escorted back to the house, where she often expected to find the doors barred against her. Could it be the sight of the composed, clever lawyer—the friend of her youth, who knew more of her history than most others (but not the whole)—which had awakened recollections she generally contrived to put away from her when they strove to intrude upon her present, calmly prosperous, uneventful life ? Something in the gleam of the low sunlight on the water, in the glitter of the upward floating rays on the many windows of the Hall, on the distant hill-top, might recall the days of old—those long banished thoughts.

Not so ! neither the flashing lights on hill and dale, nor the brief allusion made by Mr. Haywarden to the misfor-

tunes of her former friends, had first roused the reminiscences which swept over the shuddering woman. The train
had been lit by the spark which shot from the eyes of the
old soldier as he sat on the broken wall, disdaining to rise
as she passed. What was the spell that made the usually
undaunted Maud Langdale fear as well as hate him? Even
at this moment Maud resolved to let him stay in the niche
he coveted. She did not dare to dislodge him. In the
heart of this proud woman were depths into which she seldom cared to look. Out of these sources welled up sometimes waters of bitterness; at others sweet womanly impulses. Perhaps as a wife and mother, Maud might have
been tender and affectionate; but she chose to tread her
way in solitude, without seeking to find happiness, or to
impart it; yet still the sweet waters, though kept back from
sight, were there.

One of these softer emotions was stirred when the old
woman spoke of the veteran's hopeless malady, bravely borne
in solitude. She saw him, in fancy, battling with his foe,
and honoured him for the conquest. Had the man doffed
his cap as she passed, Maud would have befriended him ever
after. Kind impulses were in her heart when she left the
Hall, and saw him sitting patiently in the sunshine, on the
very spot where, in her happiest hours of girlhood, she had
often lingered, rejoicing, when life was in itself a joy.

Why had he confronted her so insolently, when her intention was to be charitable and compassionate? and yet, on
consideration, Maud felt half ashamed of her vindictiveness.
Mr. Haywarden must be right. What motive could the
man have for wilfully annoying her?

Maud rode on quietly, full of kindly thoughts. She was
not angry now with the poor old General, as the children
called him, when she thought of him as she had last seen

him, sitting on the courtyard wall, wrapped in his blue
roquelaure. She would almost like, if the man were more
civil, to see the two chambers which Mr. Haywarden—a
man of taste and refinement—said he had contrived to fit
up skilfully, and where the old dame said he would, on
some wild winter night, be buried in the midst of the
rubbish.

At all events that must not be. Maud sent stringent
orders to Mr. Haywarden to have the necessary repairs set
on foot. Although some evil memories clung about the
place, Maud had no wish to see the home of the ruined
Noels crumble to decay. It might yield shelter to a few
otherwise houseless peasants, and the obscure, afflicted
soldier.

CHAPTER VIII.

THE work-people employed in repairing the dilapidated
building at the head of the valley, soon fraternised with the
old soldier who was always ready to lend a helping hand to
anyone who stood in need of assistance. In return, the
men gave him, good-humouredly, pieces of the rotten wain-
scoting for which they were substituting plain, serviceable
deal, unmindful of the scriptural injunction not to mend
old things with new material.

In like manner the broken panes of stained glass, precious
to an antiquarian, were replaced by green-tinged diamond
or square-shaped panes of the commonest description; but
the smallest of the curious antique fragments on which

4

bird, flower, or heraldic sign, had been emblazoned was
carried off in triumph by the General.

He scarcely looked his age when, in the heat of excitement,
he cast off his coat and worked lustily with the masons and
carpenters, incurring great risk, to take out with more
care than the workmen would have bestowed upon it a
cracked window-pane. In the heat of battle, the men said,
he must have learnt steadiness of eye and hand; they could
fancy him mounting a scaling ladder in the teeth of the
enemy's guns. On one occasion a boy had turned suddenly
faint and giddy, just as he gained the top of a ladder reared
against one of the twisted chimneys of the old house; the
General, who was on the scaffolding, hard at work removing
some curious bits of sculpture, saw the lad's danger just in
time, saved him from falling, and bore him down in his arms
to the ground. The workmen cheered him heartily as he
deposited his burden on the turf; but the veteran stalked
off at once, as though unwilling to be thanked or noticed,
and was seen no more that day.

Next morning he came out, looking aged and weary,
wrapped in his cloak; and sat apart in his favourite corner
of the courtyard where the father and mother of the boy
came to thank him. No need of that, he said, but he was
glad the boy was none the worse, for at first he feared it
might be a sun-stroke. When he saw the danger, he forgot
for the moment, that he himself was not so young and
active as he had once been.

The father, a master-mason, from that moment was the
General's staunch friend. He even ventured to speak about
the matter to Miss Langdale, when he went up to the Hall;
telling her how bravely and coolly the old man had borne
himself; and that he owed his son's life to him, but he
would scarcely bear to be thanked. From that day the

General became a prime favourite among the workmen; any choice bits of carving, panelling, or glass which they came across were reserved for him.

He was almost wild with delight when, on the inside of a board used to stop up a chimney-place, a picture was discovered. The General carried away his prize; and after washing and scraping off all impurities, fitted it into a frame of his own making, out of bits of antique oak-carving. Then he set it up on high above the great sculptured mantel-piece in his own den, and worshipped it. Truly it was a quaint chamber on which the eyes of Lady Barbara Noel (for such was the name and title at the back of the canvas) looked down with aristocratic contempt and wonder. A haughty dame, clad in rich satin and lace, her hair looped with pearls, and a page holding up the train of her court dress.

The picture was not of ancient date; but then the people located at the Hall were mostly strangers; few traditions hung about the place, and no one assisted the republican soldier in discovering the appellation of the lady. He said that in clearing the dirt off the picture, he had detected some writing at the bottom of the canvas, among the weeds in the foreground on which she looked too proud to set her dainty feet; the centre of the ground on which she stood was covered with rich crimson cloth, over which she was supposed to be stepping to her carriage through the gateway of the Hall.

With infinite care and skill, the man fitted bits of old painted glass into the framework of his diamond-paned case-ment windows. An antiquarian might have found amuse-ment for hours in studying these singular devices; birds, such as never flew over land or sea—fish, that swam in no waters—coats of arms worn by no one now living—brave colours faded—outlines fast disappearing!

4—2

Through these motley transparencies the autumn sunlight
fell on the dark oak boards of the floor, polished daily till
they shone like glass, on massive beams, and curiously
painted borders of panel and wainscot, joined together and
fastened to the wall in the fashion of olden times. Hither
had been brought, honestly purchased, or exchanged for
common useful articles with the other inmates of the Hall,
a few choice pieces of furniture which had survived the
general wreck, a bed on which King James slept when he
made a crusade against the Yorkshire Witches—a chair with
the royal arms and cypher on the back—probably used on
the same occasion—and a harpsichord, much older than the
picture, which might have responded to the touch of the
fair fingers of an ancestress of the Lady Barbara Noel.

When the fit was upon him the old soldier would sit,
with his hands clutched convulsively, as if stiffened by
cramp, in the twisted woodwork arms of the antique chair,
his glance riveted on the eyes of the picture above the fire-
place. Thus would he remain for hours, uttering now and
then a groan or shriek of pain audible to his compassionate
neighbours. All the colour would die out of his weather-
beaten face, and strange hues of age and sickness would
creep over it ; not a morsel passed his lips, not a tear de-
dewed his eyelids, till the paroxysm was past. He would
then get up and go about as though nothing had happened.

Sometimes he remained entranced for days together ;
only moving, at intervals, to fetch a fresh jug of water from
the outside of the door, which he would, in his fiery thirst,
drain off at a draught. No wonder, if, after such terrible
attacks, white lines were more numerous in his still thick
hair and beard, in some places black as night, or that the
eyelids drooped wearily over orbs at other times full of fiery
light. Years of prosperity might pass over a man's head

without ageing him as much as these periods of intense tor-
ture.

Often at night, when every other occupant of Noel Hall
had been long in bed, a light might be seen burning in the
gateway tower, through the window that overlooked the
valley of the Lang ; or, if all was still and dark within the
old walls, a worn, haggard face, nailed to the glass, would
turn its wild eyes eastward, in the direction where the young
moon silvered the tops of Miss Langdale's trees. As the
planet rose higher and higher, glancing rays fell upon the
stream, and weird shadows were cast on the hill-side.

Perhaps the baying of a watch-dog at the neighbouring
farm, or the hooting of an owl, would disturb the hearer's
reverie, and he crept shivering to his lair, like some hunted
animal ; throwing his ponderous limbs on the old oak bed-
stead, which creaked and groaned as a ship's timbers moan
when about to part in a storm. The tired soldier would
draw his cloak over his weary frame in vain ; shivering
with cold, sleep far from his eyelids, he would lie awake till
dawn broke over the landscape ; or the first sun rays stole,
through the high uncurtained window, athwart his couch.
Then at last he would close his aching eyes and sleep dream-
lessly until the sun was high in heaven. The cheery song
of the workmen, the tap of the hammer, the driving of the
saw, after a time would dispel the enchantment, which had
banished alike the sense of present desolation and the
memory of the past.

PART THE SECOND.

CAUGHT IN THE SNOW-STORM.

PROUD words are graven in the stone,
  O'er my portal grey and low,
Boasts of the sons who have left me lone,
  Where tempests round me blow.
"Ours is the soil of the old West-Riding !—
  While sunlight gilds the dale :—
So long as the beck flows down from the moor
  And the swallow flies over the vale."

The children cluster at my door,
  The beck flows darkened past,
Dim shadows flit across my floor,
  Cold blows the wintry blast.
Through cracks and chinks the rain-drops steal,
  Moss clings upon my walls,
And the stamp of labour's heavy heel
  Upon my pavement falls.

Where, oh where are the Mighty hiding
Who dwelt in the Halls of the old West-Riding ?

CHAPTER I.

 WINTER of unusual severity had passed away at Godley Grange, and although Easter was close at hand, the frost-bitten earth showed no token of advancing spring. Hard and cold, the soil yielded little encouragement to vegetation, and the March winds blighted the shrinking buds and blossoms.

Mrs. Lang had suffered very much from the intense cold of the season during the three winters spent at the Grange, although she never quitted the two rooms facing the south, which were appropriated to her use, and where every effort was made to equalize the temperature. Bitterly had her husband repented of his rashness in bringing the invalid into Yorkshire, though his principal motive had been to obtain for the delicate mother of his children more comforts in the old family mansion than were provided in temporary foreign homes. The addition to his not over large income, which his position afforded as principal clerk in the largest house of business in the neighbouring manufacturing town, was also an important consideration.

Fritz had not remained long at Godley, nor often visited Yorkshire. He was not so persevering as his father, and the prospect of being eventually Miss Langdale's heir, helped to unsettle him. An invitation to visit the elder brother

of one of his fellow-students, the head of one of the usually
exclusive aristocratic families of Germany, afforded irresistible temptations, and was followed by many similar courtesies.   The splendid hunting-grounds of the Austrian and
Prussian nobility, the perfect freedom of a sportsman's life
in those extensive domains, offered a striking contrast to
the circumscribed precincts hemmed in by Miss Langdale's
park fences and prerogatives.

Mr. Lang had pressed urgently upon his son the duty of
choosing a profession, and not depending upon uncertain
expectations ; but Fritz steadily refused to enter a counting-
house ; and felt no disposition towards any of the learned
professions.   He was a great favourite with foreigners, and
had made friends in circles to which the generality of
Englishmen were not admitted.   His German education,
and ardent love for, as well as skill and daring, in all manly
exercises and pursuits, made him popular with the owners
of the princely territories seldom visited by English sports-
men.   His greatest friend, Count Max von Berliegen, possessed large estates, where he could roam at will, chasing
the deer or chamois.   Fritz greatly preferred such a life to
being cooped up at Godley Grange, within the narrow ring
of Miss Langdale's preserves.

The twins were growing up into pretty fair-haired girls,
so alike, that it was difficult to know them apart.   Gertrude
and Frances attended alternately upon their mother or
managed the household.   They knew more of the difficulties
of their father's position, and entered more fully into his
anxieties now than their invalid mother.   Frances, her
father said, was a capital woman of business.

Florence was more altered than any of her sisters.   She
had shot up suddenly from the little slender child into a
tall, dark-haired girl.   Her manners were singularly self-

possessed, considering that she had lived in no society, and enjoyed few advantages. She was still a great favourite with all, and very good-tempered; but there were points on which her elder sisters were wont to say, if Flo had made up her mind, it was of no use to contradict or argue with her.

One of Flo's fancies was on all possible occasions to call and sign herself Langdale, although it was in opposition to her father's desire. As she had few correspondents, the matter at present was of little consequence; but her sisters were right in blaming her, and in considering that it might occasion inconvenience, if she persisted in the practice after she was grown up. She would undoubtedly excite her father's anger, if it were brought under his observation.

When quite a little child, if strangers asked her name, Flo would answer "Langdale;" and Meredith, her nurse, a worshipper of the old family, always encouraged her. "Miss Florence," she would say, "is a real Langdale, the image of the lady at the Hall, who had been the greatest beauty in all the country side." Her little lady, Meredith would say, when gossiping with her especial crony, the wife of the head keeper, was the only regular Langdale amongst them. She had a will of her own—just the same as Miss Langdale. Truly, humility and dutifulness were not likely to be inculcated by the old family servant, and in one, at least, of these virtues, Florence was naturally deficient. She now looked as much older than her age as she had previously appeared to be younger. The little one, as she was still called, although she had ceased to deserve the name, was undeniably the beauty of the family.

The first person who noticed the alteration in Florence's manners and disposition, which had more than kept pace with her growth, was her mother. Mrs. Lang perceived, with one of the sharpest pangs which had ever pierced her tender heart, that the little one came less often and less willingly than of yore, into her apartments—hitherto the sanctuary into which all the hopes and fears of childhood, as well as its fleeting joys and sorrows, had been carried. The mother, with patient, watchful tenderness, tried to discover the cause of Flo's alienation, but the young girl's reserve was impenetrable. She came, indeed, at proper times to enquire after and attend upon her mother, and was always attentive and affectionate; but she no longer crept in unbidden, or waited tearfully at the door, or sat quietly behind the curtain, during her mother's worst attacks of pain. Often, formerly, had Mrs. Lang put back the chintz hangings, feeling instinctively that the little, sweet, anxious face of her youngest-born would be revealed; and gathered the loving child to her bosom, comforted by her sympathy. Now, when startled by some indistinct sound, she looked round longingly, if Florence were the appointed watcher, her mother would see her sitting unoccupied, with a book in her lap, gazing into the fire.

When the invalid spoke, Flo would rally back her thoughts, and attend upon her devotedly, with more than a child's consideration; but, as soon as she was released from duty, she would fall again into a reverie. When away from her mother's apartments, she would ramble about alone for hours in the now leafless plantations; forgetting to bring home to gladden the sick-room, as had been her wont, the earliest primrose or violet.

Mrs. Lang's medical attendant warned her husband that some wearing mental disquietude aggravated her sufferings, and prevented the remedies he prescribed having the proper effect. For the first time since her marriage, the wife did not confide this trouble to her husband. She knew that Flo was not her father's favourite child, and she feared that he might exaggerate the failings which, even to herself, she was not willing to admit existed in her darling.

To her father Flo was always submissive. In truth, she was very much afraid of him. Her little ebullitions of pride, vanity, and self-will, were carefully hidden from his view, for her sisters still regarded her as a complete child. Not one of the household would make a complaint which might bring the little one into trouble.

Florence took her own course unchecked, save occasionally by a mild remonstrance on the part of her eldest sister, when she persisted wilfully in signing herself Langdale, thus making an inconvenient difference between herself and the rest of the family. Why should she give up a name which had come down to them through generations? Flo argued passionately. Fritz signed his name as he liked, why might not she? No one but herself ever touched the books on her own shelves, where she had written her name properly, as she considered, and as she liked to see it.

"You may take my word for it, an English winter is not the only reason for Mrs. Lang's increased sufferings," said Dr. Forsyth, an old friend of the family, as he walked by the side of the grave, anxious husband of his patient, up the long winding avenue, leading from Godley Grange, towards the gate where his carriage waited. "Yorkshire is not such a bad place after all, and the thick walls of your old house, together with your admirable daughter and excellent nurse's care, keep out the cold winds and draughts, as well as damp. Nothing amiss, I hope, with that pretty little girl of yours, Miss Florence?" added the good doctor, with professional acuteness, quickened by very sincere regard. "She has grown wonderfully of late, and I cannot help fancying she is rather delicate. Mrs. Lang looks a little uneasy about her, and says she wants air and exercise. She sighed as she said so, after sending the young lady to take a long walk with Mrs. Meredith. By the way, what a treasure that good servant of yours is; I never saw a better nurse."

"No, no; Florence is all right," said Mr. Lang, impatiently. "Thank goodness, none of my girls are delicate. She has been growing very fast this winter, as you say, and my poor wife thinks of, and takes care for, everybody. Of course, she has anxieties. What mother of six children can be free from them? But we share them together. My wife has never kept a secret from me since the day of our marriage."

"So much the better—I am glad to hear it," said the acute physician, who, nevertheless, had visited too many households, and travelled too far in the West Riding for many years, to take for granted the most confident assertion. "I suppose, as you are quite sure that Mrs. Lang has no hidden, wearing subject for uneasiness pressing on her mind, and retarding our efforts, we must trust that the approach of a more genial season will bring about a pleasanter state of affairs. Speaking of weather, I don't like the look of those blackish-blue clouds on the top of our great hill. The Beacon is certainly putting on his night-cap. I think there will be more snow and hail before night-fall. March is going out, as he came in, like a lion. I wonder in which direction Miss Florence is walking? I might be able to give her a lift."

" Meredith was going to take some wine and warm clothing to a pensioner of ours who lodges at the old Hall at the head of the valley, where the Noels once lived," said Mr. Lang, after a moment's consideration. "We—Marina and I —owe him a good turn, and my wife never forgets a friend or a service."

"I know whom you mean, and a strange creature he is. He saved a boy's life last September, and got laid up with a sprained back and acute rheumatism," said the doctor, "I am afraid merit is its own reward here below, though we will hope it has its guerdon in the courts above. But what on earth could the old General, as the people at the Hall have named him, ever have done for you and Mrs. Lang?"

"He saved Marina's life," said her husband, "a life most precious to us all. But for the General, as you call him, Marina would have been drowned. The ship in which she and her parents returned to England was lost, as you well know, and only one little girl, my wife, was saved. But for the old man at the Hall, she would never have known me, or become the partner of my indifferent fortune, and the mother of my children."

Dr. Forsyth looked at him sharply. "Come, come, man, it is only right to give the devil his due. If that poor fellow, Cuthbert Noel, never did another good deed, he pulled that child out of the wreck of the *Hesperus* at the risk of his life."

"Neither will I stand by and hear the old General defrauded of his dues," said Mr. Lang, hotly. "I do not deny that Cuthbert Noel had a share in the work, but that old soldier at the Hall brought her to shore in his arms. He saw a black speck on the raging waters, and swam out. That speck was Marina, wrapped up in an officer's cloak. He has it to this day."

"I do not suppose that, excepting the great lady at the Hall, there is a soul now living who cares much for Bertie Noel," said the doctor, as he stepped into his gig. "And yet he was no one's enemy so much as his own. You and he were never the best of friends."

"I am not his enemy now," said Mr. Lang. "Death

settles all scores—even the longest—but the old man at Noel Hall is the only living being to whom I can manifest my gratitude for Marina's preservation from shipwreck."

"Well, be it so," said the doctor, giving his reins a vindictive shake, and drawing his plaid rug over his legs, as he settled himself in the driving seat. "I think gratitude should survive even death itself; and I have no notion of transferring the remembrance of a benefit, like a ticket for a raree-show, to a person who had, I firmly believe, no more to do than I had in rescuing your wife from the cold embrace of the water. For that matter I had a great deal more to do with her preservation, for, as I will do you the justice to admit, you have never forgotten, I brought the child back to life and warmth, and got rid of the cold water out of her little body. But I never heard till this moment that yonder old pauper had any share in the business."

"Pardon me, Forsyth, in this matter, I am not likely to be mistaken; and I assure you, on my word of honour, that the General took part in the brave and efficient aid rendered to the beloved woman whom you and others rescued from a watery grave," said Mr. Lang, shaking hands warmly with his friend. "Now if you are going over the hill, look out for my little daughter. My wife is sure to see those snow-laden clouds, coming up from the direction in which she has sent her."

"You will have to give up calling her 'The Little One' soon," the doctor said, good humouredly. "Miss Flo will be a beauty like her cousin, Miss Langdale."

"I trust she will be a better woman," said Mr. Lang, sternly; "I do not like them to be named in the same sentence."

He walked quickly back to the house, and up to his wife's room, where, as he expected, Mrs. Lang was anxiously

watching the weather. Mr. Lang assured her that Dr.
Forsyth had promised to bring Florence back with him, and
judging by the pace at which his fine old mare had started,
and by his usual rate of progress, it would not take him long
to reach the ancient house of the Noels.

CHAPTER 11.

THE wind blew strongly and right in his teeth, after Dr.
Forsyth parted from Mr. Lang at the sheltered gate of the
Grange. Accustomed as she was to encounter on those
bleak hills the fiercest extremes of weather, his fine old
black mare shuddered, as after breasting the steep ascent,
she came full into the sweep of the gale.

The good doctor looked sharply over the hedges, or stone
enclosures, at the clearly defined pathway across the fields.
Grey slabs laid down between bright green grass, and stone
walls indented by narrow apertures, or with steps on either
side, afforded easy means of crossing on foot those verdant
pastures. At intervals the path dipped down into thick
coverts of foliage, as yet leafless; and narrow foot-bridges
were laid over a brawling beck, hidden among trees; but he
could see no one on the footway.

He touched the mare with the whip when they reached
the higher level overlooking the valley of the Lang, and
drove on fast; hoping to be in time to prevent the young
lady and her attendant from leaving the shelter of the old
Hall; still far above him.

Another sharp ascent obliged him to slacken speed, and,
at a turn in the road, a close carriage passed the doctor's

5

gig. Accustomed to being out at all hours and seasons, pacing the same monotonous round of professional duty, Dr. Forsyth knew most persons on his beat : but though he was quite familiar with the appearance of Miss Langdale's equipage, liveries, and servants, it was almost the first time he had ever met her driving out in her carriage on a weekday.

The wind nearly blew his hat out of the Doctor's hand, and played roughly with his grey locks, as he uncovered them, to salute the ladies seated opposite to each other in the carriage. Dr. Forsyth almost forgot to put his hat on again, when his sharp eyes noticed that Florence Lang was seated side by side with the lady of the Hall, whilst Meredith, bolt upright, occupied the opposite place next to Miss Ellinor Langdale.

"The little one" looked flushed and happy, not in the least awed by her formidable companion, and the first smile Dr. Forsyth had seen there since the days of her beaming, beautiful youth, sat on the lips, and lighted up the dark eyes of Maud Langdale, as she listened to her young cousin.

Not one of the party inside the carriage noticed Dr. Forsyth's polite salutation. The servants touched their hats, and in a moment the vision, stereotyped in the Doctor's retentive memory by that one quick glance, had swept past him.

"No occasion to call for 'the little one' at Noel Hall," he muttered to himself. "Miss Florence is better off inside that snug close carriage, than she would be in my old gig, facing this hail storm. Strange though! I should never have thought that Miss Langdale would have given a lift to one of the family at the Grange. That was one of her old smiles! She looked quite handsome. Come, come, old lady," he added, addressing the mare, to whom, in his long,

lonely rides, he constantly talked. " We can take the lower
road now, and the sooner you are in your warm stable, this
rough evening, the better."

The good Doctor drove on quickly after this colloquy, or
soliloquy ; visiting many a remote homestead on his lonely
round of country practice, where he chatted pleasantly with
the families of his patients. He was known and loved
through all the country-side, and could have told many a
tale which would have surprised his hearers ; but he was
equally discreet and intelligent.

He was by no means devoid of curiosity, and his next
visit to Godley Grange was paid earlier than might otherwise have been the case ; owing to his intense desire to ascertain what effect his usually haughty kinswoman's courtesy
might have had upon its master.

Mr. Lang, however, was not at home ; and the Doctor,
who always acted cautiously, said nothing to the invalid
respecting the occurrence he had noticed. His visit was
most welcome. Florence, her mother said, was ill. She
had caught a severe, feverish cold the day of the great hail
and snow storm. Mrs. Lang had been on the point of sending for him, when his gig stopped at the gate.

" Oh, indeed," said the Doctor, while the vision he had
seen of the flushed face, just visible through the carriage
window, returned to his recollection. " What a pity I did
not fall in with her a little sooner. If she had waited at
Noel Hall she would have escaped the storm altogether. It
passed over much more quickly than I expected. My mare
could hardly keep her legs at one time. I was glad to turn
into the lower road."

" Flo is a tender plant," said her mother, with a sigh.
" I am never quite easy about her. She did not seem more
wet than she might have been after running up the avenue,

when caught at the gate in a shower ; and our children are accustomed to going out in rough weather. Nevertheless, she has been unwell ever since. Last night she was very feverish. Gertrude will take you at once to see her."

Dr. Forsyth followed Miss Lang silently to the room called the nursery, which of late had belonged especially to "the little one." The door next to this apartment opened into the work-room, where Meredith was sitting diligently occupied with her needle. She did not even look up as they passed.

Florence was lying on a small couch by the fire, with her eyes full of tears. The feverishness had passed off, and she looked very pale and languid. An open book lay beside her, but she was not reading.

"Leave me alone with your sister for a few minutes," the Doctor whispered to his companion. "She looks very far from well. I should like to have a little conversation with her."

Miss Lang complied immediately with his request, and waited for him in the next room. Dr. Forsyth entered the old nursery alone, closing the door carefully behind him.

Florence, who had not at all expected this visit, started nervously. Her pale cheeks were flushed instantly with crimson, as she rose to greet him.

"Lie still, my dear, I am sorry to see you so poorly," said the Doctor kindly, making her resume her recumbent position, and taking her hand in his own, as he sat down beside her. "So you caught cold from getting wet last Saturday. How did that happen ? I meant to have brought you home in my gig, but you seemed still better off, when I passed you on the road. I thought you looked very happy and comfortable in Miss Langdale's family coach. Did she take you up too late, or set you down too soon ? I should like

to hear all about it. Perhaps your boots were wet before
you got into the carriage ?"

"I don't know—I don't care!" exclaimed Florence, bursting into tears. "Oh, Dr. Forsyth. I hope you have not
told them that you saw me in Miss Langdale's carriage ?
It was against papa's orders. He will never, never, forgive
me."

"Nonsense, my dear," said the Doctor, patting kindly the
little hand that trembled in his grasp. "Why, if your
worst enemy had offered you a lift in that hail-storm, you
would have been a goose not to accept it. So this has made
you ill ? I thought you could not have had much of a
wetting! You were afraid to tell your father and mother
who brought you home. Take my advice, and always tell
the whole truth at once. It is much more difficult to confess
it afterwards."

"Oh, I dare not, I cannot tell my father and mother how
kind Miss Langdale is to me. They would not believe it.
I am afraid they hate her," said Florence, starting up from
the couch. "Promise, dear, kind Dr. Forsyth, not to say
a word. I will take as much physic as you like. Indeed,
indeed, I have told no stories. No one asked me a single
question, except whether I had seen you, and I said, no. I
really, and truly, did not see you on the road at all. Meredith and I had just left the Hall, when the carriage overtook us, and Miss Langdale said 'Jump in, little one,' and I
got in. Meredith sat opposite to me. Miss Langdale was
as pleasant as possible. I cannot help loving her. It was
as warm and soft in her carriage, as it was hard and cold on
the road and across the fields. Meredith said that papa
would be very angry, and he would tell my mother. Perhaps it would bring on one of her terrible illnesses. Oh,

please, please, say nothing about your having seen me in Miss Langdale's carriage."

"Well, for my part, I hate petty mysteries," said the Doctor testily. "I can keep a really important secret, but trifles are sure to ooze out. There, now, I did not mean to set you off crying again. I don't want to vex you. We will see about it. Let me feel your pulse."

As Flo timidly held out her hand the Doctor noticed on one of her small fingers an old-fashioned ring.

"That is a gem of the first water," he said, with the enthusiasm of a connoisseur. "When I have a little daughter of your age, I shall not let her wear such valuable ornaments, especially when they are so large that they will hardly stay on her fingers. That ring might drop off any moment, when you were running about in the garden. It ought to be an heirloom."

Flo pulled off her ring, hurriedly. "Oh, I only wear it when I am here—all alone. You gave me such a surprise, Dr. Forsyth, I forgot to take it off. Please not to mention my ring any more than your having met me with Miss Langdale."

"I wonder how many more secrets you expect me to keep, young lady?" said the Doctor. "Did Miss Langdale give you this ring?"

"Yes;" said Florence, colouring violently. "Papa would not let me keep it, I know, and I could not bear to give it up. It would break my heart if it were sent away."

"You may depend upon it I will tell no tales while you are my patient," said the Doctor kindly, anxious to quiet her increasing excitement. "It all depends on your good behaviour, afterwards. Try and get better, and we will have another talk over this matter. I make no promises, remember, for the future, excepting that you shall have fair

warning before I say a word to any one else. At present
you can get into no more scrapes, for I forbid your leaving
your room, and you must take some medicine that I will
send you. It shall not be very disagreeable. Do not think
about Miss Langdale more than you can help, and lock up
your ring in your trinket box, for a fortnight. Do not look
at it once during that time. I do not believe that it will
seem such a loss then, if you think it right to part with
it, as it would be to forfeit the love and confidence of your
sweet mother. Now go to sleep if you can, or read your
book. To-morrow I will bring Nina to see you. Don't
make troubles for yourself causelessly, about what will be
just the same a hundred years hence, whether we worry
ourselves about it, or not, in the meantime."

With this philosophical conclusion the Doctor took
leave of his patient. Flo obeyed him implicitly, so far
as locking up her ring was concerned, and after a short
time she went to sleep over her book : thoroughly worn out
with fatigue, but relieved from the dread of immediate be-
trayal.

The first point, in the Doctor's opinion, was to keep his
excitable patient quiet. He thought her looking extremely
delicate, and felt considerable alarm respecting her state of
health. "Just the subject for brain fever," he muttered, as
he descended the stairs, after noticing that Mrs. Meredith's
room was vacant. He found her waiting upon her invalid
mistress, with the attentive care which made her services in
the sick chamber so invaluable.

For the present, at all events, the Doctor considered
himself bound in honour to keep his patient's secret. He
told her mother and sisters that Flo wanted perfect quiet
and soothing care. Medicine suitable for her condition
should be sent immediately, and must be regularly adminis-

tered. Should any change of an unfavourable nature take
place, it would be desirable to let him know without
delay.

Florence was greatly relieved when Gertrude's tender
manner convinced her that her secret was undiscovered.
The draughts arrived in due course of time, and assuaged
her nervous irritability. At the end of a week her health
seemed to be re-established, though her mother and Dr.
Forsyth still regarded her with considerable anxiety.

It was in vain that Flo tried to gain courage, day after
day, to reveal the trifling deception which, as her kind
friend and confidant ·tried to persuade her, bore with it· an
excuse; as in such a storm any shelter was not to be despised. Florence knew, in her heart of hearts, that this was
not her first indiscretion; and that, over and over again, she
had disobeyed her parents' orders. She instinctively feared
that one disclosure would lead the way to others.

Dr. Forsyth renewed his solicitations, and Florence's
favourite friend and companion, his invalid niece, who was
in her confidence, also urged upon her the advantages of
candour; but it was entirely without success that they
pleaded the cause of truth. The little lady could not see
the matter from their point of view, and remained obstinately
silent. Nevertheless, and in spite of the inutility of his
.counsels and arguments, Florence wound herself into his
affections.

"After all," he murmured, as he drove along, after leaving
the Grange, "perhaps the little lady is right; and, be that
as it may, I will not be the means of getting her into dis-
grace. If Frank Lang has a fault, it is too great a resentment of injuries. Everything comes to an end in time; and
so, if he would meet her half way, or even a quarter, there
might be a termination to his cousin's vindictiveness. He

is such a peculiar fellow—no wonder my little friend, Miss Florence, is a trifle obstinate. What nonsense he talked the other day about that old fellow, at Noel Hall, saving Mrs. Lang's life; when everybody knows that it was poor Cuthbert who swam out to the ship and brought her to shore. But it is of no use to attempt to turn him from his conviction. Lang will tell the story in his own way to the day of his death."

PART THE THIRD.

THE RUINED NOELS.

As snow in April, sudden falling,
  In its fair graceful mantle veils
Flowers, leaves, and blossoms, just recalling
  That Spring-time upon Winter steals.

Half hidden by that ivy wreath
  The rocks, and streams, and woods abide,
While Nature bright and warm beneath,
  Shows like a veiled and blushing bride.

R. M. K.

CHAPTER I.

ELLINOR LANGDALE was standing at one of the windows of the Hall, looking out at the white flakes of snow, falling on terrace and wall. At no time did the old house look so beautiful as during the first days of the frequent storms of snow, in that northern county, before its purity was dimmed by passing footsteps or the soft breathing of the thaw; at this season the frost seldom lasted long.

The ice on the pond below was covered with a soft white carpet; the trees in the clough, hooded like nuns, shook off, ever and anon as the March wind swept past, their heavy cowls; and, here and there, on the borders of the parterre, a timid spring flower peeped out through the snow.

"You are not going to ride to-day, Maud!" said her sister, turning from the window. "There is a strong wind, and the drifts will be deep in the valleys. I am glad we made our annual round of visits yesterday."

"Yes," said Miss Langdale, laying down her riding-hat and gloves, and joining her sister at the window. "The weather is not worse than it was when you objected to going out last Saturday. It was most fortunate I did not yield. I would not for worlds have missed the opportunity

of taking that pretty, delicate girl, home. Her parents
should be more careful.

Ellinor looked at her sister with surprise. Many a snow-
storm had whirled round her—many a hurricane had she
encountered on the plains and hills, darkness had fallen
upon her in the valley, without Maud's troubling herself to
send even a dog in search of her. The sudden outburst of
womanly tenderness was quite unusual.

"I wish, Maud, if you feel so kindly towards this young
girl, you would shew some sympathy with the rest of the
family! Her poor mother has been sinking gradually ever
since they came to live at Godley, and we have never sent
even a civil message of enquiry. I would have given much,
in the summer, to be allowed to take a basket of fruit, or
to send game in the winter to the invalid: but I fancied
your prejudice, against the whole family, was so inveterate
that I did not venture to propose the smallest act of neigh-
bourly kindness."

"My prejudice, as you call it, does not extend to Florence Langdale," said her sister, sternly. "I warn you,
Ellinor, that you have a formidable rival in that child."

Her sister's face flushed slightly as she answered. "Do
not sow enmity, Maud, in that poor but united household,
by instilling ambitious hopes in the mind of that young
girl. I confess that I like her less than her sisters. Her
face has not the same open expression. She is vain and
ambitious, if I am not mistaken, longing for luxuries and
splendour above her station."

"You are jealous, Ellinor," said Miss Langdale, "and
not without cause. That girl has, as you say, ambition
and vanity. She has also a strong character, and will one
day be a beautiful woman, worthy of wealth and station.
For that matter, she comes of a good stock, and has our

blood in her veins. Next to yourself, the Langdales of
Godley Grange are my nearest relatives; nay, perhaps,
nearer than we are to each other, since we are only sisters
on the father's side. Frank Lang, as he chooses to call
himself, is the grandson of my grandfather and grandmother."

"I am quite aware of it, Maud," said Ellinor, drawing
up her fair head haughtily. "To what end is this discussion?"

"To prepare you for what may happen, if you persist in
refusing the terms on which I offered to make you my
heiress," said Miss Langdale, impetuously. "I do not
wish this property to go away from the Langdales, but I
will not suffer a chance to exist, that I can prevent, of
Marina Lang's being ever mistress of Langdale Hall. If I
were to make the proposal to that girl which you, three
years ago, would not condescend to accept, Florence would
not reject it: and, ultimately, when I am in my grave, and
after her life tenure ceases, young Frederick Langdale,
against whom I entertain no rancour, would inherit all. I
am not old; but I want to put a life between me and him;
and that life shall not be his father's."

"Better at once leave the property to Frederick Langdale," said Ellinor. "I would far rather give up my
chance of inheritance to him than to his sister. What
heartburnings and jealousy it would cause! Her young
life would be blighted, as you wished mine to be; and he
might, probably would, waste his whole life in dreams of
hopes deferred. Maud, you are preparing misery for us all."

"No, Ellinor. It was your own romantic, unruly fancy
which made you reject real, tangible good for the sake of a
happiness which existed only in your imagination. As yet
you have never loved. Be warned in time. Take the gift

I am ready to give to-day—to-morrow it may not be in your power or mine to offer or to accept it."

"That must be as you please, Maud," said her sister, looking out over the snowy landscape, with eyes blinded by tears. "I may never love. I may never marry. The future lies in God's hand; but I will not bind myself by the conditions you impose."

"On your head be the consequences," said Miss Langdale, taking up her hat and gloves, and leaving the room, while Ellinor knelt down, laying her head on the oak wainscot, and crying like a child. What would the young, tender girl have given at that moment for the love of a living mother, for the protecting care of a father—that father and mother whom she faintly remembered the master and mistress of Langdale Hall,—where she now felt like an interloper!

Deeper and deeper fell the snow, drifting into the valleys and stopping all communication. For many days people were imprisoned in their houses, and then, with a burst of joy, Spring broke over the land. Brooks swelled into torrents with the melting of the snow; at the old Hall, at the head of the valley, the workmen were again engaged, mending the damage caused by the heavy floods that poured down from the high roofs and chimneys of the dwelling and out-offices; but the genial warmth and fresh winds soon dried up the deluge, and on the coping-stone corner of the old wall, wrapped in his blue roquelaure, the General sat, like "the monarch of all he surveyed," enjoying the April sunshine.

CHAPTER II.

A FAIR youth, staff in hand, was walking quickly through one of the romantic gorges which intersect the hills between Lancashire and Yorkshire. In summer, these rocky highlands are full of sunshine and beauty, whilst the melting of the winter snows, or the violent floods of rain which accompany the severe thunder storms which often break over them, convert the narrow valleys into channels for rushing, roaring torrents.

At the present moment the bed of the Calder was full, but not overflowing : birds were building in the tufted branches overhead, and the voices of the peasants, busy with their spring crops in every overhanging croft that would allow of cultivation, were borne upon the breeze that swept through the hawthorn and hazel bushes.

" When the trout darted and the pigeons cooed, humanity was sparse," says a clever modern writer. " Now it teems o'er dell and hill-side. Yet there is something more deserving admiration in Calder Dale now than formerly. There is token of prosperity, there is work for nimble fingers, work for active brains. Intelligence which before lay dormant has been elicited. Energy which before was undirected finds now a legitimate field for exercise." *

Centuries ago the traveller in these wild recesses of the hills, or on the moors above, might have been bewildered among winding paths through heathery wastes and tangled thickets—at a later date he would have found the people weaving and spinning in their own houses ; now the roar of factories fills the air, and mill after mill spans the stream

* "Through Flood and Flame."—By BARING GOULD.

6

and casts down, nightly, the reflection of its serried rows of
blazing windows into the water.

Just over the road a crag seemed to start out from a wall of
rock, like an eagle in the act of springing on its prey; whilst,
as if in contrast with the sublime features of the natural
landscape, a train rushed through the valley, filling it with
clouds of smoke; and the screech of the signal-whistle overpowered the sweet notes of the thrushes and blackbirds. A
large factory filled up all the space left by the railway, the
bridge over the river, and the road through the Eagle's Gorge.

Accustomed to the free range of wide domains where commerce has not laid her disfiguring touch—flinging the
smoke-wreaths of trade over the beautiful arches of Kirk-
stall, and blackening the glad rejoicing streams that rise to
the light of day only to fall back dimmed and polluted—
the young man looked angrily at the visible tokens of
industrious prosperity everywhere surrounding him: all
along the course of the river, mills, hamlets, and factories,
had sprung up. The water-privilege had been used and
abused to the fullest extent; and neither his age nor his
disposition prompted him to look for good under the unsightly mantle which had fallen upon a grand and beautiful
scene. Had it been Sunday, the atmosphere would have
regained its natural purity; or had he been wandering in the
lovely valley of the Riburn, the mills would have consumed
their own smoke; but, here, the wind, blowing from the
west, sent the smoke before it down the dale, and the sound
of the machinery at work echoed from the rocky overhanging
crags.

A great bell rang out suddenly, and the mills poured
forth their busy hands. In a moment the valley was full of
life—over the high bridge—along the winding road—here
pausing to gossip—there delaying to meet, or hurrying to

overtake some favourite companion—came pretty young girls with bright-coloured shawls drawn over their heads and pinned beneath their chins. For a moment, as, one after another, merry groups passed him, the youth thought there were some adjuncts of picturesque beauty in the workings of commerce.

When the mills stopped, the smoke for a while cleared off—the great piles of rock stood out against the clear sky —here and there a gleam of scarlet, crimson, purple, or magenta showed the presence of the mill-girls, returning homeward, to cottages clustered in the roughs above the wooded valley. The last faint gleam of colour died away— the last whirl of black smoke cleared off—the puff of the engine of the six o'clock train, with its curl of white vapour wound out of sight, and the youth for half-an-hour seemed to have the Eagle's Gorge to himself.

Fritz climbed up a steep path that led away from the dusty high-road, and cast himself down under a clump of trees. The first news of his mother's increased illness had brought him home;—away from his sporting friends—from his free life at the Chateau in Upper Austria, which was like home to him,—back to the narrow, circumscribed orbit of domestic life. He had unhesitatingly obeyed the summons, but now, though deeply thankful to find immediate cause for anxiety past, he liked Godley Grange less than ever.

His sisters were too much engaged in attending upon their mother, and in household matters, to be as constant and amusing companions as formerly. Gertrude, his especial favourite, now seldom left Mrs. Lang's room for more than an hour in the twilight, when Fritz usually took a little walk with her. The pale, patient girl will miss him this evening. He is miles away from home, lying in a lazy discontented mood under the birch trees at Todmorden!

Fritz was just beginning to think of his long walk home, when the last of the stragglers from the mill came, suddenly, round the corner of the rocky pathway towards him. A young, dark-haired girl, her bright locks covered by a Rob-Roy plaid, fastened under her chin with a Scottish pebble; her short black petticoat revealing small feet and delicate ankles. She stopped shyly for a moment on seeing a gentleman, then, modestly and quietly, passed on, with a slight respectful gesture, full of natural dignity.

The young man rose slowly after the girl had passed him, and followed her at a distance. He did not for a moment think of addressing her; for he was of a chivalrous disposition, and the girl's dress showed her to be of humbler station than his own; one to whom the open expression of his involuntary admiration would be insulting. Neither was there anything in her manner to encourage a stranger in taking a liberty. Still, almost unconsciously, he yielded to the desire of knowing whither her light, buoyant footsteps were carrying her. The path wound upward and onward through thickets of blackthorn and hazel, and larch, with tassels hanging from the boughs and bursting leaves; then it dipped down suddenly into an orchard full of budding blossoms, with the sweet scent of hidden violets perfuming the air, and banks starred with primroses.

Fritz wandered on, though he had lost sight of the bright shawl and black skirt,—past old crumbling walls of out-offices, fallen completely to decay, and overgrown with stonecrop and ivy,—till he came in sight of one of the few small, old stone Mansions which may still be found in that district.

The one in front of which he suddenly stopped, conscious that he was trespassing, was square-built and solid, with marks of wind and weather on its venerable front, which was mantled by a large-leaved creeper, framing in a bay-window and an escutcheon, beneath which was the date of the erection of the building.

Another long low window—with stone mullions and curious antique painted glass in the upper panes, whilst the lower ones were left clear—overlooked the gravelled court in front of the old house. The narrow casement between the deep mullions stood open, and Fritz saw the scarlethooded maiden gazing from it. An older female in black, with her hair drawn off her face under a white plaited muslin cap—evidently a widow—was standing in the doorway feeding poultry.

The low sunlight glanced on the bright wings of the fowls as they fluttered about, picking up their food. White pigeons came down from the roofs and settled on the woman's shoulder and sleeve, cooing, and receiving a portion of the banquet. Two little blue terriers with their long hair blown back and shining like silver, ran out barking at the stranger; as he stood still for a moment, admiring the pretty rural scene, and anxious to apologise for trespassing upon it.

"Bertina," said the woman at the door, looking up from satisfying her clamorous pensioners, "come out and tell the gentleman the way. I know nothing about this part of the country, sir; I never leave home from one year's end to another."

Her eyes filled with tears as she spoke, and she smoothed nervously the wide lappets of her cap hanging down over her black dress. The girl came forward bashfully, and stood in the ancient portal beside her. In feature and figure, making allowance for difference in age, the mother and daughter were very much alike.

"You must go back all the way, to where I saw you sitting under the birch trees," she said. "The road to the

station runs just below. I am sorry you did not ask me
when I passed you. It would have saved you the long
walk."

"Indeed I do not régret it," said Fritz. "I am a stranger
in this part of the country, and I have seen few quaint old
houses like yours. I hate these mills and factories, and the
ostentatious dwellings of the merchants and mill-owners;
and I regret the ruin which has fallen on the fine old houses
of the gentry of the West Riding. Yours is the only one I
have seen in good order, excepting, indeed, the one in which
my family have recently taken up their abode."

"We can scarcely call ourselves gentlefolks," said the
widow. "Come in, sir, if you like, and rest a while, and
see our old house. It *is* curious, and we try to keep it in
order, but it is a struggle. My daughter has a position of
responsibility at the Mill—though she is so young she is
steady enough to be one of the Overlookers—and she
manages to keep order among girls older and more unruly
than herself. I fancy it is often difficult, but she is too
good to worry me with complaints for which there is no re-
dress, since she cannot afford to give up her employment."

While she was speaking, the widow led the way indoors,
and into the principal sitting-room, the one looking out into
the court-yard. At the further end was a high chimney-
piece, curiously inlaid with foreign woods, and wide steps
on each side of the hearth. Above was the same date as
the one over the door, and a Latin inscription, with a coat
of arms.

"That is the crest of the Noels," said Fritz. "I have
seen it often in the old Hall, near my father's house, which
once belonged to that family, but is now utterly dilapidated."

"Yes," said the widow, while the colour, which seemed
to have utterly deserted it, suddenly flushed her pale face;

"this house still belongs to the Noels. It is pretty nearly all they have left. And this young girl, who has to work for her bread at the Mill in the valley, is Bertina Noel, the last of the race."

The young man, thoroughly aristocratic in his tastes, and rendered more so by association with the exclusive nobility of Austria and Bavaria, looked, with increased respect and admiration, at the descendant of the ruined Noels. The girl did not manifest as much emotion as her mother. She stood, calm, quiet, and dignified, in her virgin modesty, as though the innate loftiness and integrity of her character lifted her above worldly pride, and said, gently—

"Do not speak of that, mother. Since it is God's will that we should be poor, it is no degradation to work for our livelihood."

"God's will and man's wickedness," said the mother, with more anger and less resignation. "But the child is right, as she always is, for that matter; and I must ask you to forgive me, sir, for troubling a stranger like yourself with my woes. 'The heart knoweth its own bitterness,' and there are times when I think, 'no sorrow is like unto my sorrow,' but it passes off, and I remember that I have still many blessings to be thankful for. Bertina, fetch some milk, and a crust of the loaf. I have no wine to offer you, sir; but of such as we have you are most cordially welcome to partake. You must have had a long walk, if your house is anywhere near the old Hall."

Fritz willingly accepted the proffered hospitality, and thought that the cool sweet milk was like nectar, when handed to him by the pretty Overlooker at the Mill. The home-made loaf, set before him with some preserved strawberries, tasted deliciously, and the repast was one fit for the gods, with Hebe for their cup-bearer.

CHAPTER III.

THE pale blue sky was set thickly with stars, which, in the deepening twilight, shone forth more and more strongly, as Fritz retraced his way along the path towards the Factory. There was no gleam of scarlet, no light footstep now to lead him on; the road seemed much longer and duller than before.

At last he reached the spot above the river where he had cast himself down to rest; and, hurrying on, was just in time to catch the evening train to Hazeldon. The carriage into which he hastily leapt as the bell rang out, contained only one lady, and it was now getting so dark that he scarcely noticed whether she were old or young, plain or pretty. Most probably she was handsome and youthful, for her veil was drawn closely over her face.

One of those prolonged unearthly whistles, followed by short sharp shrieks, which often foretell danger, and always make timid hearts quail, caused the lady apparently some uneasiness. She put back her veil, and looked out of the window; but nothing was visible, excepting the sides of a deep excavation, a railway signalman flourishing a flag frantically, and clouds of escaping steam.

"We are all right," said Fritz, encouragingly. "There must have been some impediment on the line. The train does not usually stop here. Now we are off again," he added, as the line of carriages was again put in motion, slowly at first, then rushing at full speed through the darkness. "I do not think there is any cause for alarm."

The lady thanked him courteously. Something in the voice seemed familiar to his ear, and it was low and sweet.

Now that her veil was raised, and the lamp in the carriage burned more clearly, Fritz noticed a fair pale face, framed in by smooth bands of light hair; resting upon the sunny tresses were some blue flowers, corresponding with a muslin dress of the same colour.

He contrasted mentally the black hair and eyes and glowing complexion of Bertina Noel, the Overlooker at the Mill, with the blonde young lady, and decidedly preferred the warm, gipsey-like colouring, set off by the scarlet shawl and short black skirt, to the flowing draperies and forgetme-nots, which relieved becomingly the paler countenance of the refined looking girl sitting opposite to him in the railway carriage.

Though by no means conceited respecting his own appearance, Fritz could not help fancying, after a time, that the young lady bestowed some attention upon him. More than one furtive glance met his own, with a reflective, melancholy expression—and more than once his companion sighed audibly. At last, in a voice that trembled slightly, she said :—

" Are you not Mr. Frederick Langdale ?"

Fritz assented, and the young lady went on, speaking in somewhat tremulous accents,

" I have seen you in church with your sisters, and I longed to speak to you all, but I dared not. Everyone at Langdale knows me, and would have thought it strange,—might have mentioned it—in short, I dared not. But since accident has thrown us together, and you have been kind to me, I may venture to thank you otherwise than as a stranger. I am your cousin, Ellinor Langdale. It is not by my wish, nor is it my fault, that we are so completely estranged. I would give the world to know your mother and sisters ; but I have not the power—perhaps I have not strength of mind, to act

independently. Still, I should like your sisters to know that
I feel kindly towards them. I hope you find your mother
better than you expected? I was told in the village that
you had been suddenly summoned from abroad, during her
recent illness."

Fritz was somewhat embarrassed by the knowledge which
the young lady possessed of his proceedings, but she was
quite pretty and interesting enough to make him consider
the acquaintance desirable. The two young cousins shook
hands, and appeared to be as devoid of enmity and jealousy
as though no hopes of inheritance, no family prejudices,
existed to impair their friendship.

Fritz learned, during their short journey, that the younger
Miss Langdale had been spending the day with a school-
friend, whose father was the proprietor of the Mill where
Bertina Noel was employed. The beautiful scenery of the
Gorge supplied them with subjects for conversation, till the
train stopped. A carriage was waiting, and an elderly man-
servant, who had attended the young lady, came from the
other end of the platform to assist her out. Fritz, however,
performed that service. He perceived that the moment
Ellinor Langdale was under the surveillance of the sharp-
eyed domestic her manner changed; and, in obedience to
what he believed might be her wishes, young Langdale com-
ported himself as a perfect stranger might have done; handing
her out of the railway carriage and into her own equipage with
the most formal courtesy, and raising his cap silently and
respectfully, as he took leave of his timid and pretty travelling companion. More than once during the long walk
home, the carriage with the Langdale liveries overtook him,
after he had shortened the way by cutting off angles in the
winding road, and crossing fields and meadows, but he took
care not to look that way; uncertain whether any mark of

recognition would be bestowed upon him by its fair occupant, and unwilling to subject himself to an affront.

Gertrude and Frances were walking together in front of the old house at Godley, as he approached it. They ran to meet him. "How late you are, Fritz." "We have been half way to Hazeldon to meet you, but it became so dark we turned back." "Have you enjoyed yourself?" "How hungry you must be. Let us go in to supper."

These ejaculations, alternately uttered by the sisters, having been affectionately responded to, Fritz went indoors. He told them frankly of his meeting with the pretty young Miss Langdale in the train, and repeated her kind messages; but he did not say a single syllable respecting Bertina Noel and her widowed mother, nor acknowledge that he had been hospitably welcomed at the old stone Mansion in the Eagle's Gorge.

CHAPTER IV.

MR. LANG was spending one of the few holidays his busy life afforded, at home with his family; and amusing himself working in the large old-fashioned garden, which needed more hands to keep it in order than he could afford to pay; when Mr. Haywarden rode up the avenue, and, catching sight of him through the trees, threw the reins to his groom, after dismounting, and joined him.

The horses were led away to the stables, and the two gentlemen, who had been friends from their youth, walked up and down together. Mr. Haywarden, since Mr. Lang's return to England, had frequently ridden over to Godley, and it did not occur to Mr. Lang that his present visit was one of business rather than of pleasure.

Mrs. Lang, since the fine weather set in, had slightly improved in health, and the whole family were in better spirits. Fritz and his sisters were practising archery, excepting Florence, who was sitting with her mother.

Mr. Haywarden looked at the young people critically, made some good-humoured remarks on their proficiency, and then resumed his walk with his old friend, declining for the present to enter the house. "Upon my word, Lang, you have a goodly row of olive branches! what a splendid young fellow your son is—thoroughly English in spite of his foreign education," he said, as they turned away from the archery ground; "you have, I think, one other daughter whom I do not see now?"

"Flo is with her mother," said Mr. Lang. "We never leave her entirely alone, and the little one, as we call her, has been rather delicate since she was caught in a snow and hail storm last month. She is not at all like any of her sisters. Some people call her the handsomest of all my children, and yet they are, as you say, a goodly flock. I do not —I admire fair women. Florence is dark, like me."

"Well, I do not know that the resemblance would mar her prospects," said Mr. Haywarden, laughing, and glancing at the regular but now severe lineaments which he remembered well in their first youthful beauty, when Frank Langdale was the handsomest man of his acquaintance. "I confess I have a great desire to see your youngest daughter, Miss Florence."

"Oh, presently, presently will do," said Mr. Lang. "Don't tell her you think her a beauty, Haywarden; the little maid is vainer than her pretty grown-up sisters already, and much more forward than my little Saxon twins, perfect children

still, though they are four years older than Florence, who
has shot up suddenly almost into a woman. You will see
her when we go indoors to luncheon."

"I am afraid I cannot stay so long to-day," said the lawyer, looking at his watch. "Another time I shall be most
happy, but now I am limited to an hour, and we have some
business matters to discuss. Upon my word, Lang, I am at
a loss how to begin."

His friend looked at him with surprise. "It is the first
time I ever heard you confess yourself at fault, Haywarden.
What on earth are you come to propose? Anything new,
and, of course, disagreeable, on the part of my amiable
cousin at the hall?"

"I scarcely know how you will take it," said Mr. Haywarden. "Some persons might consider it a concession,—a
very fair offer—but I told Miss Langdale it was a proposal
I scarcely advised her to make. As usual, however, she
considers her own way the best, and chooses to take it."

Mr. Lang walked on silently for some moments. "Out
with it, man," he said at last. "Nothing pleasant ever came
to me from that quarter. Let me know the worst at once."

"It is rather a strange coincidence that you should have
mentioned the strong resemblance between yourself and
Miss Florence," said the lawyer, turning towards the house.
"I did not know that it existed, and I was just thinking
how singularly unlike you were to your other daughters and
to your son. If I were a believer in gossip, I should say
that it was this close resemblance between your youngest
child and yourself, which leads to the proposition I have to
make, on the part of the woman who is said never to have
forgotten or forgiven your preference of a fair-haired Saxon
beauty. Let us go indoors for half-an-hour. I am certain
I shall make myself more intelligible between four walls,

than among these flowers, and within sight of the young people and the targets."

Mr. Lang led the way at once to his own study, a rather dull room at the back of the house, looking into the avenue, and full of books and papers. Mr. Haywarden, with a sigh of relief, sat down with his back to the window.

"This will do," he said, taking up a paper-knife, and twisting it in his fingers. "A capital business room; nothing to distract one's attention from work. The fact is, Miss Langdale has taken a wonderful fancy to your youngest daughter. She wishes to leave her that life interest in the property which is at her disposal. Afterwards the estate would revert to yourself and your heirs."

"*After Florence?*" said Mr. Lang, opening his dark eyes wide in astonishment, whilst his cheek flushed angrily. "After the little one? I cannot understand your meaning."

"It is nevertheless very simple," said the lawyer, warming to the subject, now that he was no longer distracted by outward circumstances. "Miss Langdale has an undoubted right to bequeath a life interest in her large property to any person she may choose to select. In the present case her proceedings are less eccentric than usual, and will benefit your family considerably. Instead of the property going away from you all, as it might do, for an indefinite number of years, you will have the prospect of keeping it in your own family, and I am empowered to say you will have an immediate and not inconsiderable increase of income."

Mr. Lang remained silent for some minutes, and his friend took care not to interrupt his meditations.

"How can Miss Langdale reconcile to her own conscience such an injustice to her unoffending half-sister?" he said, at last.

"That is her own affair, not yours," said the lawyer.

" Miss Langdale affirms that she has offered to make her half-sister her heiress on certain conditions, which have been rejected. Perhaps this is an atonement for past injustice to the elder branch, on the part of your ancestor. She is quite free to act as she pleases, and Miss Ellinor Langdale is amply provided for, as she has her mother's fortune settled upon her—a large property at the other side of the county, in the North Riding. With regard to the estate in the Dale, of which we are speaking, Miss Ellinor is entirely and absolutely out of the question."

" I cannot accept favours from my cousin," said Mr. Lang, haughtily. " Had she treated me like a relation, my whole position might have been different. My wife's ill health may be attributed to inconveniences and hardships consequent upon a narrow income ; and, as you know, in every possible way Miss Langdale has circumscribed my powers, and refused to treat me as her heir-at-law, and nearest relation. I cannot bend to her now."

" Neither is there the slightest necessity to surrender one iota of your independence," said Mr. Haywarden, earnestly. Now that he was fairly under weigh, all the advantages of the offer he had made seemed to gather strength. " Lang, I know your character. I am aware that you have strong, perhaps well-founded, prejudices against Miss Langdale. But in this matter, I confess, I think she is willing to act most generously. If you continue in charge of Miss Florence, a large annual sum will be allowed to be spent, exactly as you desire, for the purpose of her future maintenance and education. If you decline these terms, Miss Langdale wishes me to say that she will adopt the young lady herself, and bring her up in a manner suitable to her position."

A brief sharp ejaculation, that sounded like a cry of bodily pain, burst from the father's lips.

" She would rob us of our child !" he said. " Haywarden,
if *I* were to consent, this would be Marina's death-stroke !"

" Nay, nay ; you take it too strongly. Mrs. Lang would
see the immense benefits to be derived from this proposition," said Mr Haywarden. " If you dislike one course,
another lies open to you. Certainly it would be hard to
deprive Mrs. Lang of her daughter, though you have a large
—rather a trying family. Many parents would rejoice in
having one girl out of five handsomely provided for."

" The seeds of dissension are easily sown. Maud Langdale will take care that we reap the crop," said Mr. Lang,
bitterly. " You must let me think the matter over, Haywarden, and consult with my wife. What time is allowed
us for deliberation ?"

" Oh, there was no limit mentioned," said Mr. Haywarden, rising. " Take time, by all means. I have set down
on this paper the exact terms of Miss Langdale's proposal,
and I will leave it with you. I cannot help thinking the
more you reflect upon it, the more you will realise that her
scheme has its advantages, and very strong recommendations."

He shook hands with his friend, and, without repeating
his request to be introduced to the young girl, who had suddenly become an important personage in his eyes, Mr. Haywarden mounted his horse, and rode away.

There was no more work done in the garden that day by
the master of Godley. He sat in his dull study, alone and
unoccupied, the rest of the morning ; hearing, occasionally,
the voices of the young people, as they passed in and
out of the house, but not attending to them. The iron had
entered into his very soul, and he shrank from inflicting the
same pain upon his suffering wife : yet he knew that he could
not come to any conclusion without consulting her.

Willingly, most willingly, would he have left the inherit
ance of the Langdales in its present vague ‚uncomfortable
state, and worked night and day to keep his family independent. It was true the struggle was a wearing one, but
at present they were all, as he believed, united in heart and
mind—poor, but well satisfied. He did not suspect that
already, without his consent or knowledge, the thin edge
of the wedge had been inserted; and that it was even now
beyond his power to keep the crack from widening through
which jealousy and discontent might, ere long, find entrance
into his quiet home.

CHAPTER IV.

"Come nearer to me, Florence. Why do you keep so far
away? Where is the little chair you used to draw close to
my knee?" said Mrs. Lang, that same fine spring afternoon,
to "the little one," as she sat somewhat sadly by the fire-
side.

The windows of the invalid's room were open, and all
sorts of cheerful sounds, the notes of birds, the hum of
voices, came in with the soft westerly breeze.

Florence obeyed her mother listlessly. "Are you cold,
darling?" said Mrs. Lang, tenderly putting over her shoulders
one of the numerous wraps laid on the sofa. "The sun is
warmer than the fire on a day like this. I do not think you
have been quite yourself since the day of the snow-storm.
Ring for Meredith to bring her work and sit with me if you
like to go to your sisters. I hear their voices, and the
arrows striking the targets. It is a shame to keep you a
prisoner on such a lovely day."

7

"No, thank you, mamma; I would rather stay here till Gertrude comes in," said Florence. "Fritz begged her to come and shoot with him. They do not want me."

"That is a silly fancy, Flo. Your sisters and Fritz always like to have you with them. He and Gertrude shoot more equally, but there is room for you at the other targets. I can quite well spare you."

"No, no, please let me stay with you," said Flo, laying her head down on the invalid's couch, close to which she had now drawn a high footstool. "There is a gentleman in the garden with papa."

"I thought I heard a stranger's voice," said Mrs. Lang; "stay here by all means, if you like it best, my love; I am always glad to hear you say that you wish to be with me, but I should be sorry to keep you an unwilling prisoner. Do you know who it is that I hear talking to your father?"

"Yes," said Flo, colouring, "it is Mr. Haywarden, the lawyer, from Hazeldon."

"I remember him years ago, but he is too busy now to come often to Godley. Have you seen him lately?—How came you to know his voice so well?" said Mrs. Lang, with some surprise.

Flo did not answer. Mrs. Lang put her hand affectionately round the young girl's neck. As she did so, Florence suddenly burst into tears. "What is the matter, my darling?" said her mother, tenderly caressing her. "I am not angry; there was no harm in what you said. Why are you crying?"

Florence was quite unable to speak. Mrs. Lang drew the slender girl within her arms, and soothed her passionate grief. "Never mind answering me, love, it is of no consequence," she said, mixing for her from one of the small phials and a decanter close at hand, a little salvolatile and water. " I know you were not well this afternoon; lie still, and do not attempt to talk. You will feel better presently."

Florence took her advice and lay quietly beside her, her cheeks flushed with emotion, her dark eyes full of tears. Mother and daughter were thus found lying together on the invalid couch, when Mr. Lang entered the room.

He looked at them fixedly. "Is Florence ill, Marina? What has she been saying to you?"

" She is not quite well this afternoon," said her mother, tenderly. "Something has troubled her. I scarcely know what it is, but she will be better out of doors. Go, darling," she said, tenderly kissing her, " your father is come to stay with me for a little while. Go and enjoy yourself in the garden with your sisters."

Florence had turned pale at sight of her father's grave countenance. She slid down from the sofa, after kissing her mother, and stole quietly away. Mr. Lang did not speak until the last sound of her footsteps died out of hearing. In truth he knew not how to begin, and the sight of the mother and her youngest born, with their arms interlaced, had not made his task more easy.

"You have had a visitor;" his wife said cheerfully; " Flo told me you were talking to Mr. Haywarden in the garden. What brought him to Godley?"

Mr. Lang still hesitated. "He came on business—nothing pleasant—business seldom is agreeable. I could not persuade him to stay for luncheon."

" I hope it was nothing very serious," said his wife, alarmed at his grave accent. " Nothing wrong at the office. Oh, Frank, tell me at once. What has vexed you?"

" No; there is nothing wrong at the office," said Mr. Lang, slowly, anxious to give his wife time for preparation. " All my annoyances come from the same quarter. Hay-

7—2

warden brought me a message from my cousin, Maud Langdale."

"From Miss Langdale! Does she wish for a reconciliation? I thought she must unbend at last," said Mrs. Lang. "Oh, Frank, though it is very bitter to make any concession to that hard haughty woman; sometimes, for her own sake, and for the sake of the children, I feel tempted to ask you to overlook the past and forgive her. She is so utterly lonely."

"Yes, she feels that at last," said Mr. Lang, "she is very lonely. I fancy there has been some disagreement between her and her half sister. Ellinor Langdale has given mortal offence by rebelling against her arbitrary temper. She is set aside from the succession to the Langdale property."

"That is very hard upon her," said Mrs. Lang, compassionately; without, however, seeing that this fresh eccentricity on the part of the owner of Langdale Hall called for any peculiar mark of indignation on her part. "But after all, Frank, *you* are Miss Langdale's heir-at-law. Your parents ought to have inherited Langdale. If she restores the right order of succession at last, as Miss Ellinor Langdale is well provided for, I do not see that we of all people need complain. You see I am leaping to a conclusion like a very woman; but since you say she has made some overtures to you, I cannot imagine that she means to leave the life interest in the property to a stranger."

"No, Marina, it is not to a stranger, neither is it to me, the rightful heir, nor to Fritz, that my cousin Maud wishes to leave the life interest in the property," said Mr. Lang. "Both these courses I have often foreseen, and considered what would be the result: but the plan submitted to my consideration now, by Mr. Haywarden, never entered into my mind."

" Did the child know what he came to propose ?" said Mrs. Lang, sharply, her woman's instinct prompting the conclusion, that in some mysterious way, Florence was connected with this question, though she was far from guessing its nature.

" Florence ! what made you think so ?" said Mr. Lang, in an agitated voice. " I hope not, I think not : surely even Maud Langdale would not tamper with her—with that young creature—before consulting me ; and yet who can tell what course a jealous vindictive woman will pursue ? Marina, this rich, childless woman has cast a covetous glance upon our darling—upon our little ewe lamb. Must we give her up ? Haywarden thinks me a fool for hesitating. Miss Langdale wishes to adopt Florence, and to bring her up as the heiress of Langdale. If I consent, she will not object to my becoming, after her own death, protector of the estate, which, ultimately, will be, when she can no longer prevent it, at the expiration of the life interest, mine or my son's ; but can we any of us look forward so far ? What will be Fritz's feelings ? He has counted more on these expectations than I have ever done. It will be a dreadful disappointment."

Mrs. Lang listened to her husband with dismay. " Fritz will indeed be deeply wounded," he went on. " The worst of this trial is, that I dread the effect it may have on the dispositions of our children. Hitherto the struggle has been ours. Must we tell Florence ?"

" Are you sure she does not know it already ?" said the mother, more calmly than her husband expected. "She has been crying, because I startled her by asking how she knew that it was Mr. Haywarden who was with you in the garden. She could not answer me. For some time she has been mysteriously agitated, and she has always had a

great liking for Miss Langdale. I fear that our haughty
neighbour, though she has not condescended to notice us,
has won our child's affections. Ever since she met Flo at
the Crags, the child has been possessed by a strange love
for this cold, hard woman. Of late she has been much
changed. I am afraid hidden influences have been at work."

Mr. Langdale got up and began walking up and down
the room, striving vainly to subdue his irritation. "I believe you may be right, Marina, and that the mischief is
done. Dr. Forsyth dropped a hint the other day about
Florence's wonderful power of keeping a secret. I thought
him in joke, but I believe now he spoke in earnest. Miss
Langdale must have seen and spoken to her oftener than
we have any idea of, to have formed this plan. Not one
of the other children ever kept back a thought from us,
but Florence has a shy, proud, inscrutable nature, which
has been proof against even your tenderness and integrity.
She is, after all, a Langdale, and will have her own way."

"Do not be hasty," said Mrs. Lang, while her soft eyes
filled with tears, as, worn and weary, she lay back on her
couch. "Florence is of a different disposition to her sisters,
and you have never understood her so well, but I have
great confidence in her affection. Leave me to deal with
her to-morrow, when we have thoroughly mastered all the
circumstances of the case. It would not be fair to leave
her in ignorance of the brilliant destiny offered to her; but
t is quite possible that she may prefer a more lowly one
rather than be separated from her family."

"There is another alternative, Marian," said Mr. Lang,
placing in his wife's hands the paper Mr. Haywarden had
left with him. "Florence may be Miss Langdale's heiress
without leaving her home; but, I confess, I do not think
that plan would answer. There would be heartburning

between her and her brother and sisters, if the youngest were suddenly to be placed in such a different position. Fritz, I am certain, would never submit to it. I am of opinion that it would be far better, if we can but all agree upon the matter, to reject this insidious proposal altogether, than to agree to it in part."

Mrs. Lang sighed deeply.

"Let us think it over till to-morrow, and then consult the young people," she said. "After all, they are none of them children, and they are more interested in the matter than we are. Their fresh feelings may teach us sorrowful worldlings, lessons of wisdom. What can Flo know about the advantages of wealth and station?"

"If they would but listen to you," said her husband, tenderly embracing her. "The world has not laid a speck on the fair truthfulness which first won my love. I only hope 'the little one' may prove as pure-minded and disinterested at fifteen, as her mother is still."

The entrance of Meredith interrupted the conversation, and Mr. Lang went down stairs. Perhaps Mrs. Lang would have questioned the attendant, who was often Florence's companion in her walks, but the young girl crept in after her with a bunch of violets, which she laid silently in her mother's lap.

Florence still looked flushed, but her manner was more composed. She waited affectionately upon her mother, after the servant left the room, with more of her old coaxing, caressing affection than she had of late exhibited. Her dark eyes were full of tears, and Mrs. Lang felt as if a spell was laid upon her, and that she could not disturb the serenity of the hour; as the long shadows fell across the lawn, and the birds thronged on the window-ledge, where Florence was accustomed to feed them, before they went to roost.

CHAPTER VI.

LANGDALE HALL had never looked more beautiful in the eyes of its haughty mistress than it did on the day when she expected her cousin's answer to the proposal that she should make his youngest child her heiress. The old thorn-trees in the park were covered with blossom, and the bright tender spring green enlivened what sometimes was a sombre prospect.

Masses of flowering shrubs, white and coloured lilacs, laburnums, guelder-roses, azaleas, gold-tinted and white, filled up the angles of the stone terrace, or streamed over the dusky balustrades—shrubs which had grown into a magnitude never seen except in the vicinity of some time-honoured mansion, where they have been carefully cultured and yet have attained freedom and dignity which emulate nature. The sweet notes of the singing birds,—of the cuckoo by day and the nightingale at night,—made the old place resonant of music, whilst the flowers filled the clear air with fragrance, and decked the dark rich soil of the recently upturned beds and borders. Up and down the garden walks, under the arches of lilac and syringa, through the hawthorn-scented glades of the park, Miss Langdale wandered restlessly. There was an unwonted light in her dark eyes, a flush on her usually pale cheek, which showed that the woman's heart was strangely moved. Contrary to her usual custom she found no fault, and her whole soul seemed alive to the beauty of the scene and of the day. She had ordered Christobel back to the stable, and seemed for once satisfied that no place on earth could be more like Paradise than the home appointed for her.

Ellinor Langdale, on the other hand, was depressed and unsatisfied. The air, laden with perfume, bewildered her; and she shrank from meeting her half-sister, as she had done twice, unexpectedly,—wandering restlessly to and fro, with that flush of excitement on her face. Though unacquainted with the exact nature of the steps Miss Langdale had taken, Ellinor knew that a crisis was impending.

Very little had been said on either side since Ellinor had rejected the conditions offered by her elder sister. Mr. Haywarden had been summoned, and, on his departure, he had spoken a few kindly words, expressive of regret, at the decision which had robbed her of a rich inheritance, but he had not argued with her. Evidently he considered that the time for consideration was over. Now, as Ellinor Langdale looked from her own window over the beautiful garden and wide-spread park, and caught, ever and anon, through the spring green of the foliage, a glimpse of the dark cloth dress of the mistress of the domain, as she hurried along the winding walks, she knew that the wilful woman had in her own wayward pride cut her off from what she had from childhood been taught to regard as her inheritance.

Over and over again Miss Langdale had declared that she should never marry, and urged Ellinor to take a more active part in the superintendence of the property; and, although the younger woman knew better than to oppose her will even in trifles, she had grown up in the firm belief that Langdale Hall would (if she survived its present possessor) eventually be her own.

It was impossible not to regret the change which was impending, although it was with no covetous thoughts that Ellinor contemplated the future. Her own home in the

North Riding situated on a bleak sea coast, was quite unfamiliar to her. The place had been let on lease to strangers, and she had never seen it, or thought of residing there; the tenure would expire in less than a year, but, until the last few weeks, she had been willing to renew it. Now the first exercise of womanly authority she had ever put forth without consulting her sister, had been to give notice, through Mr. Haywarden, to her tenants, that she required them to leave Moriscombe at the end of six months.

The thoughts that filled her eyes with tears and her heart with sadness were connected with the rupture of the many ties which bound her to the home of her infancy. Come what might, Langdale could never again be to her the safe refuge—the untroubled sanctuary—which home, whatever joys may be outside its walls, should be to the young.

In all her restless wanderings that day, Maud had never gone beyond the sound of the great entrance bell. Now, when it rang out sharply, she stopped short—the unwonted colour faded from her cheeks—in a moment she turned deadly pale, faint and sick. Could it be that her hopes were to be disappointed? That the girl's hand would never pluck the spring flowers—the girl's feet never wander over the blooming sward? The gardeners had been forbidden, for the first time, to put their scythes to the lawn, where the orchises were sending up spikes of purple blossom. Miss Langdale had seen Florence gathering them, as a child, on the edge of the park, and fancied she would like to see them flourishing; or that she might sorrow if they were humiliated, swept away, and forgotten—cut down in the height of their glory?

It was the first doubt of success which had assailed her; and the proud woman thrust it away from her. Was it likely that Frank Lang, as he chose to call himself, would hesitate? The only doubt was whether he and his Marina would give up their child—as she hoped and wished—entirely to her. Florence, she felt convinced, would be as glad of the change to affluence and independence, as herself.

Maud walked slowly to the house after this momentary struggle with her feelings. She did not cast another glance at the shrubs and flowers—all the beauties of the Garden of Eden would have been lost upon her. Her whole nature was strung up to meet the crisis. Perhaps the woman's fate, for good or evil, might hang upon the turn of a die!

Mr. Haywarden, anticipating her impatience, and having learnt from the servants that their mistress was in the flower-garden, came to meet Miss Langdale on the terrace. The pale girl at her high window could see the two dark figures walking backwards and forwards, though she did not hear their words. The lawyer's tones were always low and measured—Miss Langdale's rather loud, clear accents were subdued by strong inward feeling.

Calm and cool as Mr. Haywarden usually was, he dreaded this interview. He knew Maud Langdale better than most men; and his step was slow as he crossed the grass in front of the windows of the Hall, and advanced along the wide gravelled terrace to meet her.

"How slowly you walk—I thought you were never coming!" the lady said, quickening her own steps. "You do not look like a messenger of good tidings."

"I have, I assure you, done my best. It never was my fault to be lukewarm or dilatory; and no one can fail to see the immense advantage to Frank Lang of the plan you propose;" said the lawyer, standing still for a moment beside her. "Unfortunately, he cannot see the matter as plainly as I do."

"You do not mean that he is fool enough to refuse my

offer, said Miss Langdale. "He must be a madman. What right has he to say that I shall not do what I like with my own?"

"That point is of course open for your own decision," said Mr. Haywarden. "All that Mr. Lang can do is to reject your kind offers; both as regards your adoption of his daughter, or your appropriating an annual sum for her maintenance and education whilst she remains under his roof. He says he will have nothing whatever to do with this scheme, and that he hopes you will alter your mind about the disposal of your life-interest in the property."

"He does not know me as well as you, or the meanest hind on the estate, do, or he would not think it," said Miss Langdale, all the softness dying out of her countenance and her voice. "Did you tell him I was not one given to change?"

"Yes," said Mr. Haywarden. "I said so, but he only replied—'Tell my cousin, Maud Langdale, that I am as firm as herself. Nothing she can say or do will alter my resolution.'"

Miss Langdale remained still and silent for some moments. Mr. Haywarden did not interrupt her meditations.

"And the child—" she said at last, her voice breaking as she spoke—"Florence!—Is she to have no voice in this question? she whom it most vitally concerns! Are all her future prospects to be obscured and blighted by her father's dogged obstinacy?"

"Miss Florence is at present a minor—under her father's control," said Mr. Haywarden. "I understand it to be her wish to remain at Godley, and to submit entirely to the wishes of her parents."

"Ah, you do not speak so confidently," said Miss Langdale quickly, while a burning flush rose to her cheek.

"This man has no right to destroy his child's future. Florence is old enough to think and to feel—to know the difference between wealth and poverty, luxury and a narrow competence. If she has consented to throw me over, it is under compulsion. Her father and mother,—Marina was always artful—have over-persuaded or frightened her. I will not take their answer."

"Miss Florence Langdale," said the lawyer, unconsciously giving her the family name which her father had relinquished, "was not well enough to see me this morning. I cannot speak from my own observation; but her father said the whole family were of one opinion as to the undesirability of accepting either of your propositions. His great fear is, that by placing his youngest child in such a position, dissension might be caused; and he hopes that you will not be tempted to throw such a fire-brand into his hitherto peaceful circle. That was his own expression, though he did not exactly tell me to repeat it to you."

"He is afraid of me," said Miss Langdale. "His nest is straw-thatched, and will ignite easily! That is his look out. He might have made a friend of me easily, if he had chosen, but, if he prefers to have me for an enemy, he must take care of his own property. Let him look out for sparks! Impossible to say where or when they may fall. His mercantile avocations must have taught him to warehouse his goods safely, and insure them sufficiently. Well—I will think it over, and let you know my intentions."

Mr. Haywarden was somewhat relieved by her apparent calmness. He had seen her more chafed outwardly, by a branch lopped off in an unsightly manner, or an injudiciously felled tree. He bade her good day; and, remounting his horse, rode down the long avenue, thankful that his morning's work was over.

Miss Langdale stood still, on the spot where he had left her, looking over the valley. The landscape in its lovely spring green, was as blooming as ever; the birds sang as sweetly, but she neither saw nor heard the sweet sights and minstrelsy. If a torrent had rushed along the vale she would have been equally insensible. The heart within her seemed suddenly turned to stone. All the sweet impulses, which the thought of the young life she wished to bind in with her own had called forth, were at once summarily blighted. She stamped upon the blooming orchises furiously, as she strode across the grass, desiring one of the gardeners whom she encountered to have the grass mown immediately, and commenting severely on the untidy appearance of the daisy-enamelled, purple-streaked mead; though it had been kept unshorn by her orders.

A wild turmoil of vengeful memories, of mortified hopes and unruly passions, woke up in Maud's ill-regulated heart and mind. Foremost of all was a proud selfish satisfaction, in the thought that her cousin feared her influence with Florence. After all, the contest was not over. It had as yet scarcely begun; and it remained to be proved, whether the man's firm authority, and the mother's love, would win the victory over a wilful woman's wayward will.

CHAPTER VII.

MRS. LANG reproached herself bitterly for the relaxation of her former watchfulness, which had made it possible for Florence to grow up in a realm of fancy, to which even her mother had not found entrance. In the tortures of her self-reproach, when questioned by her parents as to her intimacy with Miss Langdale, Florence had confessed that,

over and over again, with Meredith's concurrence, she had
transgressed their orders, and crossed the prohibited boun-
daries of the Langdale property. It was true that she had
never actually visited the Hall. Meredith had made a sort
of compromise with her conscience, by stopping at the
pretty Lodge which gave entrance to the Park ; but there,
and at the old Hall of the Noels, and at other trysting
places, the great lady had meanly condescended to meet
them—had flattered, and praised, and caressed the vain
little daughter of Eve, whom she was trying to win over,
by artful gifts and lavish promises, to enliven her more
splendid but desolate home.

Awakened, as if from a dream, by her father's anger and
her mother's grief, Florence cordially united with them
in repudiating the thought of a final separation. Mr. Lang
had made up his mind, before submitting Miss Langdale's
proposals to her consideration, that, if Florence chose to
profit by them, it must be at the cost of leaving her home.
Nothing would induce him to consent to receive the offered
allowance, nor to sanction what he regarded as an act of injustice. If Florence elected to be Miss Langdale's heiress,
she must resign her own family ties, and abide altogether
with her.

It needed only one look in her mother's pale, tear-stained
face, to decide the affectionate, though erring, girl's choice.
Florence threw her arms round Mrs. Lang's neck, and positively refused to leave her. The mother and daughter clung
to each other, in an embrace which seemed as if it would
last for ever.

The only plea she made was that her attendant should be
forgiven. Meredith had such a reverence for the Langdales,
that it seemed almost like sacrilege to disobey the arbitrary
woman who was the representative of her master's family.

Gratitude for her faithful service to herself made Mrs. Lang
support her daughter's petition. Her husband gave way reluctantly, and on condition that the waiting-woman should
attend only on her mistress for the future, and that she
should have no control over, and no connection with, the
young people.

After this point was settled, by common consent the subject was dropped; and the family at the Grange became, to
all appearance, the same happy and united household as of
yore.

The first disturbance of this blessed tranquillity came, as
might have been expected, from the direction of the grey
turrets of the old Hall. Miss Langdale sent a formal intimation to her cousin, through the medium of Mr. Haywarden,
that she had altered her will; and that she had left the life
interest in the Langdale estate, of which she had the disposal, to Miss Florence Langdale. Should her father see fit
to reconsider his harsh resolution, the allowance she wished
to make for her young cousin's maintenance and education
should be paid into his banker's hands; or, if he preferred
it, Miss Langdale would at any time be willing, and happy,
to receive its future mistress as a permanent inmate of
Langdale Hall.

Many an anxious deliberation ensued between the husband and wife, before the contents of Mr. Haywarden's
letter were submitted to the young people; but, on the
whole, it seemed best and wisest that the family should be
informed by their parents of circumstances which otherwise
might be learnt by chance. Miss Langdale was not likely
to observe secrecy respecting the fresh disposition she had
made of her property; and the subject would be freely and
widely canvassed.

Florence did not speak when her mother told her of the

change effected in her prospects, warning her, at the same time that, from a person so eccentric as Miss Langdale, constancy was not to be expected ; and that it would be in her power to alter the present arrangement if she wearied of it, after finding that it did not give her access to Florence's society. The mother saw the large dark eyes fill slowly with tears, and wondered what were the thoughts that made the deep waters rise; but Florence silently kissed her and went away. Fritz, on the contrary, flew into a violent passion, vowing that the matter was decided in a way which injured everyone and benefited nobody. Perhaps, in a worldly point of view, he was not absolutely wrong, but his father remained fixed and firm.

After the first turbulent emotion aroused by Mr. Haywarden's communication had subsided, Fritz manifested a steadiness of purpose which hitherto had been deficient in his character. He had always shown a taste for mechanical science, and he now announced his intention of becoming a civil engineer.

Preparations for his leaving home to devote himself to study were immediately commenced. Only Mrs. Lang detected a shade of bitterness in Fritz's raillery when he found his sisters, as usual, busily occupied with his outfit. Florence was too great a lady now, he said, to be set to mend and make shirts and collars. It was, perhaps, scarcely in human nature that Fritz should not, for a time at least, feel some jealousy regarding the youthful heiress of Langdale.

8

CHAPTER VIII.

ELLINOR Langdale had exerted the independence, which her rejection of Maud's proposal had won for her, to make the acquaintance of Mrs. Lang, and now frequently spent an hour with the invalid. Maud acquiesced in the change silently. She was wise enough not to murmur when the conviction first dawned upon her that her half-sister, if not likely to be her successor at the Hall, was no longer inclined to be her slave.

For the present Ellinor agreed to remain at Langdale, but preparations were going on at the mansion in the North Riding for the reception of its mistress, whenever circumstances arose which might render it more agreeable for her to dwell in a house of her own.

A great regard had sprung up already between Ellinor and Gertrude Lang. Fritz was very proud of having brought about this intimacy, and quite disposed to share in it. Mrs. Lang's improved health, and Florence's constant companionship, enabled her to dispense, more than had been the case for years, with Gertrude's affectionate attendance ; and the three cousins took many pleasant excursions together among the lovely cloughs and carrs, and in the valleys of the Calder, the Hebdon, the Ryburn, and the Hebble.

Gertrude Lang was interested especially in the great manufactures and prosperous industry of the North. The voices of the mill-girls, as they sang at their work, stirred her heart deeply. Her own sweet yet practical disposition made her long to be of service, and many of the young girls of the neighbourhood came to her for instruction, after the hours of labour.

This interest seemed strange to the prosperous girl, who had been too much accustomed to see the daily routine of trade for any strong impressions to be roused by it. Ellinor constantly declared that she could take part in the joys and sorrows of cottage life, but not in the more bustling existence of the mill-hands and factory-girls; whilst Gertrude, to whom all was fresh and untried, longed to pour light into the dark corners of the city, or the crowded, whirring, whirling, perilous, often unhealthy structures, filled with the clang and clamour of machinery, the heat of steam, and heavy odours. Never did the fair girl pass under the tall buildings, with rows upon rows of windows, from which issued the beat and tramp of the ceaselessly-pulsing engines; and hear, high above all, the shrill clear voices of the girls singing at their monotonous work, without longing to befriend them. Her simple training in Germany—her own life of constant quiet usefulness and self-sacrifice—her knowledge of sickness and suffering, and their best alleviations—soon made her acquainted with the wants of her humble neighbours. If a man met with an accident, or a child was injured by the machinery, the parents came to Gertrude for help, counsel, and sympathy. She knew more about the troubles and calamities, incidental to the mechanical existence of the poor people among whom she had recently been planted, than Ellinor; although the young lady at the Hall had led the choir in Langdale Church, and distributed charities among the villagers, since her childhood.

Ellinor, nevertheless, felt no jealousy of her new friend. She acknowledged, at once, the superiority of Gertrude's practical knowledge of the best modes of alleviating human suffering, and the two girls often visited the sick and poor together. Ellinor's well-filled purse was open to every call upon her benevolence; and she learned, while bestowing

8—2

lavish alms, that her friend, poor as she was in worldly goods, yet had at her disposal gifts which wealth could not bestow, and even heavenly-minded charity like her own could not supply—the power of entering fully and completely into the minds and wants of others, inferior to themselves in station.

Arrangements had been made that Ellinor and Gertrude should visit together, under Fritz's escort, the week before he left home, the great Mill in the Eagle's Gorge. The owner, a friend of the Miss Langdales, whose daughter had been for a time at school with Ellinor, showed them the whole of the vast establishment. Gertrude's intelligent interest pleased him, and he paid her particular attention; affording all the information in his power, and keeping close beside her, as they moved from room to room; with the busy wheels and beating hammers plying incessantly.

Fritz coloured deeply, and respectfully lifted his hat, as they entered a long room, where a number of girls were at work, under the charge of one, younger than most of them, who acted as overlooker.

Ellinor Langdale glanced at him quickly, and then at the lovely young woman who quietly and gravely returned his salutation. The owner of the Mill, meanwhile, said to Gertrude, "Miss Noel will explain this part of the operation to you. This is all women's work, as you see, and she has the entire charge of this room. Excuse me for a moment, whilst I give an order. I shall be back directly."

He said a few words in an undertone to Bertina, treating her with marked respect; and left the room for the purpose of obtaining specimens of the fabric they had seen in the process of manufacture, to give to the two ladies.

Gertrude looked with much interest at the young girl, about her own age, who seemed to occupy such a responsible

position. In some respects the occupation struck her as not
being altogether disagreeable. The long rows of bobbins
were set in motion, or stayed in a moment, at her will; as
she explained clearly the part of the process which went on
in this room. A slight sign of disapproval on the part of
the young monitress, checked the inclination among her
subordinates to talk together and look at the visitors. In
one corner was a small table, on which stood account books,
ledgers, and an inkstand. A volume that looked like
poetry was carelessly laid down. Gertrude, as she passed
close by, saw that it was " The Lord of the Isles," and a
marker showed where the reader had left off on their entrance. Over the table, on a hook, hung a shawl of Rob-
Roy Tartan, the same Fritz had followed through the wind-
ings of the gorge. His heart beat a little more quickly as he
recognised it. Bertina Noel's dress was black, slightly relieved by a simple collar and cuffs of snow-white linen.
Over the heads of some of the workwomen, against the wall,
hung similar shawls, bonnets not being allowed in the mills.
All sorts of colours, patterns, and textures might be seen.
The only difference was that Bertina's shawl was larger and
softer than the rest.

Not one syllable was exchanged between Fritz Langdale
and Bertina Noel. The young man saw that she did not
wish him to address her; and, beyond the slight salutation
on his first entrance, he did not venture upon any mark of
recognition. Bertina explained quickly to the two young
ladies all that was necessary, and then returned to her usual
station. Gertrude, full of interest in the beautiful girl,
could not help following her. Ellinor, on the contrary, paid
less attention than usual to this part of the labour, and wondered audibly why they were left in this room so long, when
there was so little to be seen there. She turned her back on

the workwomen and winding bobbins, and stood close to the
open door, complaining to Fritz of the noise and heat.

"You are sufficiently accustomed to these sounds not to
be disturbed by them in your reading," said Gertrude,
touching the book that lay on the table close to Bertina's
chair. "I see you love poetry, and of the best description.
What a comfort you must find in it here!"

"Yes," said Bertina, lifting her large dark eyes gratefully
to the fair face of Gertrude Lang. "It makes me forget
much that is painful, and soothes many discordances. I am
so accustomed to reading poetry here, that the noise of the
machinery, which that young lady dislikes so much, seems to
me rather a pleasant accompaniment—like the sound of running water."

"That shows you have a poetical imagination," said Gertrude, smiling. "Sir Walter Scott, or any true and good
poet, would be glad to be so appreciated. But you are
very young to be so much trusted. How long have you held
this position?"

"Three years," said Bertina. "Since I was seventeen.
I am older than I seem, and I am much older in disposition
than my actual years. My mother is more impetuous; she
says that she is more of a child still, in many respects, than I
have ever been."

The girl sighed deeply. An early acquaintance with
sorrow had aged her prematurely. Gertrude, whose young
life had been clouded by anxiety for her mother, felt deeply
interested,

"I wish that we lived nearer to each other," she said.
"Even as it is I could send you some books, and, if you
will permit me, I should like to see your home and your
mother. My brother and I sometimes come to this pretty
lace by train. Will you tell me where you live?"

"If you ask for Bertina Noel, any one in the town will tell you the way to our old house in the Gorge. That gentleman—I am sure by the likeness that he is your brother—once found, or rather, lost his way, and came there," said the young overlooker, colouring as she glanced shily at Fritz, who was standing just outside the door, conversing with Miss Langdale. "Ours is a curious old house. There are not many like it now in this part of the country. My mother will be very glad to see you there, even if I am not at home. I am at the mill all day, but, after six o'clock, I am always with her."

Gertrude renewed her promise of visiting the young girl, and then rejoined the party, and completed her round of inspection. The deep Gorge was darkened by heavy clouds as the two young girls and Fritz walked to the house of the gentleman to whom the Mill belonged, where refreshments were awaiting them.

An hour passed away, and still the same deep gloom hung over the beautiful valley. Suddenly the clouds broke asunder; and, with a crash, which sounded more like an explosion than thunder, a deluge of water descended from the skies. In villages but a few miles distant, not a drop of rain fell, though over the whole district hung the ominous darkness of that heavy canopy of clouds.

Down the deep narrow Gorge swept the rain flood, meeting the seething Calder waters, which seemed to rise in wrath at its approach. The white foaming cataract filled to overflowing the narrow bed of the river; bearing down with it planks, trees, machinery, and every obstacle that impeded its raging course. Smiling cottage gardens, full of summer flowers, bee-hives and vegetables, were swept bare in an instant. Calder in flood at winter time, or filled by autumn tempests, had never presented such a spectacle.

Standing out into the river, the very image of prosperity, was a little dwelling, and surrounding acre of garden ground, of which every yard had been utilised. Now it was a picture of desolation. The out-buildings thrown down, the cottage wall overthrown, a stream of white raging water passing through the lower rooms, bearing along with it tables, chairs, crockery, kitchen utensils, and a litter of young pigs, all squeaking and choking in the torrent; such were the signs and tokens, which the river was bearing away, of one single hour's work of havoc and destruction.

Within this oasis, laved at all seasons by the Calder waters, and often trespassed upon and ravaged by winter floods, but hitherto not irreparably damaged, two tiny children had been playing, when the torrent bore down full upon the little territory on which so much care and industry had been bestowed. The mother, looking out of her lattice window, saw the white rolling wave of water bearing down upon her house like a monster; the children, at play in the garden, looked up and laughed, ignorant of danger. The next moment the flood was upon them, whirling, blinding, bewildering, defying all efforts to save life and property. The wall built up to prevent inundation split in twain, and the water, passing through the breach, dashed against the walls of the small house, flinging foam and spray against the higher windows. The man, who had hurried home, was busy putting up the shutters, striving to make all safe, and did not notice the children playing in the garden, till the woman's wild, despairing shriek roused his attention. The water rose like a white wall in front of him, dashing over everything. The cowshed at the end of the walk was carried down the stream; the coops for poultry, pea-sticks, furniture, whirled past. Blinded as he was, when the father lifted himself from the ground, he saw, through the mist of raging waters, and heard, through the surging of the billows in his ears, the little hands and voices of his children, vainly uplifted for succour.

No mortal man could stem the flood. Onward it swept, bearing all before it, and leaving behind a desolate wilderness : but, as the mighty wave tore along, it cast upon one of the platforms of rock on the other side of the river-bed, a little white heap, that lay there almost like foam shed from the water—motionless, save when the wind lifted and fluttered a tiny rag of clothing, and then laid it down again, as if tired of its plaything. The mother's eyes rested upon the tiny white speck on the bank, and descried the outlines of two childish forms. None dared to tell her that, tossed about by the raging waters, dashed against sharp stones, and drenched with cold showers, what she saw, if indeed it proved to be her children, might be only their lifeless bodies.

At present it was impossible to ascertain the fact. High and dry above the bed of the Calder; where no foot could reach them, it was said, till the water subsided ; lay the shrouded heap, which only a mother could have supposed consisted of her lost babes ! Men gathered together, looking wistfully across, as minute after minute went by ; but no one ventured over.

The tidings of the disaster spread far and wide. The owner of the Mill had come down to the spot ; and a large subscription was speedily raised amongst his friends, for the sufferers. Fritz had been actively engaged helping to save the poor people's property. Gertrude and Ellinor, with other young ladies, were going from house to house, rendering comfort and assistance. The mill-hands, set free from work, were busy and useful. A train came into the station from Hazeldon, bringing men who had families or relatives within reach of danger. All were anxious to be of service.

Fritz recognized some of the work people who had been
employed at the Hall on the summit of the hill, and, in their
company, the old soldier, wrapped in his blue roquelaure,
who had made for himself a home on the ruinous Gateway
Tower of the Noels.

"I tell you, sir," said the builder whose son's life had
been saved by the veteran, "that old fellow scents danger
as a dog scents game. He has been restless all day; and
when it grew so dark, he was neither to hold nor to bind.
He borrowed the money for his fare from me—the first
favour he ever asked, after saving my boy. If he did not
reach Calder Vale, he said, he should have the worst fit he
ever was in for in his life. There was mischief brewing,
he knew, and it was *there*, when the clouds broke, that the
bolt would fall."

CHAPTER IX.

THROUGH the crowd which had collected on the brink of
the swollen torrent pouring down Calder Vale, a slender
black-robed girl, with a scarlet tartan fastened under her chin,
forced a way to the spot where the mother was swaying
herself backwards and forwards in mortal agony, sometimes
hiding her face with her apron, at others staring across the
river with wild wide-open eyes.

"Oh, don't ye see them?" she exclaimed; "don't ye see
the children? That's Meg, and yonder one is Jennie, my
little children. Where else would they be? There never is
an inch, if they can help it, betwixt them. I can see a bit
of Meg's frock when the wind stirs their pinafores,—that's
what looks white. I made 'em myself, long and wide, to

keep the darlings clean, and now they're wrapped round
in them as if they were shrouded. Oh, will no one go
across and bring them over?"

Her voice rose to a shriek as she concluded. Her husband tried to sooth her. "I'm going, Jane. 'Tis but a
minute since we were both of us in the raging water. Bide
patient till we find a way to cross it."

"Oh, don't go, don't leave me," cried the poor distracted
woman, sobbing yet more wildly. "The water 'll take ye
off your legs, and ye'll be drowned before my eyes. Better
leave the babes to perish than lose my man. What would
I do without ye?" She wound her arms tight round his
neck. "Is there no lad or man, without wife or child, that
will venture?"

"Aye, aye—I'm your man," said the old soldier, throwing his blue cloak into her arms. "Just take care of that,
my good woman, whilst I go over to fetch the babies. I'm
alone in the world, with none to care whether I drown or
hang, if ever a fellow was."

Just as he spoke the old man caught sight of Bertina,
who had pressed eagerly forward. A leaden hue spread
over his face, he threw up his arms with a wild cry, and
but for the support of one of the men near him, he would
have fallen to the ground. The girl drew near pitifully to
aid him.

"He's got one of his terrible fits, poor fellow, I suppose,"
said the builder. "Don't come too close, young woman;
he might strike out hard, or clutch ye: I don't know exactly what sort of seizures he's liable to. He hides himself,
mostly, when they come on him."

Bertina bent over the pale face fearlessly. "He has
fainted. Bring water, some of you. Is there never a drop
to be had, when it's pouring down from the skies and driving
you out of house and home?"

A boy brought a hat full of water and dashed it in the old man's face, to which the colour soon began to return. When he came to his senses he stared up wildly at the beautiful girl bending compassionately over him.

"Why do you pin your shawl that way, mistress?" he said sharply. "Who gave you that cairngorm brooch? Are you a ghost or a mill-girl? What in the name of Heaven, or the devil, brought you across my path just when I wanted all the little strength I have left?"

He struggled to his feet and swallowed a few drops of brandy, which some one in the crowd had procured for him.

"Now stand out of the road all of ye—men and women —dead or alive. Here, tie a rope round me, Will Hathaway; it might help me to get back if the fit came on. Stand out of the road, I say."

Resolutely turning his back on the girl, whose sudden appearance had so strangely affected him, the old soldier knotted and reknotted the rope furnished by the father of the children, and descended to the edge of the torrent, which was roaring down the rocky bed of the river. As he set his foot on the first jutting stone which rose above the flood, he said in a hoarse voice, "Afore I start I should like to know what that young woman, with the Rob-Roy shawl and cairngorm pin, chooses to call herself?"

Through the roar of the cataract and the rain floods it came to his ear distinctly, "Bertina Noel."

The next instant he was struggling with the mad rage of the torrent, dashed against rocks, blinded and bewildered by the din of angry water, threatened with death from the huge logs of wood, limbs of trees, and numberless articles of furniture borne down the stream. No one who had not known the Calder well, in all its moods, could have made way; now swimming like a water dog, now springing on some upstanding rock, now diving under wide-spreading boughs, and deftly avoiding the various perils of the passage. Half-way across, a small island, on which grew two large trees, divided the stream, some distance lower down than the spot where the children were supposed to have been thrown on the bank. To this halting-place the swimmer directed his efforts, gaining strength, by the pause thus afforded, for renewed efforts. It was wonderful how a man so apparently worn and aged, could resist the force of the torrent. Men shouted encouragement, women's tears rained down, but the poor mother neither spoke nor wept. With eyes strained and fixed on the white speck, which her heart told her hid her little ones, she clung to Bertina Noel, who watched every brave effort of the swimmer with an emotion never felt before. She did not herself understand the feeling, deeper than compassion, more absorbing than the dread of death or love of life, which filled her whole soul; though her slender arm was bruised and blackened, for days afterwards, by the agonised grasp of the terrified woman beside her, Bertina did not feel it, as she watched the tall form struggling against the immense power of the water, now seen, now lost, amid foam and spray.

"Hurrah!—God bless him!—he's done it!" exclaimed the men, as, across the widened river, twice its natural span, came a faint shout, and a tall form was visible on the opposite bank. "Is it them?—is it Meg?—is it Jennie?" burst from the mother's hitherto closed lips, as the first doubt assailed her. She took courage as she saw, dimly, through tears, that the swimmer had lashed the rope round the bundle on the bank, and bound it firmly to his own person. A low wail of mingled agony and thankfulness burst from her. She hid her face in Bertina's lap, unable to watch the yet more dangerous return of the man thus burdened, through the raging waters of the Calder.

In the father's heart the revival of hope—for Hathaway had not shared his wife's belief that the children were cast ashore—awoke a different spirit. He gave the rope he had been holding to another looker-on, and, following the course taken by the soldier, plunged into the river.

His wife, if she saw the action, made no attempt to stop him. She remained with her head down and her face hidden, sobbing convulsively, all the time he was struggling through the encumbered bed of the river. The old man had not stirred. He was probably much exhausted, and glad to see that assistance was approaching. From the other side it was impossible to perceive, through the blinding mist and rain, how tenderly the old fellow was chafing the cold limbs of the half-perished, terrified children. He had forced a few drops of spirit, from the flask handed to him, between their blue lips; and they were gradually returning to life and consciousness. Full well he knew—the practised swimmer who had saved many a human life—how much it would aid in their rescue, if they could cling with warm living grasp to their preserver, instead of hanging a dead weight on his shoulders, palsying exertion.

Hathaway, though in the prime of life, hale and strong, was longer in crossing than his predecessor. At last he touched the land; and, much exhausted, was glad of a helping hand to pull him up the bank on which, oh joy!— lay his reviving infants.

The two men aided each other in making fast the burden which they must carry back through the raging flood. Fortunately the wrath of the elements was now subsiding. The rain fell less violently, and the course of the river was not so heavily encumbered. The shattered homesteads on

its banks had been rifled, and their contents swept away
farther down the stream. Hathaway was astonished at the
superior knowledge of every turn in the bank—of each
shoal and current, and submerged stepping-stone or coign of
vantage, possessed by his companion over himself—though
he was a man born on the banks of the Calder, who had
lived in the same place all his life.

"You be a Yorkshireman, surely," he said, as they rested
for a moment on the island. "You do know Calder to a
turn. Were ye bred and born in these parts?"

But the veteran vouchsafed him no reply. Probably he
was aware that he required all the breath left in his old
body, to help him through the remainder of the passage.

The women, when danger was over, had gone into a
neighbouring cottage, to prepare beds and comforts for
those just rescued from the cold embrace of the water.
There were only men on the bank when the exhausted
swimmers got back to the starting point.

CHAPTER X.

BERTINA NOEL, when the shouts on the bank proclaimed
that the children were rescued, hurried home to her mother.
She knew that the day must have been long, dreary, and
anxious, to a woman who never, under any circumstances,
stirred beyond her own small territories.

The extraordinary emotion shown by the old soldier
when he first saw her, had made her unwilling to expose
him again to an attack of illness, after his recent exertions,
by another view of her face. Strange to say, her own feelings had been almost equally excited; and, until he returned

in safety, Bertina had found it impossible to tear herself
away. She tried to persuade herself that it was only his
brave effort to save the children that interested her; but
some mysterious sensation at her heart contradicted this
impression.

As the young girl pressed on through the wet brambles
and blackberry bushes, which fringed the narrow path
through the gorge, she suddenly overtook Fritz Langdale
and his sister, on their way to the station.

Had she come upon them less abruptly, just at a turn in
the path, Bertina would have waited for them to pass on;
but she was absorbed in thought, and Fritz and Gertrude,
hearing footsteps behind them, stood aside under the trees
to let her go by. Fritz had been one of the most active
assistants in rescuing people from their submerged cottages,
and saving some portion of their little property, and he had
contributed handsomely to the sum raised by subscription; but he had not heard of the accident to the children,
nor seen the dangerous exploit crowned by their rescue, as
it had taken place lower down the river.

Gertrude held out her hand to the young woman who
curtseyed respectfully. "How wet you are," she said compassionately. "I hope you have not far to go, before you
reach your home. My brother has been telling me how
pretty it is, and what a hospitable reception you afforded
him."

Bertina mentioned briefly the peril of the children and
their parents' terror. "I did not even know that I was
wet," she said, unfastening her shawl and shaking the rain
from its folds.

"That is the best and the most becoming head-dress and
mantle combined, I ever saw," said Fritz, taking the tartan
from her and placing it once more over her dark hair, as

respectfully as if she had been a princess, or one of his own fair sisters. "An old soldier, you say, who came by train from Hazeldon, rescued the children, I hope he will go back with us. I should like to shake hands with him. Can you tell me his name?"

"No," said Bertina, "but I heard the people on the bank say that it was not the first brave deed he had done, nor the first life he had saved. One man told me that his son would have been dashed to pieces before his eyes, having become giddy on a scaffolding, if this old soldier had not, at great risk, rushed to his side, supported, and brought him down the ladder."

"It must be the General!" exclaimed Fritz. "He aided in saving our own dear mother, when a child, from shipwreck; and has been a pensioner of my father's ever since. It appears that he has a passion for rescuing people from dangers by flood and fell, and deserves the Victoria Cross, or some insignia of merit. You ought to be interested in him, Miss Noel," he added, "for he has taken up his abode and redeemed from dilapidation a portion of the old Hall belonging to your ancestors, near the head of Langdale."

Bertina coloured deeply. "I did feel interested in him—more so than even the sight of his brave action could account for," she said with emotion. "I wonder what made him take up his abode at Noel Hall, and why he was agitated at seeing me? Can he have been an old servant in the family, during better days?"

"Very possibly," said Fritz. "I do not at all know what his position was when he won my father's life-long gratitude, but he is poor enough now. I fancy he has known fairer fortunes."

"Here I must say farewell," said Bertina, at a spot where the path separated into two. "That is the way to the

9

station, and yonder to the right, among the trees, lies our
old house. Unless, indeed," she added, simply, "you and
your sister will condescend to rest there."

"Not to-day," said Gertrude, shaking hands cordially.
"We are all wet and weary, and Mrs. Noel must be anxiously looking out for you. Fritz shall bring me another
time to see you."

Bertina stood still on the spot where they parted, until
the two figures were lost in the woodland.

Mrs. Noel was standing at the gate, looking out anxiously
for her daughter, when Bertina came slowly up the path.
The lappets of her cap were thrown back, and there was an
angry flush on her face.

"How late you are, child! With whom were you
talking on the high ground yonder? I have heard voices
this half-hour."

"Nay, mother," said the girl, quietly. "I stayed only a
few moments speaking to Mr. Langdale and his sister.
They were visiting the family at Mill Hall, and came down
to see the cloth-making just before the great storm. I
think it must have been a water-spout that burst over Calder Vale."

"Never mind about the water-spout," said Mrs. Noel,
stamping her small foot impatiently on the gravel pathway.
"Bertina, why do you evade my question. What brought
Mr. Langdale to the Gorge again? He does not come to
watch the cloth-making. Was it an excuse to see you
once more?"

"He scarcely spoke to me," said Bertina, colouring
deeply. "Mother, I have not deserved this from you. I
would not bear it from any one else. Have I ever behaved lightly, that you should question me so sharply?"

Mrs. Noel's high spirit broke down: she burst into

tears. Her daughter soothed her tenderly. "Forgive me, mother; I did not mean to vex you; I only hope you do not blame me."

"No, it is I who am wrong and foolish. I never was steady like you," said the penitent woman. "Bertina, it was a gentleman like Mr. Langdale, one of the county gentry who saw me at work among the girls in that very room where you sit, who turned my brain—my weak, silly head. He followed me through the copse, just as that young gentleman pursued you the other day, and admired my scarlet shawl and black hair. It is grey enough now, but then it was long and shining' like yours. It all came back to me to-day while I was waiting for you; and, when I heard your voice, and his deep, low tones, such as one never hears at the Mill. Oh, my darling, if you knew how I have learnt to hate such courtly accents as once made music in my hearing! If you are good and virtuous, still such wooing unfits you for your station; and if you yield to the temptation to listen, as too many poor girls have done, why, then God help you! See what a life of misery mine has been; and I might, but for *him*, have been a humble, happy, wife and mother in the station appointed for me."

"Have no fear, mother," said Bertina, proudly. "Whatever you have suffered, I am a Noel—poor enough, certainly, but never likely, any more than yourself, to depart from a virtuous path. Young Mr. Langdale was not thinking of me;" she added, with a slight sigh. "He was quite devoted to a beautiful fair girl, his cousin, Miss Ellinor Langdale, from the Hall. I believe she is a great heiress, and I daresay he wishes to marry her. I am quite sure she likes him. His sister was very kind, and talked a great deal to me. She has promised to come and see us. Mr. Langdale did not even speak to me this morning, and, when we met

among the trees above, he was only asking about poor
Hathaway's children, who were saved from drowning by an
old soldier from Hazeldon."

She told her mother of the brave deed, carefully ab-
staining from mentioning that the old man had shown any
particular emotion at sight of her; or that he lived at the
old Hall belonging to the Noels. Her mother's excitable
temper might have been roused by these circumstances
being mentioned. Any reference to the Noels brought back
the memory of sufferings which her undisciplined character
had lacked strength to endure. Her education had been
very faulty, and she had never striven to improve.

Even as it was, her daughter's narrative accidentally lit
a spark which blazed up fiercely.

"*He* Mrs. Lang's preserver from shipwreck!" she said,
indignantly, as Dr. Forsyth had done, when Mr. Lang
made a similar communication. "Bertina, your old hero is
an audacious impostor. It was your poor father, Bertie
Noel, who swam out to the ship, when no one else would
venture, and brought back the poor little lady in his arms.
I have heard him tell the story a hundred times. There
was an aya, an Indian nurse, rescued. Perhaps this man
brought *her* to land, but he never laid a finger on Mrs.
Lang. And yet her own son told you this! So much for
people's gratitude!"

Bertina strove in vain to calm her mother's indignation.
Mrs. Noel, a beautiful brunette of low birth, had captivated
the spendthrift heir of the Noels—the last of the old line.
He had carried her off from her companions at the Mill;
but her virtue was proof against temptation, although
passion and vanity aided her lover's pleadings. It was said
that Cuthbert Noel was the victim of his own wiles; and
found himself, most unexpectedly, the husband, lawfully

wedded, according to Scotch law, of the beautiful peasant he had carried across the border. Both were lost sight of for years, and the property went to wrack and ruin; but on her return to her native place with her child, Bertina's mother produced papers which gave her a right to the name of Cuthbert Noel's widow, and the remnant left of his property, including the old house in Calder Dale.

PART THE FOURTH.

THE VICTORY WON.

Set like a gem in the green valley's breast,
Flecked by the gold of the burnished West,
Shadowed with russet, and purple, and pall,
Brightened with flash of the oars' gentle fall;
Warmly reflecting the sun's latest blush,
Lies our lake in the Evening's tremulous hush.

Red and white roses on terrace and wall,
Stars of white jasmine illumine our Hall;
Old checker'd woodwork, cream white and dark brown;
Moonlight o'erflooding the clough and the down,
Lights sparkling out on the hillside and crest:
Fountains at play, and all nature at rest.

R. M. K.

CHAPTER I.

LORENCE LANGDALE, willingly or unwillingly, and in spite of the positive refusal on the part of her parents to accept any present advantages, was acknowledged by the whole neighbourhood to be the heiress of her cousin's property. Miss Langdale mentioned on every possible occasion the decision at which she had arrived ; and spoke of Frank Langdale's young daughter as the future possessor of the Hall, and of her large landed estates.

The only alteration which the owner of the Grange permitted in the habits of his family, was that the abbreviation of the name ceased to be insisted upon. Florence had carried her point even in childhood, and it was impossible to insist now upon her calling herself by any but the unaltered family name belonging to the property which would one day be her own. As this was the case, it seemed unfair to her sisters that they should not share the same advantages. Mr. Langdale had always allowed his son to use the name, considering him to be the future Langdale of Langdale. Now his prospects were altered, it was right that no unnecessary difference should exist among the young people. The great commercial house in which Mr. Langdale had acted for several years as senior clerk, had recently offered him a junior partnership, thus removing one some-

what fanciful reason for the simple style he had adopted
on first settling in his native county.

Not even to her mother, since the day when she rejected
with horror the proposal that she should abandon her home,
had Florence mentioned her feelings on the subject of Miss
Langdale's adoption of herself as her heiress. She had become very grave and silent, but all her duties were scrupulously performed, and she attended diligently to her studies.
Mr. Langdale's accession of income enabled him to afford
the means of improving the education of his daughters. The
best masters in various accomplishments now attended at
the Grange, and Florence applied herself diligently and con-
scientiously to her different tasks. She had a fine ear for
music, and a melodious voice, but no taste for drawing.
Frances and the twins continued to take long excursions, for
the purpose of sketching the lovely scenery of the West
Riding. Gertrude cared most for acquiring foreign languages. Whatever might be her favourite pursuit, each of
the girls was now encouraged to prosecute it, and every advantage was afforded to bring it to perfection.

Little as she cared for worldly wealth, Ellinor Langdale
often found it a hard task to command her countenance, and
to silence the expression of her feelings, when her sister
spoke in her presence of the changes she had in contemplation ; as though she were a totally indifferent person, unin-
terested in these arrangements.

Ignorant as she was of the tastes and wishes of the young
creature whom she had arbitrarily constituted her successor,
Maud constantly alluded to Florence's supposed inclinations
and future plans, as though she could map out the whole of
her life. Whilst she disregarded entirely the feelings of the
sister who had spent her whole young life under her roof,
regarding Langdale Hall as her own fair inheritance ; Miss

Langdale studied every imaginary fancy of the almost unknown cousin, who had so strangely captivated her fancy.

One of the few traits of character which she had seen exhibited by her future heiress, was Florence's intense admiration for the antique carvings, and picturesque architecture, of the old Hall on the hill overlooking the valley. On this foundation Miss Langdale had raised a lofty structure, still further embellished by the few inwardly clinging predilections and fancies of her own long past girlhood.

Mr. Haywarden shook his head doubtfully, when his rich client consulted him as to the possibility of restoring to its ancient style the ruined edifice, which of late had yielded shelter to labourers, and even paupers.

"You want to restore Noel Hall!" he said. "Far better let it alone. It will take an enormous slice out of your young favourite's fortune; and, after all, it is not an old family property, like the one in Langdale. *I* never advised you to buy it; but in that, as in most other matters, you like your own way the best."

Maud smiled gravely. Mr. Haywarden was a privileged mortal.

"I mean to have my own way now; and, depend upon it, Florence will not grudge the outlay. The child is as liberal as the day."

"She is not a child—you made her a woman long before her time," said the lawyer, gravely. "People do not go back into childhood. How can you answer for her liberality, or for any part of her future character, after placing her in a false position?"

"Cultivation improves good plants," said Miss Langdale. "Weeds grow rank, but the tender vine—the rich blossom—needs good soil, and profits by fostering. I tell you Florence Langdale would have pined and died in the arid ground at the Grange. Now, with hope and affluence in prospect, she will flourish like a young palm tree. But never mind about my responsibilities : I will take care of myself and of her. What will it cost to repair Noel Hall ?"

" I cannot possibly answer you without going fully into the subject. We must have a builder's estimate, and you are sure to prefer the most expensive plan. Upon my word I hope you will be advised, and give it up. If you wish to leave this young lady a fortune, why spend thousands and tens of thousands on an old place for which she cannot really care very much, instead of embellishing Langdale Hall ?"

" I do not mean to lay out a penny unnecessarily on Langdale Hall," said Maud with increasing obstinacy. " Florence is perfectly satisfied with it, and so am I. Get me the estimates, plans,—whatever is desirable—and I will find out what she likes best. There are always ways and means of discovering what one really cares to know."

" I will have no hand in deceiving Frank Langdale and his wife," said the lawyer, pushing his papers away from before him, and confronting his client boldly across his writing-table. " If you have any underhand dealings with their daughter I will wash my hands of the whole affair."

" Nonsense, old friend," said Miss Langdale, soothingly ; " if I were about to enter into any unlawful traffic I should not let you into my secrets. For once in my life, I have changed my mind. To tell you the truth, it is for my own pleasure principally that I wish to restore the old place on the hill-top, where some of my happiest days were spent. You need not remind me that it was in consequence of a whim of my own that the place has been neglected. I cannot bear to see paupers airing their rags on the once hospitable hearth-stone. When all is done that I contemplate,

there will be enough for Florence. Why, in ten years—and
I mean to live as long—I could pay for it out of my income.
The first step is to give notice to quit to every one of its
present wretched occupants. How long will that take?"

"You had best not meddle with the General," said Mr.
Haywarden. "Let him alone, I beseech you."

"On the contrary, he is the very person I wish to eject.
Let his be the first notice served," said Maud, blazing up
with wrath. "An insolent, ill-bred beggar! I cannot think
why you allowed him to lodge there. We have spoken about
this before, and I yielded to your wish to give him proper
notice. I was even sorry for his lamentable condition. But,
if the rest are to go, why should he remain?"

"Because he may give you trouble if you aggravate him.
At present he has done no harm—nay, he has served you
well. Neither you, nor Miss Florence, nor the clever architect who may execute your behests, will work harder, or
strive more lovingly, to do honour to and reclaim the old
house of the Noels, than this poor feeble creature. It is worth
your while, before you proceed further with your whim, to
view the Hall and inspect the Gateway Tower. With his
own hands he has laid stone to stone—mended the old
stained glass—in short, done wonders. It would be a
burning shame to eject the old veteran."

"I shall certainly not suffer him to remain," said Maud,
icily. What can a half-senseless vagabond have effected
that will stand side by side with high art?"

"Listen to me, Miss Langdale," said Mr. Haywarden, earnestly, "and for once be ruled. I know very little about
high art, but I do understand law and common humanity;
and I tell you that, if you offend thus recklessly and cruelly
the honest occupant of the Gateway Tower, you will never
restore the Hall of the Noels."

"This is some superstitious fancy; I am not to be frightened by any Meg Merrilies threats. Of course, all those wretched creatures will cry out and threaten my roof-tree if I meddle with theirs; but I am not like the weak Laird of Ellangowan, neither is it my intention to act cruelly or recklessly; you ought to know me better. I shall trust to you to make proper and reasonable provision and compensation, to all who may suffer from my resolution to restore the old house of the Noels. But it must be cleared of the foul crew who are now housed in the ancient Hall. Let them have cottages built for them, on any part of my property you choose to point out as fitted for the purpose—all except the man you call the General. Make him what compensation you like—I will not have him as my tenant."

"He will lodge nowhere but in the Gateway Tower, and he will take from you neither money nor favour. Let him alone; I believe he was once in Bertie Noel's service. At all events, he loves the old place for his sake. Will that appease you, Maud?"

A very striking change passed over Miss Langdale's face as the lawyer, who had known her from a child, pronounced the last words; but she hardened her heart against him.

"No," she said, deliberately; "I will not tolerate his presence there."

"Then you may as well give up your new scheme," said Mr. Haywarden, drily. "I have hitherto abstained from telling you my real reason for advising you to let this poor fellow alone. If you do not disturb him he will not trouble you; but, if you tread on him, he will, like any creature provided with a sting, use it in self-defence. This man maintains that Cuthbert Noel is not dead. With his usual wayward inconsistency, finding himself utterly ruined, and being unwilling to bear the burden of his own follies and vices, he determined to have done with the world, and with his few still remaining friends. The woman whom he had never acknowledged as his wife, received, as his widow, some small competence, and the old house in the Eagle's Gorge, where the widows of the Noels have always resided. The rest of the property was sold, but, had the last of the Noels been known to be living, this could not have taken place. The title to Noel Hall would not hold good. There would be no end of complication and trouble. There might have been much difficulty sooner, for Bertie Noel's death was never legally proved; but few cared for him, living, sufficiently to deny the story of his death in some far away nook of the New World."

There was a long silence. At last Mr. Haywarden's words had taken effect, but still Maud would not own that she was conquered. She rose from her seat, leaning with her hand heavily on the table before she lifted from it her riding-whip. "Do nothing at present. I will see this man; I may not find him so difficult to deal with as you anticipate." Then, after shaking hands with the lawyer, she hastily quitted the office.

CHAPTER II.

NOEL HALL bore little trace of its once stately aspect, when Maud Langdale rode more slowly than usual, up the long ascent. Ragged children were playing and shouting in the courtyard—long rows of coarse garments fluttered above the battlements—and, niched in his sunny corner, wrapped in his blue roquelaure, the General was basking in the warm rays, and looking down over the valley.

Maud drew in her rein sharply, and sat motionless in her saddle, when she came in sight of the place. Thoughts which she had kept down forcibly, now, whether she liked it or not, rushed upon her; making the strong woman tremble with emotion. Girlish vanities, to which she fancied herself dead for ever—womanly feelings, which had been outraged and crushed and repented of bitterly, turning the milk of human kindness to gall and wormwood—re-awoke as she contemplated the ruinous structure.

Although she was too far off to see his features, Maud fancied that the old veteran was gibing and mocking at her. Brave as a lion usually, she trembled now with fear as well as sorrow. Something in the man's looks and bearing, poverty-stricken as he was, daunted her haughty spirit.

Determined as she was not to endure his presence, Maud felt as if she dared not tell him to depart.

Why had he chosen that spot of all others for his favourite station? Other eyes had gazed upon her from that place, as, in her proud fearless beauty, she rode up the hill to Noel Hall. Other hands had lifted her from the saddle, at whose touch every nerve vibrated then—the very memory of their light yet tender clasp still set her pulses beating—the only assistance she had ever cared to accept, saving from one other who never proffered to her now, aid or courtesy, had been extended, in greeting and welcome, when she reached the Gateway Tower where the old pauper had taken up his abode.

Miss Langdale noticed for the first time, as she rode on, the glimmer of the stained glass in the high narrow window of the room above the archway, and the careful training of the ivy boughs. The place where the old soldier sat looking down upon her was near the entrance into the courtyard.

She must pass close by him, and underneath the gateway tower.

Her voice seemed to die away in her throat as she essayed to speak; an unwonted faintness oppressed her. One of the urchins playing in the courtyard ran forward on hearing the horse-hoofs on the stone, and threw open one side of the great gates—the other would not move. Maud rode forward silently.

Mr. Haywarden had as yet said nothing of her intentions. He hoped that for once Miss Langdale would give way. The women who were busy hanging up their clothes, stood still and curtseyed as she passed. An old crone, bolder than the rest, came to meet her with a complaint. Maud coldly referred her to the steward. The black cat, as she lay basking in the sunshine, glowered at her, arching her back and bristling all over as the lady disturbed her slumbers. Her mistress came to the door, and asked whether Madam would please to get down and rest a bit. The woman stood on the very stone where, over and over again in former days, Maud had been helped from her saddle by that well-remembered firm clasp. Often as she had since visited the old hall, she had never till now felt the past return to her so vividly.

With a sharp touch of pain, which made her manner haughtier than usual, Maud repulsed the offer; saying she had ridden over to see if the repairs she had ordered had been executed. She had not expected to be met with fresh complaints, as had been the case the moment she passed the gateway. If people were not satisfied, it would be better for them to leave. She should certainly lay out no more money on the place for their benefit.

Meg's great green eyes dilated, as if she read in the lady's disdainful words threats of summary ejectment; but her

10

mistress did not take the hint. She grumbled about the
workpeople not having finished their task properly; and
showed the lady where the new spout let the rain into the
building, instead of carrying it off. Something was out of
order where the water-works and fountains used to play.
There were no end of grievances to be rectified, some real,
some fictitious. Maud listened with a frowning brow in
ominous silence. When the old dame had finished her sorrowful list of evils, from wind and water, smoke and damp,
Miss Langdale rode away from the door, without bidding
her good day.

A gloomy shadow crept over the busy group as she
passed. The children stopped playing, and huddled together in a frightened group, as if anticipating chastisement :
a cold blast fluttered among the rags, the women stood still,
curtseying, but no one ventured to address her. The
General drew his cloak tightly round him, as if suddenly
chilled, and looked down upon her from his now gloomy
coign of vantage, without lifting his cap.

Maud's courage rose at last, and she rode straight across
the yard, and accosted the man who had not deigned to
salute her.

" Come down," she said, without any attempt at courtesy ;
" I wish you to show me what alterations you have made in
your lodging in the Gateway Tower."

The old man did not move. He beckoned to one of the
scared children, and leaning from the wall, whispered a
word in the lad's ear. It was the curly-haired boy who had
held the rein of Miss Langdale's mare on her previous visit.
He came close to the lady, and pulling one of the fair locks
on his forehead, said, " I be to show it you, he says, it
don't suit he to move just now."

Miss Langdale curbed her impatient temper with difficulty.

It was, perhaps unconsciously, a relief that her curiosity might be gratified, without her being oppressed by the presence of the object of her passionate dislike. Without a second glance at the old man, she dismounted; and, leaving Christobel in charge of the oldest of Ned's companions, she followed the boy across the courtyard.

A dark, steep stair led up to the room over the gateway; winding round and round inside the thick walls, and lighted only by narrow loopholes deeply set in the luxuriant ivy. The boy stood back to let the lady enter the room above; gathering in his sunburnt hands the folds of a heavy curtain which was let down over the wide portal. As the lad stood, with his fair curls relieved in light against the dark velvet hangings, bending under their weight, the glow of the painted glass above his head, and a bright smile on his face, with the dark steps winding down in front of him, an artist might have kept him there to make the foreground for a picture; but Maud did not even look at him.

Before her—seen dimly through the narrow shadowy opening of dark Ypres velvet, seemed to lie the land of her youth; the only scene where she had known a girl's bright dreams of love and happiness :—a very lofty chamber, panelled and painted, with gleams of broken bars of burnished gold, here and there lit up by rays of many coloured light falling from above ;—strips and scraps of velvet pile carpet, laid down, as if for votaries to kneel upon and worship, beneath rare shrines and statues and relics from far-off southern climes, full of surpassing beauty. On high, wreathed with elaborate carvings, picked up among the ruins by the workmen, and tendered to the old man in gratitude ; arranged in semblance of a frame, hung a picture which made Miss Langdale's breath come fast and short, and her eyes fill with tears. To her, that proud woman had

10—2

been like a mother; the only tenderness her youth had
known had been shown her here,—where she now stood, a
lone woman, hard and cold, and blighted,—by Lady Barbara
Noel and her wild son, Cuthbert, Maud's early lover.

The boy, who was peeping into the chamber, suddenly
felt the curtains snatched from his grasp, and let down
between him and the lady, as she harshly bade him go
away and wait for her below. He was too much frightened
to linger; and not a soul credited his assertion that he heard
the lady sobbing and crying, as he ran down the turret
stairs; or would have recognised, in the form prostrate
before the life-size portrait of the once haughty Mistress
of Noel Hall, the equally proud, equally feared, Lady of
Langdale.

Maud looked round timidly, as though fearing to be confronted by spectres, after the first long sorrowful burst of
emotion.

The room was not large, though very lofty, and within it
seemed assembled all the best remembered tokens of the
vanished pride and taste of the Noels. Where had the old
pictures and cabinets been hidden? Who had unearthed
those long slender glasses—the many curiously moulded
relics of antiquity. Maud gazed round her wonderingly as
she recalled each token and memory of the past.

Miss Langdale started and shivered as she heard a heavy
footstep on the stair. She would have given the world to
be alone for one hour in that room—to hold in her hand,
and study lovingly, the various signs of a time for ever past;
—but it was not to be. In vain she strove to rally back her
pride, to recover her self-possession. It was with difficulty
that she stood erect, with her hand trembling as it rested
on a small ivory slab, fixed in the wall beneath the picture
of Bertie Noel's lovely mother; when the tenant of the Gate-

way.Tower entered the room in which she felt herself an
intruder.

There was a kind of dignity in the man's air as he
advanced towards her, a sort of rude courtesy. He drew
forward an antique chair, with the crest of the Noels set in
dark carving and velvet, and motioned to her to be seated.
Miss Langdale even fancied there was a compassionate
glance in his eyes which angered her, but she had not
power to remain standing; her shaking limbs refused longer
to support her.

Her host—for she felt herself to be his guest—seated himself without craving permission. Through the painted glass
a soft light fell on the man's figure, and on the dark lines of
drapery which he gathered round him—ennobling the form
of the old soldier, as he cast himself down among the relics
of the past, which, with so much toil and trouble, he had collected. Maud felt inclined to view him more respectfully;
and the recollection returned to her mind of Mr. Haywarden's
words, that it would be a shame to turn him out of the Gateway Tower; and that not even she herself could have done
more honour to the ruined family, whom perhaps he had
served and loved, than this forlorn wanderer.

"You knew her?" she said, with an effort, pointing to the
large picture beneath which her strange companion had
seated himself. "What was your connection with Lady
Barbara Noel and her son? Were you once a servant in
this house? I do not remember ever to have seen you here,
and yet you must have known and loved this place, as I did,
formerly."

"Ladies like yourself, Miss Langdale, do not much notice
those who wait upon them, though we were to serve you on
our bended knees. I mind you well enough; you have seen

me here often before," said the old man quietly, without looking at her.

"Indeed, I do not recollect it," said Miss Langdale, in a softer and kinder tone than usual. "Had I guessed—if you had told me that you were an old servant of the Noels, I should have been interested about you."

"Nay, I never said I was a servant at Noel Hall. If I had been, service is no inheritance, and what's done is done and ended. I have served my country, and I have served ladies, but I never wore a livery. Of late I have lived in free countries, where men are men, and not obliged to bend their backs when great people go by. You don't like such manners ; but let me tell you, Miss Langdale, there are those who think that your own might be altered with advantage."

"This insolence is not to be borne," said Miss Langdale, starting up, with her eyes full of fire. "By what right have you ventured to make so many changes—and to gather together things which belong to me—and then, when I speak kindly, to insult me ? My steward has instructions which I shall not rescind—to give you notice to quit these premises."

"Sit down—there are two words to go to that bargain," said the old man, without moving. "By what right, do ye say, did I pick all these family relics of the Noels out of the dust-heap and cinder-pit where you had left them ? By what right did I, with my own hands, mend and make and join them together ? Is that what you want to know, Maud Langdale ? By the right given to me by Bertie Noel, the man who loved you once better than his own soul."

Maud sank back into the chair she had quitted, covering her eyes with her hands. "He *is* dead, then?" she said, hoarsely. "Was it his last wish that you should act as you have done ?"

"Nay, I am not going to say whether he's dead or living," said the old man, cautiously. He was not dead, leastways, when we foregathered in the colonies, and he told me what a wrack and ruin had been made of Noel Hall. *That* hurt him sorely. I was coming back to the old country, and, as I had a liking for this place, I promised to look it up, and see what the rats and the owls had left fit for use. I saw him living then, and it's for you to prove he's dead since; but it was not his will, nor is it mine, to trouble you, Miss Langdale, as long as you let me bide quietly in the Gateway Tower."

"I believe you to be an impostor," said Miss Langdale, rising haughtily; "but at present I shall not condescend to argue and bandy words with you. You will hear what my further intentions are, in due course of time, from my steward, Mr. Haywarden."

"Have a care, Miss Langdale, have a care," said the old man, drawing the curtain aside for her to pass. "Don't wake the sleeping lion. Best let me bide in the old Tower."

Maud stopped involuntarily. Something in the old man's voice once more brought back the thoughts of earlier days, and softened her heart. "You have seen Cuthbert Noel since he left England—since he has been considered by all his friends to be dead. Did he indeed give you a commission to restore order—to gather together—his scattered possessions?" She hesitated, and the colour rose to her haughty brow. "Did he—did Mr. Noel—send no word, no token, to me? I would have respected his wishes."

"Nay, that he did not do, most certainly—he sent no word to you," said the old man. "Mr. Lang, as he chose to call himself—your cousin down to the Grange—*he* got a message. He'll bear witness I've told ye naught but truth.

A very good man is Frank Lang—better than most; ye can ask him about Cuthbert. He knows more about him and me than any other living man."

"I have not spoken with Frank Langdale of the Grange for twenty years. I do not care to do so now," said Maud, impatiently. "I believe, however, that you are speaking truth; and that you have known Mr. Noel longer, and better than your present position at first led me to suppose. I am grateful to you for bringing back memories of the past which will assist me in embellishing this place, and, on certain conditions, I will even suffer you to remain in the Tower to which you have so strangely attached yourself. Are you willing to enter my service, and to act as porter here, assisting the workmen in their operations?"

"No, I am not," said the veteran, sturdily. "I'll bide here as my own master, or not at all. Your servant I will not be. I am a free man, and able to pay my way. I want neither wages nor livery. For the rest, I'm right willing to help the work-people, as I've done before, without your asking me, and without fee or reward. What I do will be not for your sake, nor at your bidding, but for the sake of the dead Noels who lived here before you bought the place."

Maud Langdale remained irresolute. Under the shadow of the curtain the man stood dark and firm, as though all the pride and obstinacy of the wayward Noels were concentrated in his own person. A certain respect for his independence rose within her, and for once she yielded up her own haughty will.

"Be it as you like," she said, bending her head not uncourteously. "For the sake of Lady Barbara Noel and her son, whom I so dearly loved, I accept, on your own terms, your good offices on behalf of this place."

A gleam of triumphant pleasure shot from the General's

dark eyes. "All right," he said; "take them or leave
them as ye list. How soon will the work begin?"

"The moment we can get rid of the present occupants of
the Hall," said Miss Langdale, "almost immediately—
none of them deserve much consideration;" Mr. Haywarden will see to their removal, and that they have
proper compensation and house room elsewhere. The sooner
the whole crew are off the premises the better I shall be
pleased."

"I'd rather have nought to do with their flitting," said
the old man; "they're flesh and blood, though not of the
best sort, and the bairns will greet, and the women will
mourn over their bits of gardens and the big kitchens. But,
what must be, must. I suppose you think one place is as
good as another for the likes of them. It's little you'll
trouble about such varmint. Up on the hill-top or down in
the ditches and fens, will be good enough for the poor
devils. I can't say they've been over well housed here, but
the foxes like the hill tarns, and birds of the air their nests.
The dame's cat will not easily take to feeding at another
hearth; but they'll come round, bless ye, in time, and if
they don't, what's the odds? They've got to go, man and
maid, mother and son, cat and kitten; to go, or to bide and
starve. I reckon that's about it, isn't it, Miss Langdale? And when all's said and done, what will ye do with
the old Hall of the Noels? Are there any of the family
left in England? I've heard say Cuthbert left a wife and
child."

"Not one of Mr. Noel's friends have ever acknowledged
the low-bred woman who calls herself his wife," said Miss
Langdale, with bitter scorn. "I certainly never will admit
the validity of the marriage; and I am astonished that the
trustees allow that woman to live at the Dower House in

the Gorge. The girl works at the mills as her mother did before her."

"It's a pity Cuthbert did not get his living after the same honest fashion. But there, now, Miss Langdale, I've no mind to offend ye, and I do believe it was that connection and the dread of the woman's claiming him that kept Bertie Noel away, and made him pass himself off for dead. It looks as if he felt she and the child—'twas a girl, wasn't it?—had some sort of a right to claim him."

"I have no wish to argue the matter," said Miss Langdale, with returning haughtiness. "Mr. Noel lost himself by that ill-fated connection, but no one who knew him believed it to be a legal marriage. At Noel Hall these women will knock in vain for admission. The place has passed away from the race for ever, even if they could prove themselves to belong to it."

"Aye, aye—sure enough—you're right there. The Noels have neither stick nor stone belonging to them here, I suppose," said the old man, looking round mournfully. "Not even my lady's picture there, proud as she looks; a real lady, every inch of her."

Miss Langdale looked with wonder at the man who stood with his head bent back gazing at the picture of the friend—the almost mother—of her youth. Again a softer feeling stole over her, as she noticed the marvellous care with which the forlorn old soldier had repaired the ravages of time. Never had she felt better satisfied with herself than now, as she reflected that she had persuaded him to remain in the renovated tower.

She bade him farewell kindly, but the man did not turn his head—he hardly seemed to notice her departure. Christoble was pawing the ground impatiently in the midst of a group of half scared children. Ned held her rein cau-

tiously. This time Maud threw him a handsome gratuity.
She even recollected to thank the lad, and smiled upon him
kindly as he held open the heavy gate under the entrance
tower.

CHAPTER III:

MR. HAYWARDEN made no farther protest when Miss Langdale signified to him, in writing, her wish that the present
inmates of Noel Hall should be served with notices to quit
the premises ; with the exception of the old American soldier
who occupied the Gateway Tower, and Meg's mistress and
her grandson.

For the present these persons might remain, but, as soon
as possible, workmen were to be engaged, and plans sent in,
for the restoration of the Hall. As nearly as possible, she
wished it to resemble the place it had been in the days of
her youth.

Satisfied with having gained the point which he considered most important, the lawyer executed her behest with
alacrity and intelligence. He went over to Noel Hall, with
the plans furnished by different architects, and studied the
capabilities of the place, before submitting them to Miss
Langdale, in order to be able to give her his own advice on
the subject.

He did not disdain the suggestions of the General, who
stood at his elbow looking at the drawings, and studying
their comparative recommendations and merits. It was
wonderful how much the old soldier knew of architecture,
and how deeply his mind was imbued with reverence for
the traditional glories of the ancient Hall. Like many re-

publicans when in the mother country, the General set great store by old families, old houses, and old customs. It would not be his fault if the house of Lady Barbara Noel was not, in due time, once more what it had been in her day; before her thriftless son brought all under the hammer.

One advantage which arose from propitiating the veteran was, that Florence Langdale's taste was consulted. Ever since her earliest childhood, the old Hall on the summit of the hill had been a favourite object for a walk, and the General was a privileged friend of all the children at the Grange. Now that they were older they frequently visited him, and were always welcome at the Gateway Tower. Mr. Haywarden left the plans with him, on purpose that they might be shown to Miss Langdale's future heiress.

The news had spread far and wide that the old Hall, formerly belonging to the Noels, was to be restored to its ancient magnificence. Frances Langdale and the twins came over several times to sketch the ruins, before they were delivered over to the workpeople, and hidden by boards and scaffolding. While her sisters were at work with their pencils and brushes, Florence sat in the Tower turning over the architectural drawings. Her taste was pure and noble, though, practically, she was not an artist.

The elevation that pleased her most was one slightly drawn, and less technically complete than the others, which gave the ground plan of the house and a sketch of its future aspect. Again and again Florence returned to this drawing, which seemed to realise her own romantic dreams. Noel Hall from her childhood had been a visionary paradise; and she had seen the old man toiling away day after day, at the partial restoration of the Gateway Tower, with the deepest interest.

In the plan which she preferred, the same style prevailed

throughout the building ; a severe simplicity reigned everywhere ; less of ornament than in any other, but a sombre
grandeur, which suited equally well with the commanding
situation of the mansion, and the ruined fortunes of the
former possessors.

" Let who will abide here, this place will always to my
fancy belong to the Noels," said the girl, as she bent over
the drawing, while the old soldier stood behind her, contemplating it gravely and silently. " If Miss Langdale thinks
as I do, she will follow this plan in restoring the Hall. All
the lavish decorations, the floral emblems, the classical
ornaments in the other drawings seem to me out of place.
I like the dark old English oak and ebony—the quaint
tapestry and purple tinted glass, with here and there a stain
of glowing crimson such as lights up Lady Barbara's face at
this moment. Whoever made this drawing may not be a
practised architect, but he has the spirit of the ancient
English art to help him, and he will work out his purpose
well and truthfully. I hope Miss Langdale will choose this
plan."

The General took up a lump of chalk which lay on the
table, and made a cross on the corner of the drawing.

" I am glad you have chosen this one, Florence," he said,
calling the young heiress by her name, as he had done from
the days of her childhood. " It is mine. The others were
furnished by Mr. Haywarden. I do not like them."

Florence looked at him with surprise. " And yet I might
have guessed," she said, reproaching herself for the doubt.
" No one understands and appreciates this place as you do.
I hope you will always stay here."

" That may depend on yourself some day, little lady,"
said the veteran. " Miss Langdale is restoring this place to
please you—because you admire it—at present she has con-

ceded not to turn me out. Hereafter it will be you who
will have to say to the old soldier, Go—or—Stay."

The girl's dark eyes filled with tears—" Stay,"—she said,
softly, taking in her own the old man's brown but well-
shaped hand. " I should not recognise Noel Hall without
you."

The General pressed fondly the slender fingers. " So
then, that is settled. And I regard it as decided that our
plan for the alterations will be adopted. Miss Langdale
will not go against your will and taste."

"How kind she is," said Florence, thoughtfully. " It
seems so hard never to be allowed to thank her for all she
has done or wished to do for me ; and now, in spite of all
our ungraciousness, she means to make me rich, and will,
you say, let me have my own way in this matter, which she
knows from a child I have had at heart. How well I
remember, when she found me here in the snow, and took
me home, her telling me about the Noels, and what a grand
place the Hall used to be. I cried at the change, and asked
her why she let these wretched people live here ; and wished
I could see it all as it used to be. And now she is going to
fulfil my childish prayer. It was very wrong to try to
deceive my parents, and tempt me to disobedience and
deception ; but still I cannot help loving, and being grateful
to, Miss Langdale."

"Love her, by all means," said the veteran, energetically.
" Maud Langdale has not won the love of many human
beings. And yet, if she had not been crossed in youth—if
the blight which has withered fairer flowers had not fallen
upon her, she might have been a noble woman. Love her,
child, if you can."

"I never could help it," said Florence, simply. From
the day when she took me up before her in the saddle, to

the present hour, I have loved and feared Miss Langdale. I would not say this to any one but you. It is the only subject on which I ever had secrets hidden from my parents, but I cannot help thinking that they are prejudiced against one who would willingly, if they allowed it, be our friend."

"Maud Langdale may be *your* friend, but she is not your mother's," said the General. "Trust me, little lady, they are right to be on their guard—the velvet paw, like Meg's, yonder, has claws beneath. But they will not scratch your tender skin. Love her, as I said before, if you can. Miss Langdale deserves it of you, but do not let her detach you from your best friends."

He turned back to the drawings, explaining his views about the different parts of the structure. Florence entered into all he said with eager interest and delight. When she made any suggestion, the General, unnoticed by her, wrote it down with his chalk on a board, transferring the note, after she was gone, to the margin of the drawing; on which he also wrote in stiff characters, quite unlike those hastily put down in the chalk, "approved by Florence Langdale."

On Mr. Haywarden's next visit, the plans, neatly folded in a sealed packet, were delivered up to him. He was on his way to Langdale Park; and he did not open the parcel, but delivered it to Miss Langdale's servant; as she had directed, should be done, if she happened to be from home. The drawings were, therefore, left for her consideration. The next day Mr. Haywarden received back the plans at his office, with a letter, desiring him to carry out, as speedily as possible, the one marked as approved by Miss Florence Langdale.

Mr. Haywarden opened the packet with a good deal of curiosity. The architectural ground plans and elevations were all unmarked, and, consequently, he judged them to be rejected. The innermost of all was a very carefully but not scientifically executed ground plan, and a bold drawing in chalk, which, at the first glance, carried back the lawyer's thoughts to the time when Noel Hall was one of the show places in the county.

He knew well that this sketch and plan were not among those which he had intended to submit to Miss Langdale, and he searched them closely for any indication of the designer; but he could find neither name nor initials, only the words, "approved by Florence Langdale," and a few marginal notes, written in a stiff, business-like hand, which he did not recognise.

When he inquired of the 'General', who was the only person who had seen the plans, the old man answered succinctly that he and Cuthbert Noel had drawn the plan and sketch selected by Miss Langdale, in America. A time would come, they both thought, when the old place would be restored; and few people living remembered exactly what it had been in its best days. Satisfied with this reply, Mr. Haywarden put the plans at once into the hands of an experienced architect, to be worked out practically, in order that an estimate might be drawn up of the cost. Miss Langdale did not make the slightest objection to the sum proposed, though it was very considerable. She was one of those persons who seldom hesitate about expense in great matters; though she often made herself unpopular by holding back from some trifling, necessary, or at least desirable outlay. All that she said when the completed plans and estimates were submitted to her was, "Let the work be set on foot immediately. Life is uncertain, and, before I die, I wish to see Noel Hall restored to the aspect it used to wear when Lady Barbara and her son were its occupants."

CHAPTER IV.

JUST as she had been haunted in childhood by visions of Christobel and her rider, was Florence Langdale now pursued by thoughts of the restoration of Noel Hall. Miss Langdale could certainly have devised no better way of keeping herself ever present in the romantic girl's imagination. She felt intensely flattered when the General·told her that the plan of which she approved was the one adopted, and that the suggestions she had made would also be carried out.

From her childhood Florence had been fond of the old soldier; and, of all her father's family, she was his especial favourite. Often, in the days when she took long walks with Meredith, had she asked leave to carry some article of luxury or comfort to her father's pensioner. The service he had rendered them all, in saving their mother from shipwreck, was quite a family tradition. The young people, as well as their father, thought that they could never show sufficient gratitude, in return for the preservation of such a valuable life.

The General was not entirely dependent upon their bounty. He 'had a small income which passed through Mr. Langdale's hands, besides the interest of the sum which, in his fallen fortune, Marina's husband had insisted upon his accepting. He often said that what he received was more than sufficient for his moderate wants, and that he should one day leave a fortune to his benefactor's children.

Sometimes, Florence came with her father to the Gateway Tower; but, on these occasions, she was always very silent. More often she accompanied her sisters in the long summer

11

evenings, and then she would sit for hours with her old friend, in his shadowy room, listening to his stories of travel and adventure, or to family legends about the old Noels: while Frances and the twins sketched the Hall from different points of view; with groups of children playing, women drawing water from the deep well in the courtyard, or men returning with horses and carts from their labour in Miss Langdale's fields.

Now all this was altered. Noel Hall, after the hours of toil, was very quiet and solitary. The only figures to be seen at eventide were those of the old dame, who, as a mark of especial favour, was allowed for the present to retain possession of the old dining-hall; as she sometimes crossed the court with her scarlet shawl over her head; the bright-faced, fair-haired boy and some chance companion playing at marbles on the pavement; and the soldier, in his dark blue officer's cloak, sunning himself on the wall.

For a certain number of hours, it was true, a busy crowd of workmen took possession of the place; the air was full of sound; the ring of the axe and hammer, the creak of the saw, the boring of the chisel, went on monotonously, and the outline of the large building was obscured by scaffolding. At six o'clock work was over, and complete silence fell upon the busy scene of a few hours before.

Miss Langdale, though she spared no expense, had not visited the place again. It was whispered abroad that the strong woman's health was failing. She took much less exercise, and when she rode or walked, the pace at which she moved was slower, and her manner was less impatient and less energetic.

Often as Ellinor had winced at her sister's roughness, and rebelled in spirit against, if she dared not openly resist, her arbitrary encroachments on her own liberty and inde-

pendence, it now grieved the affectionate girl to see a
sort of mournful apathy take the place of Miss Langdale's
usually active, restless habits, and fiery temper. Many a
time had she wished and prayed that some softening influence might descend upon Maud, making her more humble,
more womanly, more tender of the feelings of herself and
others. Now the change seemed coming, the prayer on the
point of being granted, Ellinor regretted the change.

These listless moods, however, were only temporary.
Maud strove to shake them off, and rebelled fiercely against
such unaccustomed weakness of mind and body. After
being shut up in the house for a few days, succumbing for
the first time in her life to atmospheric influences or indisposition, Miss Langdale would rise up, like a lion or a
whirlwind; and rush about the place finding fault, and dis-
missing offenders who had relaxed in their diligence during
her temporary seclusion. She had never been herself, the
people about the Hall said, since her disappointment in not
getting the young lady at the Grange, to live with her.

"I assure you, Mrs. Langdale, it was a shock to me, quite
a shock as well as a surprise, to hear that Miss Langdale
had sent twice to my house for me yesterday, in my absence.
Of course she was in a hurry, and as a matter of course,
too, no one knew where to find me," said Dr. Forsyth, as
he stopped to see his patient at Godley, after leaving the
Hall.

"I never knew her to have so much as a head-ache before,
and now she is all unstrung—nervous, feverish, highly excitable; in short, I scarcely know what to think of the
case. I declare you might have knocked me down with a
feather, when I saw her sitting in the great library in her
riding-habit, grim and sombre, and, I believe, with her gold-
mounted whip close at hand; not such a thing as a foot-

stool, or a couch, or an easy chair within a mile of her;—bolt
upright, in a stiff carved-ebony sort of cushionless throne, as
hard as herself, waiting for me. How am I to prescribe for
such a woman? I thought. Will she let me feel her pulse?
Will she take my medicines? What on earth am I to do
with her? It was like attending a lioness: and the slight
delay, unavoidable as it was, made her glare at me. 'I
want you to give me something to make me well immediately, Dr. Forsyth,' she said; 'I have no time to be ill;
none of your rose-coloured draughts that suit my sister
Ellinor: she is not half the woman that I am. I never had
a day's illness in my life. What can be the matter with me?'

"'I do not know how that may be, Miss Langdale,' I
said, 'but allow me to say you look very unwell now. I
advise you to go at once to bed; and I will send you something which I hope, in a little time, may restore you to your
usual state of excellent health.'

"Not a bit of it—she would not listen to me. 'Go to
bed yourself,' was her polite reply; and she chafed, and
fumed, and pooh-poohed all my advice. I should not in the
least wonder if I found her in a raging fever to-morrow."

"It is so hard for a person who has never been accustomed to it, to bear illness:" said Mrs. Langdale, with a
gentle sigh. "I am very sorry for the poor lady, but, unfortunately, it is not in our power to be of any service to
her."

"Indeed! you are quite mistaken," said the kind doctor,
confidentially. "That poor soul at the Hall is pining away
for a sight of her future heiress. Would it be against your
principles to allow Miss Florence to go up with me to-morrow for half an hour, to see her? I promise to bring her
back safe. It would do Miss Langdale more good than any
medicine I can prescribe for her."

Mrs. Langdale turned pale. "I dare not ask my husband to allow Florence to visit her cousin. Rightly or wrongly, he entertains the greatest fear of her influence over our child. I myself fear that it would unsettle her mind. Miss Langdale has not deserved this sacrifice from us."

"Oh, well, just as you please," said the doctor, buttoning up his great coat. "Miss Langdale has a constitution of iron; to-morrow I *may* find her better. She is not used to being thwarted, and she has set her heart on seeing Miss Florence; but, if you don't like it, she must get over the fancy."

Mrs. Langdale did not speak.

"People must reconcile themselves to the inevitable," continued Dr. Forsyth, as he shook hands with her before taking leave. "Only it is harder for some than for others. Upon my word I could not help feeling a little sorry for her, though she is not usually a person to excite compassion. But she seemed so sad and lonely amid all her grandeur,—not a comfort near her; just the old family paintings and tapestry,—and old saws on her lips; much good may they avail her! One loving kiss, the clasp of a kind hand, the watchfulness which has been about you all through the long years of your trial, what a world of good they would do her! But I should like to know how a woman who has lived without love all her life, and despised it as Maud Langdale has done, can expect to find it at the time when the need of affection—the value of human care and kindness—first comes upon her? She must learn to die, as she has chosen to live, without these things——"

"You do not think she will die?" said Mrs. Langdale awe-stricken. "I wish Frank were at home. I would ask him, but I feel certain that he would not let his daughter go to Langdale Park."

"Best leave it alone—I am sorry I mentioned it," said the doctor, while all the time he rejoiced at having scattered seeds abroad which he believed would ripen in the soft soil of Mrs. Langdale's heart. "Take care of yourself, that is of the most consequence. That poor unfortunate sinner at the Hall must reap as she has sown. The rector called, but she positively refused to see him."

"Come here on your way to the Hall to-morrow," said Mrs. Langdale. "I will prepare my husband, and you can ask him. But if you meet Florence, do not, I entreat you, mention the subject to her."

"Do you think she does not know all about it?" said the doctor. "Depend upon it, your good Mrs. Meredith, or some of the allies of the great lady at the Hall, have been paying court already to her successor. I will wager my existence Miss Florence is watching my old mare at this moment, and longing to go up and nurse that grim old virago. Good day,—I can't possibly stop another minute."

He was as good as his word this time, though in general the doctor's adieus were as protracted as the close of his old friend the rector's sermons. No wonder that Miss Langdale's impatient temper chafed at their ministrations.

CHAPTER V.

THE invalid at the Grange, had enjoyed better health lately than whence she first came into Yorkshire. Her malady, though incurable, no longer caused her such acute suffering, nor did it oblige her to keep entirely in her own rooms. Some of the improvements of modern science had been brought to bear upon this tedious case by her kind and clever doctor, aided by the sudden impulses of affection, and of maternal anxiety ; which seemed, almost as if by a miracle, to have lifted Mrs. Langdale from her sick couch, and restored power to her feeble limbs, when she was first made aware of the conspiracy on foot to deprive her of her darling's affection.

Fritz was at last working hard and steadily. Perhaps his disinheritance was the best thing that could have befallen him. He had quite got over his disappointment, and dismissed the thought of his former expectations from his mind. Reason told him that Florence was not seriously to blame ; and the little one, when he thought of the loved beings at home, was as dear to him as the rest, excepting Gertrude, who had always been his favourite.

The young German nobleman, Count Max von Berlingen, the elder brother of Fritz's favourite school comrade, was now travelling in England; and at his request, Fritz obtained a brief holiday, which the two friends agreed to spend at the Grange ; arriving there, after a brief notice, on the day of Dr. Forsyth's visit, and during Miss Langdale's indisposition. The master of the Grange had gone himself to meet the young men, and bring them home from the Station.

Mrs. Langdale was very much troubled by the Doctor's suggestion. Again and again the picture he had drawn rose up before her ; of the hard, cold, unsympathising woman, unloving and unloved, ill and solitary ; with one ungratified wish at her heart. Even her joy at seeing her son was overclouded by the remembrance of the promise she had made to place the subject before her husband. She knew that it would cause him grievous disturbance.

Fritz and his father were in such good spirits. The young man was more respectful than formerly, yet with a healthy independent manliness of aspect. Mr. Langdale grew younger in spirit as he looked at his son, and heard the report of his proceedings. Gertrude, calm as she looked, was more beautiful than ever, with a slight glow of subdued excitement on her usually pale fair cheek, and a steady light in her eyes, which the watchful mother had never before seen gleaming out of their blue depths. Frances and the twins were busy unpacking photographs, which the young Count had brought from Germany, and listening to his account of his travels. Florence alone was absent.

"Where is Flo? What has become of the little one?" said her brother. "Did she not know that we were coming?"

"I am not sure that she saw the letter," said Gertrude. "The post was late; Florence had just left the breakfast-table and was gone on one of her long rambles. We ought to have had your letter yesterday, Fritz, but it only reached us this morning."

"Well, I suppose she will be back presently," said her brother with some annoyance. "I hope the old lady at the Hall has not, like a wicked fairy, carried her off! I do not think I told you Max, that, since you were here last, my little sister has become an heiress."

"Miss Langdale is very ill," said his mother, in a low voice, unwilling to lose the opportunity thus afforded for unburdening her mind in some degree. "Dr. Forsyth was here an hour before you arrived, and drew quite a touching picture of the poor lady, so sad and solitary, and chafing at her own miserable weakness. All the luxuries she can command impart no comfort, the only desire to which she confesses is unluckily one which cannot be gratified."

"If my cousin Maud has set her heart on anything, she generally brings it to pass," said Mr. Langdale gravely. "What is it, Marina, that she wishes? Did the Doctor tell you?"

" Yes, Dr. Forsyth mentioned it," said Mrs. Langdale, nervously ; " I wish he would not talk so much about his patients. After all, they might not like it ; but he is a good man and very tender hearted, and he has known Miss Langdale from a child. Her great wish, he says, is to see Florence."

Mr. Langdale's brow clouded over. Fritz, too, looked disturbed. In spite of his philosophy this allusion to the change in favour of his young sister, in his prospects, brought the future before him painfully. The moment the words had passed her lips, Mrs. Langdale regretted their utterance. No further notice, at the moment, was taken of them, and the party separated. The young people set off on an excursion to Hazeldon woods, and Mr. Langdale, without a single observation even to his wife, went out of doors. She saw him walking up and down alone in the orchard, thoughtful and sad ; and she did not venture to interrupt, unbidden, her husband's meditations.

Dr. Forsyth had judged rightly that Florence would receive early intimation of the illness of the Lady of Langdale Hall. She had gone out immediately after breakfast, without hearing of her brother's intended visit, and the first person she met in the road towards the village, informed her of the fact.

Florence turned back immediately. Sho forgot her intention of visiting a sick girl at a neighbouring cottage ; and, hardly conscious whither she was going, walked slowly along the field pathway to church, which passed in front of the Hall and across the Park. The interdiction had long been removed against using this mode of communication between two parts of the village and the church ; and now, though it was a week day, the gates stood open. The reapers were busy gathering in the corn, and the gleaners were following

the heavily laden wains picking up the ears of yellow
grain that lay in their track. Florence kept out of their way
under the high hedges, in which old trees were set. She
felt as if she could not go home, where no one would sympathise with the sorrow which filled her heart.

All through her young life—ever since she could remember
anything—this haughty woman—who now lay, as she was
told, sick unto death, for the report which had reached her
was a very exaggerated one, as is usual among the poor in
cases of sudden illness,—had been the object of her young
cousin's romantic idolatry. Florence had struggled with
herself against this passion, for it was nothing else, but it
was in vain ; opposition had fostered it, and it had grown in
silence, till it had obtained entire possession of her whole
being. Torrents of tears rolled down the girl's cheeks, as she
cast herself down on the bank ; in the middle of the fertile
fields, flushed with the harvest glow, which ere long might be
her own.

For the first time Florence realised this truth. It seemed
to flash upon her, as the sunrays flashed on the golden corn,
and lit up the windows of Langdale Hall—of the very room
where its mistress might be dying. Florence lifted herself
on her elbow, and looked, through streaming tears, at the
old house.

The park sloped down very steeply from the terraced
garden which lay on this side of the mansion. Here and
there a tall flower, a glowing lily, or dark red hollyhock, rose
above the grey walls which supported the banks of earth
of the flower garden. Miss Langdale had herself laid out
this stately pleasaunce, which was not in character with the
black and white timbered front of the house—but in their
different ways both were beautiful.

On Florence's uncritical imagination the effect was very

powerful. She loved and admired the grim, grey, smoke-blackened walls which frowned above the green valley,—the great baronial tower at the entrance—the heavy gates, flung open so swiftly at the approach of Miss Langdale's carriage. In her childhood she had often stood still to watch the lady enter her own domain. Now, with the summer heat brooding over the hills and glades of the park,—with the loaded wains and rustic groups scattered over the stubble —though the blinds of the mansion were closed, the prospect was unusually gay.

The girl lay looking at the darkened windows till a strange dread stole over her. What if Miss Langdale were dead ! Her fancy pictured the whole scene, forgetful that the blinding sun-rays alone caused the blinds to be closed, and that she had seen the same eclipse take place every afternoon at that hour.

In all Florence Langdale's dreams her own triumphant entrance into the old Hall had borne a conspicuous part ; but she had never thought of it except in connection with its present mistress. The old feud was to die away, and through her agency all were to be made friends. She was to be Miss Langdale's honoured guest, and all sorts of dimly guessed pleasures were to follow. Her own recognition as Miss Langdale's heiress had touched her feelings. Gratitude, affection, were due for the generous gift. She longed to acknowledge her deep sense of its magnitude.

Now it struck her as too painful a thought that, for all this generous love, she might never be able to thank her kind friend and benefactor. That at this very moment life might be passing away—that she might never, never, be able to pour out the treasures of her long pent up affection and sorrow.

Florence dried her tears and started up. She went nearer

to the high walls, and, as they interrupted her view, she crossed the park into the cart road leading to the back of the Hall, and slowly approached the entrance. Her intentions were quite vague. She allowed herself to drift along as circumstances might dictate.

One of Miss Langdale's servants, followed by a cart bearing refreshments for the reapers, was coming down the drive. The old butler uncovered his grey head respectfully to the young lady, pausing and drawing aside for her to pass him. But Florence stopped suddenly. The man's face was quite familiar to her. She had often seen him at the head of the long row of servants from the Hall, in church, and in her walks, as a child, with Meredith.

"Oh, do take me to your mistress," she said; "I must see her. Is it true that she is dying?"

"Nay, I hope not—God forbid," said the trusted domestic, to whom Maud Langdale had been a kind mistress. "She's altered surely, and has not been herself of late; but she'll be main glad to see you, I know. Come this way, my dear young lady."

Giving a brief direction to his subordinates, the old butler, who was quite aware of Miss Langdale's infatuated predilection for her young cousin, and of the long family feud; turned back, and accompanied Florence along the road to the Hall. In a sort of bewildered trance, dizzy with the burning heat, faint from crying, she walked by his side like one in a dream.

Not a thought of her father or mother, of Fritz, or of her sisters, at this moment entered the young girl's mind. She seemed to herself to be under a spell, and she offered no resistance. A gush of sweet scents almost overpowered her, as, through a long dark arched tunnel, which passed under the road, Miss Langdale's private garden came into view.

She felt as if another world lay under her feet, as she stepped from the gloom of the overhanging rock, through which the passage was bored, into that bright region of scarlet blossoms and shadowy fern leaves, waving boughs, and glancing cascades and fountains.

The old servant stood still for a moment, while Florence stopped under a thicket of Alpine Rhododendron, just tinged with the last remains of its crimson bloom; feeling as though the dream of her whole life was at last fully realized. Through waving boughs of lime and acacia, glimpses were visible of the jasmine-wreathed, chequered windows of Langdale Hall. Around her, in the shadowy twilight of the dusky trees, waters were flowing, ferns waving, birds singing, and the gold and silver fish darted in and out, through gloom and sunshine, across their rocky basins. There was no point in the grounds where the Hall could be seen to more advantage.

In front of the house was the bright parterre of which Florence had caught glimpses from below. Now it lay before her, gleaming in scarlet and gold, purple and crimson, in the sunshine of the last days of August. Masses of geranium, heliotrope, fuchsia, lobelia, and other numberless bright flowers of the season, intersected with bordering leaves of gold and silver, or dark brown stems and leaves veined with scarlet, domineered over by lilies of gorgeous hues or spotless white, were guarded by stone walls, balustrades, and statues. Across this flower garden, silent and darkened, rose the Hall, every window open and shaded; not a living creature was to be seen.

Florence Langdale followed the old servant across the grass that lay between the flower beds, and entered the house under a jasmine-covered porch. A wide, dark passage passed right through to the great entrance, crossed by a similar gallery leading on the one side, to the principal living rooms, on the other to the offices, a simple plan adopted in most of the ancient Yorkshire mansions.

"Miss Langdale is in the library," said Florence's companion in a whisper. "I think it will be best to take you to my mistress at once. She is very impatient of anything like preparation. I'm *sure* she'll be main glad to see you."

Florence felt surprised at the intimation. Expecting to stand in a few moments at the side of a dying bed, the idea of the library came upon her with a shock ; but it was too late for retreat. Trembling from head to foot, she mounted the winding staircase erected by Miss Langdale in that part of the building, and called, in the establishment, the Library Tower.

Lighted by loop-holes commanding a view of the lovely winding valley of the Lang, and lined from floor to ceiling with gravely bound books, the library was always dark and somewhat gloomy. What little furniture it contained was simple in character and sombre of hue. It was a place sacred to study, yet Miss Langdale seldom opened a book.

Ponderous ledgers were piled on the leather-covered table, under the largest of the high narrow windows. On a covered ebony chair, in front of an old-fashioned desk, totally unoccupied, in her usual cloth riding dress, and with her whip across her knees, sat the mistress of Langdale Hall. The expression on her face was one of profound sadness and extreme lassitude. She was not looking at the beautiful landscape far below, nor at the writings spread out before her. Her face wore the leaden colouring of disease, and her whole attitude bespoke extreme depression.

The door left open on account of the extreme heat revealed to Florence the interior of the gloomy room, before the quiet entrance of the old servant attracted his mistress's attention. The girl stood trembling on the threshold, awed by her kinswoman's silent, stony abstraction. Then a strangely soft compassionate feeling for the forlorn being before her, took possession of all her faculties; and she glided across the room, and cast herself on her knees beside her, clasping her arms round her, before the domestic could make any form of introduction.

"It is I, Florence Langdale, to whom you have been always so kind," she said. "You wanted me, and I have come to you."

Miss Langdale looked at the young girl with astonishment. Then with a wild cry of delight she returned Florence's embrace; and, laying her head on the girl's shoulder, she burst into a flood of tears, which relieved her overcharged brain and heart. Not for years had such a refreshing shower watered the arid ground of her affections. Florence did not speak, did not move. The servant respectfully and discreetly withdrew. When Miss Langdale raised her head, the leaden hue was gone from her cheeks, her eyes sparkled brightly. "Welcome," she said, as she kissed her young cousin, "Welcome to Langdale Hall, now, and for ever."

CHAPTER VI.

FLORENCE LANGDALE was not aware of the importance of the step she had unadvisedly taken until she experienced the difficulty of drawing back. It was very far from her intention to remain at Langdale Hall, but, having once entered the enchanter's ground, she seemed to herself spellbound.

It was a long time before it occurred to her family that she was really missing, for her usual mode of life was solitary and independent. Fritz's suggestion that the young heiress hàd been carried off to Langdale Hall did not alarm her parents; no one guessed that it might be near the truth.

Even this jesting remark, followed by Mrs. Langdale's communication respecting his cousin's illness, and desire to see Florence, had, however, sorely disturbed her father; but not the slightest suspicion crossed his mind, that his young daughter was at that very moment virtually quitting her home for ever.

The mistress of the Hall, meanwhile, had resolved that Florence should not leave her. She felt well and strong in a moment, and her iron will re-awoke from the stupor of indifference which had crept over, and for a time weakened it. It was as though this fresh young life had entered into her own, and refreshed the worn springs of her joyless existence.

She said not a word that might alarm Florence, after her first hasty ejaculations of welcome; but busied herself in at once placing the young girl in the position, which, henceforth, she meant her to occupy. Neither did she confess that her own indisposition had, at least temporarily, vanished, but, with a tact and tenderness hitherto seldom manifested, she seemed to rely upon Florence to sustain and comfort her in her illness.

She herself conducted Florence to the beautiful room intended for her, and showed her the preparations made for her reception; confessing how bitter had been her subsequent disappointment.

Never had the daughter of Frank Langdale, the youngest of a large, struggling family, even in her dreams, fancied herself the occupant of such a splendid apartment. Miss Langdale had arranged it for her when she altered the disposition of her property, and invited her young cousin to take up her abode at Langdale Hall. After Mr. Langdale's rejection of her proposal, she had shut up the room designed for the young heiress.

The half-hour passed in the old library, during which Miss Langdale constantly solicited some slight help which served to keep alive Florence's sympathy, and made her feel herself really useful; had sufficed for the additional preparations judged necessary by the well-trained domestics: fresh flowers in the vases; the uncovering of the delicate furniture; and the arrangement of the snowy toilette and stores of fine linen, which might have suited the satin skin of the princess in the fairy tale, whose royal lineage was revealed by its susceptibility.

Miss Langdale mounted the staircase slowly, leaning on Florence's arm. Through the old house, beautiful and venerable, full of tokens of care and taste, the two went lovingly together; while, through the cool space and open windows, the summer breeze entered freely; bringing with it the scent of flowers, the hum of insects, and the song of birds.

Florence looked round with artless admiration as she entered the low but spacious room; with its carved ceiling and panelled walls, old pictures, and some lighter, more graceful, and commodious modern articles of furniture, antique in style, and suited to the apartment, but not originally belonging to it; which Miss Langdale told her had been introduced especially for her use. One of them was a low couch, drawn close under the long window, around which, outside, and peeping in at the casement, the jasmine twined luxuriantly.

12

"We will not talk any more at present," said Miss Langdale, affectionately kissing her. "These are your own rooms, my dear, this one and the next, whenever you like to take possession, which I shall never enter without your permission. You can make what additions you like to the furniture. I shall leave you now to rest a little. When it is cooler, and you are revived, come to me in the library."

Florence blushed deeply. She said, hesitatingly, "I will come and see you before I go home, when it is cooler. I do not think they will miss me at present. No one knows where I am."

"Oh, I will send word. It would be a great pity for Mr. and Mrs. Langdale to be alarmed," said her hostess, with a shade of coldness. "Do not speak of leaving me, Florence, when you are only just come here, and I am so ill. If you like to change your dress, you will find all you require in your wardrobe. I will settle every thing with your parents. I am sure they will spare you, for a while, to nurse me."

Miss Langdale did not wait for an answer, but, shutting the door gently, left her young heiress to amuse herself with inspecting the various luxuries provided for her.

Maud sat for some time in the shadowy library with her pen in her hand, and a sheet of note paper on her desk, before any words arranged themselves in her mind, by which she could communicate to her cousin, Frank Langdale, the news that she had robbed him of his child. When completed, her note was as follows :—

"LANGDALE HALL,
"*August* 27.

"MY DEAR COUSIN,
"Florence has come of her own will and wish to Langdale Hall, hearing of my illness, and anxious to help

me to bear whatever may be God's will. I do not know
whether my sickness is unto death, or no. I feel better
since the dear child has been with me, and I implore you
to leave her here for the present. Of course, you have
legally the power to separate us, though you could not prevent my having bequeathed to her all that I possess. In
her name and in my own, I beg you not to use your legal
authority.

"Your affectionate cousin,

"MATILDA LANGDALE."

Miss Langdale sealed her envelope with the large coat of
arms of the family, and rang the bell.

"Send this letter down to the Grange when it grows
dusk ;—*no sooner.* Desire the messenger not to wait for an
answer."

The old man bowed respectfully. "Will the young lady
dine here to-day ?" he said. "Shall I lay a cover for her ?"

"Of course," said his mistress with cheerful decision.
"Let there be *always* a cover laid for Miss Florence Langdale, opposite to my own."

The butler hesitated. "That is Miss Ellinor's place,
madam ; am I to change it ?"

"Certainly. Miss Ellinor is a visitor here, and will sit
on my right hand. Miss Florence Langdale is at home : I
wish her to be treated as if she were my daughter. Let
the household understand this, Phillips. One day, perhaps
very soon, she will be your mistress here."

"Nay, madam, I hope that day may be long deferred : I
never saw you looking better. The young lady's coming
has already done you good. We shall all be glad to serve
you both. Shall you be well enough to dine at table
to-day ?"

"Yes, Phillips, I am better, nearly well, I believe, but you need not say so. Who knows what may happen? Miss Florence must not leave us again. We will try to make her so happy that she will not desire it."

The old servant withdrew, gratified by his mistress's condescension. He soon spread the tidings that the young lady was to remain ; and most of the household rejoiced in the acquisition. Miss Ellinor Langdale's former nurse, now her personal attendant, was an almost solitary exception ; though Phillips was too discreet to mention Miss Langdale's directions about the dinner table.

"The sooner my young lady is gone from here the better," she said, as she prepared to leave the room at the sound of a bell. "It is one thing to have your just inheritance taken from you, and another to sit down every day at the same table with the interloper. I hope that *I* am not expected to wait upon her, until she gets a lady's maid of her own !"

"No, indeed," said a pretty young woman, who had just entered the servant's hall. "I am to be Miss Florence Langdale's attendant ; and I quite love her, she spoke so sweetly about the new curtains and toilette-cover that gave me such trouble in ironing ; and was not too proud to praise everything, and thank me for my pains. Such a sweet, pretty young lady, the old place will be twice as lively. Miss Langdale worships her, and will not allow her to be as dull as we have often felt lately."

Phillips departed to his own sphere, and, with his subordinates, speedily arranged the dinner table according to Miss Langdale's directions. Without asking further questions the family plate was produced and polished, and much more attention paid to appearances than had been the case for years.

A new era was about to commence,—there was to be no more of the old règime. Miss Langdale, in spite of her indisposition, was actually dressing for dinner; in one· of the dark handsome silks she usually wore on Sundays.

This was evidently not to be one of the hurried, comfortless, unceremonious repasts, of which she had so often partaken standing, and in her riding-habit, or kept waiting for hours. The old house was to be swept and garnished, and remodelled, for its fair young future mistress.

PART THE FIFTH.

A WOMAN'S WILFUL WILL.

Soft winds of summer—whither away ?—
Twisting and twirling in frolicsome play ;
Leaves slightly curling of flowers on our way;
Cooling your brow as we merrily pass,
Flinging light shade on the green rippling grass ;
Softly expanding, above and below,
Till our circlets are lost in the hushed evening's glow.

Waves of the mountain stream—whither so fast ?—
Sinking and rising, rushing and gliding,
Steep rocks surprising, sunken shoals hiding ;
Inviting to bathe in some cool sheltered spot,
Kissing the stones where the sunbeams come not :
Through sunshine and shadow, with rocks overhead,
Till we find rest and peace in the ocean's broad bed.

Translated from HENRIETTE OTTENHEIMER'S " WOHIN ?"

R. M. K.

CHAPTER I.

NDER Hazeldon Crags the sunny hours of the sultry August afternoon wore away after a different fashion. Neither Fritz nor his sisters felt the slightest uneasiness respecting Florence, and the Count was perfectly satisfied with his present companions. The heat was tempered by the waving boughs and flowing water: each cool recess in the rocky woodland offered temptation to linger on the banks of the Hebdon.

Not one of the party remembered on this occasion the day, when, sitting among the reeds and forget-me-nots, "the little one" had first attracted the attention of the Lady of Langdale. No one in the least anticipated that, even now, the fine meshes of the web, of which the first was spun on that bright fine holiday, six years ago, were, at this moment, drawn close. Many a summer morning, many an autumn day, had since that time been passed happily by the young people in Hebdon valley. They were full of energy and cheerfulness now.

Through that bright vale the river ran, past rocks and shoals of sand and gravel, swiftly on its course. The shallow waters, in some parts, rushed noisily and merrily round sharp pointed masses of grey granite, or glided smoothly round great mossy boulders, reflected in the glassy mirror.

Shelving slabs of stone and slate sloped down into deeper water, and rare ferns hung from the steep banks in almost inaccessible places, like coy beauties, the best being always the most difficult to win. Fritz and Count Max were searching for the rarest specimens, whilst Frances and the twins sat on the shady bank, sketching a bright, wide reach of the river.

Gertrude alone was unoccupied. It was a real pleasure to her to stray along the broken path, or to venture to step from stone to stone, and look down into the water arched over by cool green boughs, of which each stem and waving leaf was reflected. She could not remember that she had ever been a child; and, in her earliest girlhood, life had been overcast, and her path encompassed with troubles. Mrs. Langdale's illness, and subsequent helplessness, had thrown upon the eldest daughter of the family a mother's duties; and Gertrude had adopted and discharged them cheerfully.

Now, almost for the first time, the weight was removed. She no longer felt such a fearful load of responsibility. Her sisters had all grown up: even "the little one" was sixteen; and Mrs. Lang herself superintended Florence's studies. Gertrude, of late, had felt the nearest approach to jealousy which her gentle, generous nature could experience. Ever since Miss Langdale's attempts to divide Florence from her family had been discovered, their mother had clung to her youngest born.

Relieved of the charge of completing the education of her young sisters, Gertrude had taken up her old habits of study. She was particularly fond of the study of languages, and, from her childhood, had been accustomed to speak, and to read, French, German, and Italian. Her father's improved circumstances enabled her to increase her collection of foreign books, and she had ample time now to profit by them.

Many a wild German legend came into her thoughts as
she listened to the wild song of the waters—the murmurs
of the rustling reeds—the quiver of the boughs—and the
plaintive cooing of the wood-pigeons in the thicket. Quite
unconscious of observation, believing herself to be entirely
alone, she crossed the river; leaping lightly over the wide
intervals between the stepping stones, and standing still to
look down, from time to time, into the shining stream. In
an arched recess on the opposite bank her quick eye detected
some graceful sprays of the beech fern, which she longed to
secure, before Fritz and Max came back from their quest;
but, when she reached the spot, they were high above her
head, quite beyond her reach.

Gertrude was looking wistfully at the green tufts cropping
out of the dark damp stone, when a hand was stretched out
to gather them for her; and the shadow of the tall figure of
the young foreign nobleman was cast upon the bank, beside
her own. "Why did you not call to us to help you in
crossing over?" he said, in German, the language in which
they always conversed when alone together. "Your brother
and I were quite close at hand, but yet not in time to aid
you."

"Oh yes, you have helped me now. It would have been
too provoking to lose my prize," said Gertrude, laughing
and blushing. "I did not know that any one was looking
at me. It seemed all so still, so solitary; as if only wood and
water nymphs could be within hearing."

"That is exactly what we were saying, and your sudden
appearance did not disturb our theory," said Max. "Who
would imagine that so near one of your great manufacturing
cities, in busy, wealthy England, there could be found a
place so utterly wild and solitary as this. So beautiful, and
with scarcely a pathway to mar its tranquillity! One might

expect such scenes in the Saxon Switzerland, or the König-See, or in the Schwarz Wald, but not on the borders of the Black Country. The West Riding is not spoilt yet."

Gertrude did not re-cross the stream unassisted, and the transit was not by any means as rapidly performed as might have been expected. The two light agile forms were reflected in the pools and ripples, pausing on each large stone that broke the current; with the magic glamour of the woodland whispering all around them, and the bright waters gleaming underneath.

"It is six years since I first saw this place," said the German nobleman, during one of these brief halts. "I have never forgotten the September day, when I first visited the Crags with you and your sisters, and Fritz. You said it was your first holiday since your arrival in England. Your sisters had been in Hebdon valley once before, but we came here for the first time together. Have you forgotten that day ?"

"No," said Gertrude, turning her head away, "I remember it quite well. I have not had many such bright holidays in my life as that September afternoon, and to-day, by the bright Hebdon waters."

"I am glad to hear you say so," said Max. "These days are marked with a white stone in my calendar. Your sisters have grown into women since then. You are no longer the Haus-frau—the mother of the family. You are younger than you were, six years ago—younger and brighter. Is it not so ?"

"It is cruel to remind me of my advancing years," said Gertrude, laughing. "My tall sisters make me feel quite old. Even Florence, 'the little one,' as we used to call her, is almost a woman."

"She looks older than you do," said the Count; "older

and graver. You are so fair—you will be always young.
Twenty years hence, in my eyes, perhaps in those of others,
you will look just the same."

"That is a pleasant prophecy," said Gertrude, taking his
offered hand to assist her as she sprang across the last running channel of water. "I certainly do not feel older than
when we were last at Hazeldon Crags. Sometimes I am inclined to fancy myself a child again, for I do my lessons, as
the twins used to say; and I had no time for them when I
was a girl. My vocation is taken from me. Florence is now
my mother's principal companion, and I have no one to
teach, so I have gone to school again myself."

"Does not this prove that you're free to accept another
destiny?" said the Count, drawing Gertrude's arm within
his own after they reached the bank. "Take care; the
sward is slippery here; let me help you, Gertrude. I tried
once before to persuade you that in our German Fatherland
there is a country house where your presence is needed. I ask
you now the question you prevented my uttering then. I have
not changed, but, with you, circumstances are altered. Is
this in my favour? Fritz can tell you all about me—my
home, my position in my own country, my young brothers, for
whom, as the head of the family, my house must always be a
home. Will you help me to make it a happy one for us all?"

Miss Langdale had not this time interrupted her lover.
She did not speak. Max went on:

"You know me well yourself, Gertrude. We are not
strangers to each other, and you love my country. The German tongue—the habits of our country are quite familiar to
you—we are of the same religion. What should part us?
Even when you suffered me not to address you, three years
ago, I did not think that you disliked me. I saw that you
were so necessary at home. I waited. I will wait seven years,

like the patriarch, if you tell me that in time my patience
will be rewarded."

Gertrude tried to speak but her voice failed her. The
hand that rested on the Count's arm trembled, but it was not
removed. At last she said : "I believe you are right. There
will be home now without me at the Grange, and you,"—
she paused—"you, Max, ever since you first came to our
house with Fritz,—I have loved you."

"Is anything the matter? What on earth are you about?"
were the words that startled the lovers from a very blissful
dream, as Fritz pushed his way through the bushes to join
them. "The carriage is waiting, and the girls have finished
their sketches. I have been looking everywhere for you and
Gertrude."

"And you have found us at last, together!" said the
foreigner, cheerfully. "All right, my dear boy, that is just
as it should be ;—Fritz, I cannot keep a secret from you,
and you have long known the earnest wishes of my heart.
Give me joy, at last I have won my bride. The old Castle
is to have the mistress I have always wished to install there.
And you, dear Fritz, must look upon it as your German
home." The young men clasped hands, and between them
Gertrude went her way, happily, through the valley.

Now and then the interrupted track, encumbered by rocks
and stones, forced the trio to separate ; although they had
now emerged from the wilder, entirely pathless, portion of
the woods. On these occasions Fritz fell back; suffering with a
kind of wondering magnanimity, his friend to aid his sister.
It was with a severe pang, though he cordially rejoiced in
the success of his wooing, that Fritz recognized the indis-
putable fact, that henceforth, even with his favourite sister,
he must be satisfied to take the second place.

The drive through the woods—all gleaming with sunny

light, while the red mountain-ash berries glowed scarlet in
the declining rays, and the water glittered and danced along
far down below the winding road—was a very silent one.
It may be conjectured, nevertheless, if the secret thoughts
of all could have been made manifest, that this was not
the least pleasant of the sunshiny afternoons spent in the
woods and under the crags by the Hebdon Water; before it
changes its character, and flows, dark and sombre, through
the gloomy moorland scenery beyond the Hazeldon rocks.

CHAPTER II.

MRS. LANGDALE gave some necessary orders respecting the
accommodation of her son and his friend, in the absence of
her children, with a certain feeling of satisfaction. She
even, with the aid of her husband's arm, travelled as far as
the greenhouse to see if the grapes were ripe enough to be
gathered for the late repast, which was to be laid out for
the young people on their return from the crags.

It was a pity the clusters were not quite ready to cut, the
gardener told them. Miss Florence had wanted a bunch
to take to Miss Forsyth, the Doctor's invalid niece, her
only intimate friend in the neighbourhood.

This accidental piece of information quite relieved Mr.
and Mrs. Langdale's mind of any uneasiness respecting their
absent daughter. Florence often spent a morning with her
friend, and, if the Doctor caught sight of his pretty favourite,
he was sure to make her stay to partake of the early dinner
at Langdale Cottage, and often drive her back, when he paid
his round of country visits.

Dr. Forsyth had been a naval surgeon. After various

wanderings, he had taken out his diploma, and settled down near Langdale Park, in a cottage belonging to its last owner, as Mr. Langdale's medical attendant. As long as he lived, the doctor visited the Hall daily, and, after his death, he found himself in the enjoyment of a handsome annuity. It was with difficulty, from long habit, that he and his old mare could pass the gates without entering ; and the lodge-keepers, with whom, as with most of the country people, he was a great favourite, were always ready, at the sound of the black mare's fast trot, to throw them open for him. Hitherto Miss Langdale had not required medical attend-ance, but he often visited the Hall as a friend, or if any of the household were ill; and at all times he had leave to cross the park in any direction. Langdale Cottage was at the opposite end of the long straggling village, from the Grange ; at about three miles distance by the road, but much nearer, through the fields and park.

Satisfied that Florence was safe with her kind friends, the husband and wife dined together, at an earlier hour than usual ; the excursionists not being expected back till night-fall. For years they had not been alone at the dinner table. The change, once in a way, was pleasant. Mr. Langdale was always very attentive to his invalid wife, almost like a lover. He enjoyed having Marina entirely to himself.

They did not mention the subject of Miss Langdale's ill-ness, and wish to see their daughter. Mrs. Langdale was satis-fied that the doctor would keep his promise and bring Flo-rence back safely, without communicating the circumstance. She did not wish to disturb her husband's serenity, and she left it to his discretion how to act in any emergency that might arise : fervently hoping that the invalid at the Hall might soon be better, and that no formal proposition might be made respecting Florence.

After sitting for some time together, while the intense heat prevailed, Mr. and Mrs. Langdale rose from table, and separated for the rest of the afternoon. Mrs. Langdale went to her own room to lie down, while her husband set off across the fields to the Doctor's house; intending to bring Florence home with him.

It was now delightfully cool: long shadows lay across the fields and rural pathway. The reapers were still busy, and all the gates stood open. After a momentary hesitation, when he had crossed the last meadow, and an intervening lane, Mr. Langdale entered his cousin's park.

Though one of the private keys hung up in his study, Frank Langdale had never, since his youth, crossed his kinswoman's domain. In general he would prefer to go any distance round to avoid the necessity; but, as the shadows lengthened, a slight anxiety crept over his mind about the little one, and this way was decidedly the shortest approach to Langdale Cottage.

He walked quickly on under the old trees, which rustled as the wind rose above his head. A thought which often haunted him—which hitherto he had succeeded in banishing—now kept its ground. How would it fare, with him and his, if the lady at the Hall were gone, and Florence the mistress of the land on which he was treading?

Mr. Langdale was not a man for whom the idea of living in his young daughter's house was a pleasant prospect. He was of a very firm independent character, and he had always been entirely the master in his own home. Of late—ever since his wife's illness indeed—something like sternness had grown upon him. He knew that the little one feared as well as loved him.

He stood still for a minute, under the aged chestnut trees, trying to realise the altered position in which his child, the

13

youngest born, his little Flo, would stand towards him, when she succeeded Miss Langdale at the Hall, but he could not do it—again, but unsuccessfully he strove to put the thought away from him. Supposing that even now,—he thought, as he walked on quickly, and, through the branches of the trees, Langdale Hall became visible at intervals—the haughty woman whom he had long looked upon as an enemy should be dying! If he should hear from Dr. Forsyth, or early in the morning, that the allotted time of her reign at the old Hall was over; how would it affect himself and his family? Must they leave the Grange and live at the Hall, or could he expect Florence to continue submissive and content, in his humbler home, within sight of her own woods and towers?

He was certain that Marina would never bear to part with the little one voluntarily. Here was the vulnerable point in the man's pride. This touched him to the quick—at any cost, at any sacrifice on his own part, he wished to spare the feelings of his delicate, suffering wife.

It was getting to be dusk under the trees by this time: the days were shortening. Just as Mr. Langdale reached the farther gate of the park from his own house, a man rode past him rapidly, and pulled up his horse at the Lodge—a groom in the Langdale livery. As the gatekeeper threw open the gate the servant said, touching his hat to Mr. Langdale, who came up at the same moment, that his mistress was much worse; she had come down to dinner seemingly better, but had fainted away, and been carried to her chamber. He was going to fetch the Doctor.

The horse-hoofs clattered on the stony road and died away, as the man rode on swiftly. Mr. Langdale followed him to Dr. Forsyth's cottage, which was about a mile beyond the park gates. He felt very glad that he had come to bring home his daughter. Her being with Dr. Forsyth might cause unnecessary delay, and he should not have liked her to go through the park without visiting its mistress, if, indeed, her last hour were nigh.

His thoughts took a softer turn during the last few moments of his walk. He would consult Dr. Forsyth, and hear exactly what his cousin had said. If, indeed, her illness was of a dangerous nature, and she wished to see Florence, he supposed he must consent : but he dreaded and shrank from the necessity.

Dr. Forsyth was standing at his own door, talking to the messenger from the Hall, when Mr. Langdale came up.

" This is bad," he said, " your cousin has had a serious attack. I must go at once to the Hall. I think I had better mount your horse, Robert, and let you walk home. It would take some minutes to get either of the carriages, even the gig, under way ; and my old Bess has just come back from a long round."

Though the Doctor had two other carriages in his coach house, he always preferred that now almost obsolete but convenient and pleasant equipage, the old-fashioned gig—or as it used to be called—a tilbury.

" Never mind about Florence : I will take care of her home," said her father. "I am very sorry to hear of Miss Langdale's increased illness. It certainly will be best not to lose a moment. I suppose I shall find my little girl with your niece ?"

Dr. Forsyth, who was already in the saddle, looked at his friend with surprise. " We have seen nothing of Florence, to-day," he said. " Did you expect to find her here ? A friend, whom I met at Hazeldon, said he had seen all your young people at the Crags this afternoon."

" Well, do not let me stop you," said Mr. Langdale, to

13—2

whom the idea immediately occurred, that, perhaps, her brother and sister had encountered Florence in the village and
persuaded her to accompany them. "I have had my walk
for nothing it appears. Good-night, I suppose I shall find
Flo at home when I get back. Let me know, to-morrow, how
you find Miss Langdale. I sincerely hope this attack may
not be a serious one "

The Doctor shook his head. "I don't like the appearance
of it," he said, looking after the servant, who, after surren-
dering his horse, had walked on homeward. "Now that
young fellow is out of hearing, I don't mind saying that
I have my own very serious apprehensions about your
cousin's life. Maud Langdale is not a woman given to faint-
ing, and now this is the second fit of insensibility ! Don't
you think it would be right, if she wishes it, to let that
pretty little daughter of yours see her benefactress? You
have your own way of looking at things, Frank, but I suppose most people would consider her to be so."

Dr. Forsyth was riding on, beside Mr. Langdale, who had
turned away from his door without entering ; the road,
darkened by Miss Langdale's trees, was too shadowy for the
two old friends to see each other's faces.

"Yes, I suppose it may be necessary," said Mr. Langdale,
in a tone of suppressed emotion. We will talk about it to-
morrow. Let me know how Miss Langdale is, as soon as
possible. Now I will not detain you."

The Doctor rode on across the park. Mr. Langdale took
the road through the village. He stopped at the door of
one or two cottages, where Florence was in the habit of
visiting, and asked if their inmates had seen her, but he
could gain no tidings of his daughter.

It must have been as Dr. Forsyth suggested. She had
gone with her sisters to the Crags ; although it was so little

the custom with his daughters to leave their mother alone, that her father could not but feel surprised at her doing so on this occasion. Still, it seemed the most natural explanation of her long absence.

As Mr. Langdale passed through the shadowy gateway of the Grange, another servant of the Hall came out, and, touching his cap, said that he had been up to the house with a note from the Hall. There was no answer expected. The man passed on, and Mr. Langdale did not stop to question him. His mind was in a state of perplexity and irritation, and he hurried home. Probably the letter from the Hall was a formal intimation of Miss Langdale's illness. Possibly it might contain the request he had nearly resolved to grant, that Florence should visit her kinswoman. At the present moment the chief anxiety in her father's mind, was concerning her absence; and he hurried up the long, dark avenue in order to be at home; to shield his delicate wife from some dim, vaguely foreseen, long-dreaded, calamity.

CHAPTER III.

THE lamps were not yet lighted in the large low hall, but as Mr. Langdale entered his own house, his eyes were immediately attracted by the white outlines of the letter which he knew awaited his reception. Had it been a serpent coiled near his hearth, ready to spring upon his nearest and dearest, the Master of the Grange could scarcely have regarded the foul, dangerous reptile with more abhorrence.

Frank Langdale took up his cousin's letter reluctantly, and carried it into his study without in any manner making his presence in the house known to its inmates. The hall door always stood open till a very late hour, the young people had not returned from the Crags, and Mrs. Langdale was still in her own apartments. He had a quiet time for the consideration of whatever might be the contents of the missive.

Though he neartily wished the ordeal over, Mr. Langdale did not open the letter quickly. He lighted his reading lamp with calmness and deliberation, placing it near his own favourite chair, and trimming the flame carefully. Then he turned the letter over and over, looking at the hand-writing which was less firm than usual, studying the coat of arms, though he knew it so well; at last he broke the seal.

Before he read a single word he knew that Florence was at Langdale Hall. The conviction that his cousin had triumphed over him at last, seized him as soon as he saw that the direction was in Miss Langdale's own writing. Had the letter, as he at first surmised, contained merely the formal notification of her serious indisposition, it would have been written by another person. As he stood alone in the half darkness, making his lingering preparation for reading his cousin's communication, Frank Langdale instinctively guessed its purport.

What he was not in the least prepared for was Florence's apparent share in the deception practised upon him. He had seen her, that very morning, in the midst of them all, not manifesting the slightest emotion; and yet, so at least it seemed to the angry father, she must have laid her plans for leaving them.

Miss Langdale's expression that Florence had come of her own will and wish to nurse her, and at the conclusion of the letter, her pathetic entreaty that, for both their sakes, he should not use for a time, at least, the authority to separate them, which she did not dispute, had the exact effect in-

tended. Mr. Langdale felt himself to be much more power-
less than if she had dared him to the contest. He covered
his face with his hands; and, in the solitude, bowed his head
in an agony of pain and grief which seemed to harden his
heart into stone. For more than half an hour he sat with
the letter open before him, mute and motionless. A slight
sound behind him made Mr. Langdale suddenly turn round.
"Marina," he exclaimed, starting up and trying to put the
letter out of sight. "How you startled me, love : I thought
you were lying down, up-stairs. Let us go into the drawing-
room. The young people will be home directly."

"No, Frank, let us stay here for a few minutes, I want to
talk to you," said his wife, sitting down in the chair from
which he had risen. "There is no need for disguise or
preparation. Before you saw me, I had read over your
shoulder the letter which I saw grieved you so sorely. You
are not angry with me ! Surely we are not at this late
hour of our lives beginning to keep secrets from each
other ?"

"I scarcely understand the import of this letter myself,
as yet," said Mr. Langdale, gravely. "Had you any idea
that Florence was so much affected by my cousin's illness ?
Did she hear of it from you."

"I do not believe that she had heard of it at all this
morning," said Mrs. Langdale, instinctively divining the
truth. "Perhaps the suddenness of the intelligence overcame her. From a child she has loved your cousin."

Mr. Langdale walked up and down the room in silent
discomposure for several minutes. His wife's calm tone
made him more nearly angry than he had ever been, with
her, in his life.

Mrs. Langdale took up the letter and read it over again
composedly. "Miss Langdale wishes you to suppose that

Florence desires to remain at the Hall, but we are not bound
to trust her implicitly.   At all events she is safe there for
the present; and I was beginning to be seriously uneasy.
To-morrow our child will come home and explain her own
conduct.   Do not condemn her unheard."

Mr. Langdale paused in front of his wife.   " Unfortunately Florence has not your perfect candour.   She is the
only one of her mother's children whom I do not perfectly
trust."

The invalid's pale cheek flushed.   " Rely on me, then,"
she said, " Florence is timid and reserved.   You have not
always done her justice, but, one day, you will acknowledge
that I understood her character the best.   After all, can we
blame her for entertaining very strong feelings of gratitude
and affection for one who, to her, has been most kind and
generous ?   Whatever may be Miss Langdale's faults, our
little one has seen only the bright side of her character.
She has only anticipated by a day the request I should
have proffered to-morrow, that, if your cousin was really and
seriously ill, Florence should visit her.   Some impetuous
impulse has prompted her to go at once, fearing, perhaps,
that even another day might make it too late.   Since we
cannot alter the circumstances—since Florence is, and must
be Miss Langdale's heiress, and successor at the Hall—do
not let us deny to this poor lady, in her last moments, the
comfort of expressing some natural desire, and bestowing
some token of affection, on one who will, perhaps before very
long,' be her representative at Langdale.   Depend upon it,
Florence will not forget us.   Leave her to act for herself."

Mr. Langdale kissed his wife affectionately.   " Be it as
you will for to-night," he said ; " to-morrow I shall go to
the Hall, and bring Florence back with me.   I cannot trust
my cousin to deal fairly by us."

The sound of the carriage-wheels on the gravel outside interrupted the conversation.

"Do not, I entreat, blame Florence before her brothers and sisters," said Mrs. Langdale hurriedly; " she and Fritz stand in a very awkward position towards each other, and one careless word may set them at variance. Let it appear as though Florence had gone to the Hall with our consent, in consequence of Miss Langdale's increased illness. Dr. Forsyth implored me yesterday to let him take her there, and I think he was right. At least wait till you have seen her to-morrow, before contemning her conduct. Hear both sides of the story."

Mrs. Langdale's opinions had been so often proved to be right, that her husband did not dispute the point. He gave a silent acquiescence to her brief statement, that Florence had gone to the Hall in consequence of its mistress's serious illness, and no one enquired into the exact circumstances. In truth, the thoughts of the whole party were preoccupied. The young count and Gertrude were full of troubled, happy perplexity, as to how best to disclose what, they felt, could not long be kept secret. The younger sisters already suspected the truth; and Fritz, as yet their sole confidant, was deeply interested in what so nearly affected his favourite friend and sister. The cause of Florence's absence was heard in silence; with merely a momentary, unavoidable feeling of bitterness, on the part of the young man who, until lately, had regarded himself as the future Langdale of Langdale.

Gertrude made her escape early, and went at once to her mother's room. Mrs. Langdale had retired there before supper, and was sitting in her easy chair beside the window. The room was lighted only by the moon, and the young happy maiden did not observe her mother's worn, anxious

countenance. She drew close to her mother's knee the low
chair which had been the property of the little one, and
crouched down upon it, laying her head on the soft black
draperies of the invalid.

, "You are tired, my darling. Had you a pleasant day?
I have scarcely heard a word about your pic-nic :" said her
mother, trying to appear interested. "I thought you all
seemed very silent. Did you not enjoy yourselves?"

Gertrude pressed still more closely the thin fingers laid
caressingly upon her arm. "I scarcely know—I forget what
we all did," she said. "Yes, we were happy—at least I was
—I was not much with the others."

Mrs. Langdale's curiosity was awakened. "Something
is the matter—what is it Gertrude. I cannot bear suspense
to-night. What have you to tell me?"

Brokenly, slowly, half smiling, half-weeping, the girl told
her simple love story; little dreaming how sharp a pang
rent the motherly breast against which she was leaning.
To lose them thus, her precious ones—for at that moment
Mrs. Langdale, confused and grieved, felt as if she were
parting with her two devoted attendants—was unspeakably
bitter, but she suffered in silence. She would not sadden
the innocent joy of her companion.

Gertrude, encouraged by her tender, sympathising caresses,
unfolded her whole heart to her mother. The love so long
cherished, so fully returned, so fittingly bestowed, was revealed with modest pride; and Mrs. Langdale, fully ap-
proving of her choice, would not by a single doubt or appre-
hension, damp her quiet happiness. The young Count was
to speak to her father after the family had all retired to rest.
Gertrude believed him to be so great a favourite that his
appeal would be successful. In worldly circumstances the
match was a brilliant one, and the German nobleman was

richly gifted in person and mind. The only drawback and difficulty was that she must reside with him abroad.

Mrs. Langdale soothed the agitated girl, when she burst into tears at the idea of a separation from her beloved family. For herself the case was bitter almost beyond endurance—far beyond tears—but she did not murmur. Even through Gertrude's wild weeping streamed rays of light, like sunshine in a thunderstorm. Her calmness was all broken up—her passionate sensibilities for the first time were awakened. The mother, in spite of her bleeding, half-broken heart, promised to mediate—to smooth away any possible hindrances ; and, thus dismissed, Gertrude retired, composed and happy, to her chamber. It was no novelty for herself to sit up far into the night; and, afterwards, to lie sleepless on her couch, full of pain and anxiety, waiting for her husband's footstep.

It was much later than usual before he came to her room, and her agitation was then beyond control. Tenderly he soothed her grief and pain. When she was a little calmer he told her, as of a great good which had befallen them, of the suit of the young German for their good and beautiful daughter, and of his own frank acceptance. "If they all leave us, Marina, we shall still love each other. I cannot be entirely bereaved if I have my wife," and until dawn of day they talked together, and, at last, were comforted.

CHAPTER IV.

THE lights on the dinner table at Langdale Hall had grown dim, suddenly, in the eyes of its mistress, just when she was rejoicing in the success of the grand coup which she had executed. The triumph complete, reaction set in, and she was carried to her chamber in a state of insensibility.

Ellinor Langdale and her young rival watched all night anxiously, by turns, beside that couch of sickness. Until now they had not been on intimate terms with each other, as might naturally be expected. The sudden alarm and subsequent anxiety made them friends.

In her secret heart, Florence was wounded at no notice having been taken of her absence from home. It seemed already to her a long time since she quitted the Grange, intending to return in an hour. Had no one, not even her mother, missed her ?

She knew, vaguely, that Miss Langdale had sent some formal intimation of her safety, but her vivid imagination had pourtrayed the violent indignation of her father, her mother's grief, the loneliness of all the household :—it was mortifying to feel that her desertion was met by silent acquiescence ! The girl's proud heart swelled within her as she sat in the large dreary room, beside Miss Langdale's couch, keeping watch alternately with Ellinor. She turned her head towards the silent woman, who had not spoken since she was laid down by her servants; wondering whether, from henceforward, she was to be left to fulfil the part she had rashly undertaken. Her childlike dreams all fled before the cold, stern reality, and she felt what strangers they were to each other.

Just then Miss Langdale stirred and spoke. Florence could not catch the words until she bent over the invalid, who repeated them feebly, putting her hand in the young girl's. " Why are you left all alone, little girl ? Shall I take you across the river ?"

The tall mare, the beautiful rider, the firm, kind clasp, even the reeds and flowering rushes, wet with the flowing water, on Calder's banks, rose up before Florence's imagination, just as they appeared to Maud in her feverish dream.

Years rolled away. Florence was again " the little one "—once more, deserted and afraid, she clung to the hand that had then lifted her up from her seat amid the wild flowers, and would now, if strength were restored, place her on so high a pinnacle of worldly honour, and crown her life with good gifts.

Dr. Forsyth expressed great satisfaction at finding Florence at Langdale Hall on his next visit. He had not seen her the previous night; Ellinor was then attending upon her sister, and he concluded that Mr. Langdale had sent his daughter to the Hall, in consequence of his representation of the good that might accrue therefrom to its mistress.

" This is all right—just as I wished—nothing could be better. We shall have our patient well in a week," the good Doctor said, in his low, friendly voice, as he approached the bedside where Florence was sitting. Ellinor Langdale had accompanied him into the room, but she drew back a little whilst he greeted Florence. " Your father fully expected to find you at my house last night. I am glad he sent you to a better place. I am most truly delighted, my dear young lady, to find you here. It will do my patient more good than all my prescriptions."

Having thus expressed his satisfaction at finding his young favourite where he had cordially wished to place her, Dr. Forsyth, who was really a most clever physician, gave his whole attention to the invalid. The attack for which he had visited her the previous evening, he considered, had been brought on by excitement of a pleasurable nature, and joy was seldom lastingly injurious. He desired that Miss Langdale, to whom he had administered a strong composing draught the night before, should be kept extremely quiet. " When she wakes—for this trance is changing into slumber—let my pretty little friend here be the first object that meets her eyes. Any shock or surprise might have very serious consequences. Any change in surrounding objects should be avoided. Let her be kept tranquil for a week, and her naturally strong constitution will enable her to rally. Shall I go round by the Grange, my dear, and ask Mr. and Mrs. Langdale to spare you ?"

Florence's eyes filled with tears, but she was too proud to allow them to fall. She acquiesced in the Doctor's proposal without adding a single word. In fact she felt as if it were impossible to utter more than one monosyllable.

Ellinor kissed her affectionately. " Tell Mrs. Langdale that we will take the greatest care of her daughter. It is very good of her to stay in this sad house."

" Oh, we shall have you all well and bright in a few days, now I have such a powerful auxiliary," said the Doctor, as he shook hands with her at the door of Miss Langdale's room, while Florence remained, sad and silent, by the bed side.

" There is no accounting for these fancies unless we call them monomania. I cannot say how I honour you, my dear, for exhibiting no petty jealousy of that young creature. Yes, I knew you were above that kind of thing. Forgive me, I have known you all from children, and I must speak my mind. In her present state we must humour your sister. It might bring on brain fever to contradict or vex her. You know better than most people, that she never could endure it ; and, in her present condition, it is not likely that she should be reasonable. I shall speak strongly to Frank Langdale. If he is as self-willed as I have seen him, he will be the death of that poor lady."

Professionally interested in his patient, all other considerations sank into insignificance compared to Miss Langdale's chance of recovery. Ellinor, pale and anxious, detained him as he prepared to hurry away.

"Do you think that Maud is in danger? Ought we, when she awakes from this strange stupor, in any measure to prepare her?"

"No, no, leave her to me—or rather to Miss Florence's and your own kind ministrations," said the Doctor, kindly. "I have no doubt we shall pull through this strait—though I own that it is narrow and difficult—but I know her constitution is one of iron. Next week she will be riding Christobel, provided in the mean time you carry out my system. Keep the house quiet—surround her with pleasant objects. Let her believe, at all events till I give you leave to contradict the notion, that she has secured the prize which she has for years been labouring to win. These fixed ideas make sad havoc with our brains, and there are times when they cannot be uprooted without risk of death, or even of worse consequences. There now—I particularly wished not to frighten, and I have set you crying. Good bye. Don't let my patient see any one weeping; you must all preserve cheerful countenances, if your hearts be breaking. I tell you, in a week we shall see Miss Langdale quite herself again, and mounted on Christobel."

Ellinor smiled through her tears as she shook hands with her old friend. Dr. Forsyth got into his gig, which was waiting for him under the trees at a short distance from the house, and drove on thoughtfully at a very unusually slow pace towards Langdale Grange.

CHAPTER V.

IT was still quite early in the morning. Dr. Forsyth had been very uneasy respecting his patient at the Hall; the

very great strength of constitution of which he spoke, not
being altogether a guarantee, in similar cases, that the brain
might not be seriously and permanently affected.   He now
felt more at ease, especially if the fancy, amounting to monomania, which attracted her towards Florence Langdale,
was not thwarted.

Dr. Forsyth knew better than most men that Frank
Langdale had no reason to love his cousin.   Years of un-
kind neglect of one whom nature pointed out as a proper object of kind consideration ; her own nearest kinsman,
and, eventually, whether she wished it or no, the heir to
the property, had caused bitter alienation.   The insult to
his delicate wife, contained in Miss Langdale's cold estrangement, would have sufficed to make them foes.

Rumour ascribed to Miss Langdale's avoidance of her
cousin's wife, a cause which has prompted many virulent
feminine animosities.   Before his marriage, Frank Langdale
had been much at the Hall.   In the life-time of Maud's
father, he had been treated as one of the family, and his
authority was only second to that of the master of the
house.   It was said that even Maud, then a wilful beauty,
never disputed with her cousin, or gainsaid his wishes.
At college Mr. Langdale had liberally assisted him, and his
vacations, in boyhood and early manhood, were spent as
much at the Hall as at the old Grange, where his widowed
mother, and Marina, his future wife, resided.

For many years no one suspected that the young orphan,
rescued from shipwreck when a child, and Frank Langdale,
were attached to each other.   They seemed like a brother
and sister—equally devoted to Frank's invalid mother.   The
young girl, who had been taken into the family at the death
of Lady Barbara Noel ; for whom she had been a sort óf
plaything, ever since her son rescued her from the sinking

ship, lost upon the stormy north coast of Yorkshire, had become quite like one of the family.

It was said that the surprise was greater to Maud Langdale than to any one else, when, just before the death of Dame Langdale, as she was called, Frank and Marina acknowledged that they had long been engaged to each other. The marriage took place immediately, by the side of Mrs. Langdale's death-bed. Marina had no other home, and Frank and his mother would not suffer her to go among strangers. After the funeral, the young husband and wife went abroad together.

From the day of his marriage, Miss Langdale, who had just come into possession of the family property, utterly ignored the existence of her cousin and his wife. Frank Langdale and Maud had not seen each other, face to face, since that time.

Dr. Forsyth pondered over these circumstances as he drove along. Perhaps he knew, certainly he suspected, much more than was known to the general public. Be that as it may, he was well aware that his present task would not be an easy one.

Mr. Langdale was walking up and down, impatiently waiting the summons to breakfast, when the Doctor stopped at his door.

"You will be glad to hear that I have some hope my patient at the Hall may get over this bout, but I assure you last night I was so uneasy I could not sleep a wink. Your little lady has done her all the good in the world. Langdale you are an excellent fellow. I know this poor lady has not behaved by you as she ought to have done, but she is trying to make amends. She is positively infatuated about Miss Florence. Leave her for awhile, till Miss Langdale recovers, at the Hall."

14

"Does Florence wish to stay?" said Mr. Langdale, in a cold hard voice. "What message did she send to me, and to her mother?"

Dr. Forsyth hesitated. He was, in fact, entirely ignorant of the mode of Florence's transportation to the Hall, and rather imagined it to be the result of his own eloquence, He had driven straight to the Hall, after parting the night before from Mr. Langdale. Ellinor alone had been visible, Florence having shyly shrunk out of sight; and the doctor supposed; that afterwards, in consequence of his representation of Miss Langdale's extreme illness and passionate desire to see Florence, her father had sent her to the Hall.

He ransacked his memory in vain, trying to recollect what Florence had told him to say; but, like most men, he was not famous for the delivery of messages, and, in this case, he had been entrusted with none.

"Oh, her love, of course," he said, "and all that sort of thing, and to say that she was quite comfortable. Miss Ellinor is kindness itself, that I can certify."

"Let her remain then," said Mr. Langdale abruptly. "Once before Florence had the choice between the Grange and the Hall. She then decided wisely to abide by her parents. She has now taken a different course. By all means tell her to pursue it."

Dr. Forsyth looked at him with surprise. "Come, come, Langdale, you are not quite yourself this morning. I shall not certainly be the bearer of that message to Florence."

"Just as you please," said Mr. Langdale, in the same dry tone. "Will you not come in? My children are waiting for me to begin breakfast. You are on your rounds early."

"No thank you," said the doctor, in an offended tone. "Don't wait for me. Miss Florence is all right at Langdale, I can assure you. I called to tell you that it is, in my opinion, a question of life and death with Miss Langdale if you remove your daughter abruptly. Having done my duty professionally, I can go home, and leave you to act as you think proper."

Unconscious of the mischief he had done, the doctor gave a sharper cut than he often bestowed with his whip, on the shining flank of the black mare, and drove quickly to Langdale Cottage. The master of the Grange breakfasted with his children and the foreign Count, who was now recognised as his future son-in-law. He did not mention Florence's name, and, the moment he was at liberty to leave the table, he shut himself up in his study to write to her.

There were very few occasions during his married life, on which Mr. Langdale had committed any important act without consulting his wife, but, now, he could not trust Marina's judgment. Even as it was, he found it difficult, nay, impracticable, to address the little one. After beginning half a dozen letters, and tearing them into fragments he resolved to write, not to Florence, but to his cousin, Maud Langdale. The letter he had received from her the night before, lay on his table unanswered. He read it over again, without the softening influence of his wife's comments, and detected in it a thousand painful meanings. Miss Langdale affirmed in the first sentence that Florence had come *voluntarily* to the Hall. Her father had no reason to suppose that any plot had been formed to entrap her. Of her own wish and will, discontented probably with her own humble home, Florence had gone to the house of his enemy.

Mr. Langdale had never thoroughly understood the peculiar disposition of his youngest born. He had not conciliated her in childhood, as had been the case with those who had begun life in a brighter period of his existence. The failure in his wife's health, the first knowledge of her hopeless

14—2

malady, had converted him into the austere being whom his youngest daughter loved and feared.

He had been very severe respecting her childish faults, and certainly, in respect of pride, wilfulness, and vanity, Florence erred more frequently than her sisters. Shy and sensitive, the little one shrank from his imperfectly understood railleries, which, even in his brighter moods, were sarcastic; and hid the secrets of her imaginative fancy, and really loving heart, in a reserve, which, as years went on, became as impenetrable as his own. Only her mother knew how dearly Florence loved, even while she at times dreaded, her grave, severe, yet often indulgent, father. The very effort to deserve his affection made her less able to win it than were the thoughtless fair-haired twins; who came to him in every difficulty, after their mother's helplessness prevented her assisting them, and scarcely ever found him unwilling to lend an ear to any tale of childish distress. Florence, on the contrary, would wait for hours rather than disturb him; and often went away without uttering the petition which it would have pleased him to grant.

A grave cause for dissension had arisen when Mr. Langdale discovered that Florence had carried on, unknown to her parents, intercourse with his cousin. He had never entirely forgiven this transgression of his orders, and the concealments it involved.

As he read and re-read the letter from the Hall, the conviction, shaken for a moment, returned upon him, that a long course of deceit had been practised. Each short sentence bore a meaning at first unsuspected. Whilst his legal power to separate them was undisputed, Miss Langdale and Florence seemed to have cast their lots together, and the cry uttered by both their hearts, was "Do not separate us!"

Had it been otherwise, he argued, would not Florence
have sent some message by her kind old friend, Dr. Forsyth?
Would she not have mentioned some limit to her stay at the
Hall? Ought she not to have consulted himself and her
mother as to the propriety of her remaining there? Instead
of this she had sent a common-place message of love—an as-
surance that she was well and happy—without the slightest
reference to their wishes, or to the sorrow and anxiety her
absence must have caused.

Each moment Frank Langdale grew more angry. At last
he caught up a pen, and hastily wrote a few lines to Miss
Langdale. If her cousin had realised the danger, which the
Doctor's experience taught him to apprehend from Miss
Langdale's sudden illness, he would have acted more cautiously ; but, in the angry heat of the hour, he believed the
whole to be a plot in which Dr. Forsyth played a principal
part. Over and over again they had argued the subject
without altering one another's conclusions : Dr. Forsyth
endeavouring to persuade his old friend to abandon early
prejudices, and allow his family, and especially Florence,
to profit by the present favourable intentions of the mistress
of Langdale Hall, whilst Mr. Langdale inveighed against
the injustice of Fritz's disinheritance, and refused to admit
that years had softened his cousin's animosity. Her love
of Florence, he maintained, was only another mark of her
prejudice against himself.

Under this impression, and deeply wounded by Florence's
apparent carelessness of his own and her mother's feelings,
Mr. Langdale, without reading over again his angry letter,
or consulting his wife, delivered it to a servant ; directing
that it should be sent at once to the Hall.

CHAPTER VI.

No power or persuasion could induce Maud Langdale to keep her bed when she was able to rise from it. After Dr. Forsyth's early visit she insisted on getting up ; and, after dressing herself with difficulty, and being forced to accept the unusual service of her attendant, in her customary dark cloth close-fitting habit, with her short curls carelessly clustering in her neck like a boy, she slowly crept into the library, and sat grimly erect in her tall ebony chair.

There were unmistakable signs of illness and depression in her appearance. The healthy complexion had suddenly grown wan, and the well shaped hands, laid on the carved arms of the high seat, were white and nerveless. Momentarily the fingers would clutch the hard wood, as if for support, and, after a time, the head drooped languidly. Then, as if provoked at the involuntary manifestation of weakness, the invalid would stiffen herself afresh, and glance round to see if any one was watching her.

The Doctor's injunctions were carefully observed ; and, as far as possible, Miss Langdale was surrounded by pleasant objects. The household maintained its usual routine. Florence was standing at a table covered with freshly gathered flowers, just where the mistress of the mansion could observe the graceful girl's movements. Ellinor, who sat at work in a cheerful corner of the room near the window, had suggested the occupation.

More than once the little one bent her head over the roses to conceal a tear. It seemed so strange to be so completely forgotten, and her flight ignored at her own home. Each moment she had expected to receive some message or letter, in answer to Dr. Forsyth's request that she might remain a little longer. From dread of her father's anger to intense longing for his presence, Florence's thoughts fitfully veered. It never once occurred to her that neither Miss Langdale nor Dr. Forsyth had explained the manner of her evasion. All seemed to have come to pass so naturally, that she did not in the least realize how strange and unnatural an appearance her conduct must wear in the eyes of her parents. In spite of her illness, no one in the house would have ventured, unbidden, to prevent the intrusion upon the invalid's attention of any matter of business. The old butler handed respectfully to his mistress, on a silver waiter, a letter, to which, he said, no answer was required, delivered by a servant at the Hall. Miss Langdale read it in silence.

"Come nearer to me, Florence," she said, after some moments' deliberation. "This is a letter from your father."

The roses slipped out of the trembling fingers that were striving to arrange them, and Florence went close up to the invalid.

"I am sorry he does not express himself more kindly," she said. "My cousin Frank used to regard me with more indulgence, but time and trial alter us all. He fears that association with me will render you unfit for the companionship of your sisters. He calls upon you at once to leave me, or else you are never to re-enter your early home."

Miss Langdale's cheeks, pale before, assumed a ghastly hue, and she pressed her right hand on her heart. The sudden shock was evidently more than, in her enfeebled state, she was able to bear. Florence knelt down on the footstool placed for Miss Langdale, but which she had not condescended to use, and clasped the rigid, ice-cold hand, that rested on the left arm of the chair.

"No—I cannot, I will not leave you while you are so ill," she said. "What harm can it do to me, or to any one, if I remain here while you need love and care? You have never shown me anything but kindness."

Miss Langdale's fingers closed tightly on those of her young cousin. She bent her usually haughty head low on the young girl's shoulder, and burst into tears.

"You have saved me from death or madness, Florence," she said, after the unusual burst of emotion had subsided. "My heart seemed held in fetters, while my brain was on fire. Now I am better. My love, I will not deceive you. Read your father's letter. I do not think that I have quite deserved this from him."

Florence read her father's angry words with sorrowful indignation. Her own fault, which previously she had bitterly lamented, seemed to grow smaller as she felt herself treated unjustly; and she resented the injury done to the feelings of her benefactress. Mr. Langdale did not address Maud as his cousin; the brief, angry letter had in fact no regular commencement or termination, excepting a formal signature.

"Since Florence wishes it—as she has gone there of her own free will—let her by all means remain at the Hall," he wrote. "You have made her dissatisfied—you have taught her to deceive—keep the fruits of the seed you have sown. Neither her mother nor I care to claim the casket from which the treasure has been stolen—the setting, out of which the jewel is taken. Nevertheless, if Florence *desires* to return, her home is *at present* open to her. Later—when her taste for luxury has been fostered, and the natural pride of her character has been turned into self-will—like your own, Maud Langdale—I cannot promise to receive her."

"My father will think better of this," Florence said, timidly. "I am sure he did not know how ill you were when he wrote that letter. Be that as it may, since he does not *command* me to return, I shall not leave you until you are better."

Miss Langdale pressed her to her heart. "You have given me fresh life, my child," she said. "Remember that you have always a home with me. Ring, Ellinor, and let the servants help me to my bed. Perhaps I was unwise to leave it. I did not know, till this blow struck me, how weak I had become."

She said no more; and her two companions watched her anxiously, after complying with her request. Dr. Forsyth, as soon as he could be summoned, was at her side, and remained during the rest of the day at the Hall. Miss Langdale scarcely spoke, but her eyes followed every movement of the young girl who had refused to leave her; and, from time to time, unwonted tears coursed down her pale cheeks. Florence, during the whole day and night, watched patiently in the sick woman's chamber.

Dr. Forsyth, irritated by Mr. Langdale's manner, did not call at the Grange for some days. Communication between the two mansions was never active; and the servant who carried the letter to the Hall, brought back word that its mistress was very much better, and sitting in the library.

Mrs. Langdale had learnt from her husband that Florence, through the medium of the Doctor's last visit, had sent a careless message to the effect that she was well and happy, and wished to remain at the Hall. Even her sweet temper was ruffled; and, when two days had passed without bringing back the fugitive, she acquiesced in his desire that Florence's books and wearing apparel should be sent after her.

Miss Langdale continued to receive two visits daily from Doctor Forsyth, but still her parents thought that Florence might have shown more regard and consideration for their feelings; whilst the poor young girl was mourning over their neglect and severity. Time, as it slowly wore on, widened the breach. An insurmountable dread of her father's anger, and of her mother's tenderer reproaches, took possession of Florence's mind. The sunny fields, yellow with the harvest, which she had crossed so easily on her way to the Hall, now bristling arid stubble, seemed to stretch away like the sands of the desert. She felt as completely separated from her family, now she was at Langdale Hall, as though she were in another hemisphere.

Between herself and the mistress of the Park, on the contrary, each day drew the bands of intimacy closer, Maud Langdale treated her as a daughter; relying upon her for such comfort and aid, in her weakness, as a loving child might have bestowed. She had answered Mr. Langdale's letter by a few lines, which she had shown to Florence, intimating that as her father did not forbid her remaining at the Hall, and Miss Langdale felt it inexpressibly bitter to part with her, they should, for the present, continue together. Should Mr. Langdale, on her recovery, think fit to reclaim his daughter, Maud trusted that he would find her not wholly contaminated by her society.

In this note Florence, with Miss Langdale's full and free permission, had enclosed a few trembling lines to her mother, entreating her forgiveness for the past, and love for the future.

Unfortunately she did not attempt to offer any explanation of her conduct; as she had all along imagined that her parents knew, and condemned, the impulsive action which had placed her under Miss Langdale's protection. Neither

did she offer any limit to her proposed absence. The poor
young girl, bewildered by grief and anxiety, without a
friend to advise her, simply threw herself upon their mercy.

Mrs. Langdale answered her daughter's letter somewhat
coldly. She was under her husband's influence now, and
they were both persuaded that Miss Langdale had laid a
deliberate plan to deprive them of their child. The difference in their opinion was, that Mr. Langdale thought Florence had been a party to the scheme, in which her mother
denied her complicity beforehand, but blamed her for ac-
ceding to it. Fritz and her sisters were silent; but their
strong love for their mother, and her keen sufferings, made
them, in their hearts, very angry with the absent cause of
so much pain and grief.

CHAPTER VII.

CONTRARY to all reasonable expectation, and in spite of the
fulfilment of her dearest wish, Maud Langdale did not rally
quickly. Long after the date Dr. Forsyth had named,
Christobel was grazing in the park, pricking up her ears at
the sound of an approaching footstep, and looking for her
mistress in vain. Miss Langdale had not once quitted the
house.

Air was the good Doctor's great panacea, and Maud had
lived out of doors the greater part of her life. How could
she regain strength, shut up from morning till night in the
dreary walls of the library?

Illness had softened wonderfully her arbitrary temper.
Ellinor scarcely knew her sister, and tears would gather in
her eyes as she watched her sitting by the writing table,

unoccupied, silent, uncomplaining; or sometimes at the window of her own room, which commanded a wide prospect, looking out, with eyes which pierced beyond them, at her own fields and up the wooded clough.

Dr. Forsyth was seriously uneasy about his patient. This complete change in the habits of a lifetime boded no good. He tried to rouse her by a thousand stratagems, telling her that her farms were neglected, or her work-people trespassing upon her indulgence, but she took no heed of their shortcomings.

Only at Florence's approach would the saddened eyes brighten, and a more cheerful tone denote that her granted wish had not proved a curse. Between them a very strong affection was gaining strength, day by day; and it seemed as though this tie alone kept the older woman from sinking altogether.

Not one of Mr. Langdale's family visited the Hall. Florence was entirely cut off from her home, and, since her sister's illness, Ellinor had never left her. Excepting for the Doctor's frequent visits, the trio were quite isolated.

Meanwhile, the September sunshine streamed over the land; lighting up the dark old Grange, illuminating the gay terraced flower garden at the Hall, and sparkling on the stained windows of the ancient house of the ruined Noels; which was slowly regaining the aspect it had worn in days long gone by.

"So, she's breaking fast," said the General, as Mr. Haywarden stood by his side on the summit of the hill, watching the progress of the work-people. "Going the way we must all go, sooner or later, whether she likes it or not. Seems hard where folk have money and power, which is much the same thing, I take it, that they can't stop the wasting away. Just like the rotten old wood work that has given the men yonder so much trouble, and it won't hang together. Maud Langdale's failing fast."

"She has not been well, certainly," said the lawyer; "Miss Langdale has not been quite herself for some time, but I hope her illness is not so serious as you fancy. If wealth cannot stop decay, it can, at all events, command the best means of repairing the havoc made by disease. Dr. Forsyth now recommends her travelling abroad. I fancy she will pass the winter in Italy."

"That won't answer," said the old man, doggedly. "You might just as well take up that old chestnut yonder and expect it to grow down by Langdale Tarn, when it's had to brave the winds on the top of this hill, as expect Maud Langdale to flourish if you transplant her from Yorkshire to the Bay of Naples, or Mentone. Both will die in the attempt."

"Well, I don't know," said Mr. Haywarden, who, during his frequent visits to the new buildings, had grown accustomed to, and was often amused by, the quaint old veteran's familiarity. "Miss Langdale has set her heart on pleasing the young heiress, and Miss Florence wants to see Italy. I dare say the change will do her good."

"She's had her way in this matter, as she has in most others. To be sure, what an obstinate woman can do if she gives her mind to it," said the old man, looking round him, contemplatively. "Who'd ever have fancied that Noel Hall would be built up stone for stone, as it was, and we all working to please her. Its getting as like as two peas to the old place, and what a ramshackle forlorn rat hole it was last year. Oh, Lord, if Cuthbert and his mother could only see it ! But that's what even Miss Langdale's wilful will cannot manage. She may till up the old waste places, and put back the glass in the windows, and the turrets and towers may be set straight; but she won't get the old faces, nor bring back the light hearts, nor hear the old voices, nor take the brand of the burning away, from the temple where she once worshipped in her pride."

"It seems a useless outlay. For my part I was very much against it," said the lawyer, apparently forgetful of the distance in station between himself and his companion. "None of the old family are left unless you count the girl down at the mills, and her mother, (Cuthbert's widow), as belonging to them ; and Miss Langdale distinctly told me, she would never acknowledge that marriage. When all these great works are completed who is to benefit by them ?"

"Most likely *I* shall !" said the old man, laughing, as he sat down on his favourite corner of the court-yard wall. "She's promised not to turn me out, that's something. That woman, and her daughter from the mill in the Eagle's Gorge, came one Saturday after work, to see the old Hall. I didn't trouble myself to shew it to them. She's good and she's pretty too, though, is Bertina Noel. The young spark at Langdale Grange, Master Fritz, if I am not mistaken, has a liking for her; he was showing her and her mother about, and handing the girl up the ladders. I'd half a mind to pitch him off one of them, head foremost."

"It would have been a good thing for the poor mother, if some kind friend had done as much for Cuthbert Noel; before he took her out of her own humble station, and yet never had manliness enough to lift her into the sphere she ought to have moved in. I have seen the papers, and there is no possible loop out of which his friends can pull him. The marriage was legal, though clandestine, and kept secret till after his death. Bertina Noel, though she had a scoundrel for a father, (whatever you may say about your old master), is by birth a lady. Fritz Langdale might do worse than marrying her."

"Cuthbert Noel was no master of mine," growled the General, apparently in the worst of humours. "You forget that I come from a country where freedom is the right of a white man, and as precious as the breath of his nostrils. As for Cuthbert Noel, you may as well hang a dog at once, if you give him a bad name; and so he thought, and made away with himself, I suppose, sooner than trouble his friends longer. Mind, I don't say he is dead. He was alive long after the sale of Noel Hall. That I can vouch for."

Mr. Haywarden looked at the old fellow sharply. "It will need more than your simple word to convince us of that," he said, gravely. "My own firm belief is, that Bertie Noel would never rest quiet as long as he has done, anywhere but in his grave; if, indeed, that would hold him. Perhaps, if he were living now, he might think it worth while to come forward. I have a proposal, at this moment, in my pocket for building baths and villas, and a great hotel, on that piece of ground near Filey, where Lady Barbara used to go for sea-bathing. It may turn out a profitable speculation; and if so, Miss Bertina Noel will not need to work at the mills as overlooker of the girls, in order to eke out her mother's scanty means."

The General puffed away at his pipe, philosophically.

"So you are going to start a 'Limited Liability Company' watering-place, where Cuthbert did the only good deed of his life on record, poor fellow. Don't let it be forgotten. Call the place Marina. It's not a bad name in itself, and it will hand down a tradition more creditable than some that cling to the old name of Noel."

The General drew his cloak round him, with the dignity belonging to his martial rank; and, without any mark of deference or courtesy, walked off, and joined the workmen, who had just found a curious relic belonging to the former decorations of the Hall. Mr. Haywarden followed him slowly, and found that he was listened to and obeyed like an oracle. The painted wood-work proved to be, as he declared, the bordering of the panels of the dining-room ; a small portion being still extant in its right position, though obscured by dirt and mildew. The pattern when closely compared was exactly the same.

Mr. Haywarden mounted his horse and rode thoughtfully down the long steep hill. He was revolving in his mind the changes and chances, to some of his clients, which would ensue, if there were any foundation for the old General's obstinate conviction, that Bertie Noel was still in the land of the living.

PART THE SIXTH.

TOO LATE.

Deep down in my heart—thro' fast-coming years—
I look backward and forward with eyes dimmed by tears :
Far away, Southern landscapes are gleaming in gold,
But the North holds me fast with its ice-fetters cold.
Oh, the bonds are so narrow ! The world is so wide,
And the tide flows so swiftly,—so swiftly the tide.

I remember a clime, where, round Temples and Towers,
The vine trails its clusters, mid sunshine and flowers ;
Where the ocean-waves purple the bright sands they lave,
And the laurel wreath waits for the gifted and brave.
It beckons, it lures me—the banished one—home,
But I cannot draw nearer—I may not come.

R. M. K.

Translated from Schuman's "SEHNSUCHT," (Home-sickness).

CHAPTER I.

MAUD LANGDALE bore the transplantation to a Southern clime better than those who had known her best and longest could have expected. The woman's wilful will had conquered in the strife, and, now that the prize was hers, the victory won, she would not flag. She had, indeed, made the most of her illness, in the hope of being ordered abroad, that she might carry Florence out of reach of the man whom she regarded as her foe.

Mr. Langdale made no further effort to reclaim his daughter, and Florence, bitterly offended, acquiesced in his decision. Mutual misunderstanding had gone too far for either party to retrace their steps. Nevertheless, it was with a sorely aching heart that the young exile looked at the wonders of art and nature, with which she was surrounded. A fairer and more sunshiny landscape would have revolted her sorrowing spirit, but Miss Langdale made no long halt till they arrived at Rome, where they settled for the winter. She judged rightly in thinking that the ruined city, which had once been as a Queen among the nations of the earth, must arrest the enthusiastic girl's wondering attention.

Her own mind expanded as they contemplated together

the marvellous relics of the past, and wandered among
tombs and palaces, each day choosing some fresh field for
interesting investigations. Florence understood the language of modern Italy, the country of her birth, and Miss
Langdale was an excellent Latin scholar.

Florence's beautiful voice and musical talents, now culti-
vated to the utmost, and thoroughly appreciated, caused
her society to be sought in the most select circles. Miss
Langdale had brought good introductions, and no longer
avoided company. She yielded to her dearly loved companion's suggestions readily enough in trifles; and so far
altered her style of dress, though it continued to be peculiar
to herself, as to escape eccentricity. As a wealthy Englishwoman she was privileged to be a little singular in her
tastes and habits.

Gradually, with nothing to remind her of her home, for
her sisters were not allowed to correspond with her, Florence
became acclimatised; and the dark-eyed, sparkling girl, with
her perfectly melodious voice and faultless accent, was more
than once mistaken for an Italian.

As she breathed the air of Rome, and visited its holy
and beautiful places, a love of art sprang up in the girl's
mind. Miss Langdale humoured her in everything, and
every facility was afforded for her improvement. Florence
spent hours in the studios of artists, and emulated their
industry. Her talent for drawing, though not developed so
early as that of Frances, was very considerable. She often
sighed as she thought of the enjoyment her sister would
have found in sharing her studies, and in wandering among
the picturesque ruins of the ancient city; but she had too
much tact to mention the names of any of her family to
Miss Langdale. On this point alone they were not in
unison, and Florence loved her too dearly to run the risk of

offending her kind benefactress. Every indulgence money could procure was at her command, and, as Miss Langdale's heiress, she was fêted and caressed wherever they went together.

The birthplace of Florence, that fair city on the banks of the Arno, which she had often dreamed of beholding, was visited in summer, when the climate of Rome grew unhealthy; but Miss Langdale took her young charge away as soon as she perceived, by her pensive looks, that Florence was thinking of her mother. A villa near Turin and within the sweep of the cool breezes from the southern Alps, formed a pleasant retreat where Florence quietly pursued her studies. Her education was now nearly completed, in the common acceptation of the term, and Miss Langdale longed to introduce her beautiful adopted daughter into society; but Florence shrank from notice, and begged to be allowed to continue her researches into art and nature, and to cultivate her talents for music and painting a little longer, undisturbed.

Three years had passed since Miss Langdale and Florence left England, and they were again spending the winter in Rome. It was difficult to say which of the two was the most altered. The stiff, haughty, Englishwoman, who had spent most of her life, in her own country, on horseback, roughly attired, short and abrupt in speech, old fashioned in appearance, and utterly careless of all form and routine, was now dressed suitably to her age and station, and moved and spoke like a lady of high degree; while " the little one had acquired style and grace, and was as beautiful and elegant a creature as ever basked in the warm sunshine of Italy.

It was Florence's eighteenth birthday : and, when she descended the staircase, and entered the beautiful room which

was her own, the young girl found the table laden with
costly gifts from Miss Langdale, bouquets of flowers and
trifling presents, from her acquaintances, friends, and admirers.   Florence sighed even as she took up the magnifi-
cent cameos, which, knowing her preference for objects of art,
Miss Langdale had presented to her ; and touched lightly the
flowers which made the room full of perfume.   What would
she have given for a bunch of violets from the lane at the
back of Godley Grange, such as the twins had often given
her on her birthday ; or for some little tender remembrance
of the day from her absent parents ; but no one had sent her
a present from Godley.   Perhaps they had not even remembered that it was the birthday of "the little one."

As Florence carelessly altered the arrangement of the table,
and took up a gay wreath of flowers that smelt even more
sweetly than the rest ; she saw, what had previously been
hidden under the leaves, an English letter awaiting her
perusal.   It seemed to have been laid down and forgotten.

The jewels, the flowers, the adulatory foreign compliments,
vanished from the girl's mind as she saw the handwriting.
This was no courtly scroll, no birthday token.   Ill-written,
ill-spelt, badly folded, the letter had, nevertheless, the stamp
of home upon it.   Florence had not received a line from
Godley Grange, before this morning, since she quitted
England.

Meredith's handwriting and spelling were like that of
many worthy English servants, and she had apparently
guessed at the foreign address, and written it down from
hear-say.   It was evident she had not dared to consult her
master or mistress, or the young ladies of the family.

Florence did not pause long over the outside of her letter,
although she felt a vague dread and reluctance to open it.
She knew that Miss Langdale would not disturb her.   She

was supposed to be absorbed in the contemplation of her birthday gifts. It was very difficult to find time, Meredith said, and writing was a trouble. Miss Florence might recollect how she used to come to her, to answer her own poor mother's letters. Ah well, she had not forgotten that, nor how good her darling child had always been to her. No one else had written ; and she dared not say a word to master, who was very stern now, at times, but she thought it but right to let Miss Florence know what sad trouble they were all in, at the Grange. The mistress had been very poorly all the winter. Worse than people thought, for she was never one to make much complaint, or give trouble. They all hoped she would come round in the spring, as usual, but, as the days lengthened, her pains grew worse than ever. Then came a great blot, and an apology for an abrupt conclusion, but the writer was badly wanted. If Miss Flo wished to see her mother alive, and receive her blessing, there was no time to be lost.

Flo sank on her knees, beside the table covered with flowers and bijouterie, and buried her head in her hands. All her pride and fancied injuries vanished from her recollection. She remembered nothing but the tender mother, whose death had perhaps been accelerated by her desertion. A torrent of tears flowed over her trembling fingers, and relieved her burning brain. Then she read Meredith's letter again ; together with a postscript, which at first escaped her notice. It was to the effect that " Miss Gertrude,"—which was scratched out and " the Countess " substituted—had been sent for, from Germany ; and was hourly expected at the Grange.

Florence carried the letter into the salon, where Miss Langdale was sitting, waiting to receive her thanks for the costly presents, and to hear her opinion of them. She looked at the young girl's pale, tear-stained face, with astonishment. Florence held out the letter, saying with difficulty, "This is from England, from the Grange. My mother is dying."

A dark cloud gathered on the brow, which three years in that softer clime had seemed to make fairer and younger. Miss Langdale held poor Meredith's unsightly epistle at some distance from her eyes, and, taking up her double, gold-mounted glasses, perused it slowly, wishing to give herself time for consideration.

"It is a pity that your father did not write himself to summon you," she said, coldly. "Perhaps he did not think the necessity so urgent as your poor old nurse does. Servants are excellent creatures, but in cases of illness they are always terrorists, and Meredith is a type of her class. If your mother is really so ill, you will hear by the next mail, and on more trustworthy authority."

"I shall not wait a day, not an hour, more than is absolutely necessary," said Florence, with self-will equal to Miss Langdale's arbitrary temper. "I know, I feel that my mother is dying. I ought never to have left her. Forgive me, dear, kind, friend," she added, as she saw by the expression of Maud's face, how deeply she was wounded. "I scarcely know what I am saying—I believe I am half mad. I shall never, never, forgive myself, if my mother dies before I can see her."

"It shall, at all events, not be my fault," said Maud, embracing the agitated girl. "I will order horses immediately. Go to your room at once, love, I will send your servant to you instantly. In this, as in all things, I will do my best to further your wishes."

She was as good as her word, and in a very few hours Miss Langdale and her adopted daughter were travelling, fast as money and strong will could carry them, back to their native country. The season was favourable, and, although the Alpine passes were not yet perforated by tunnels, the journey was safely and rapidly accomplished. Miss Langdale was thoughtful and considerate, taking every trouble upon herself; Florence, wrapped up in sad thoughts, and buried in impenetrable reserve, scarcely spoke. She started when her companion, on their arrival in England, said to her—

"Have you considered, Florence, how it will be best to announce your return to the Hall? Your father is very firm. He may not wish to see you at the Grange."

Florence looked at her with surprise.

"Surely you do not think he will keep me from seeing my poor mother—from asking her blessing and forgiveness. He could not be so cruel."

"Well, we will hope not," said Miss Langdale, "though you have been three years in my company. Remember, Flo, how he deprecated such contamination. But I still hope your mother may be better. In that case I should not like you to be exposed to the rude rejection of your good offices."

"I must run the risk," said Florence gloomily, her old fear of her father returning. "Oh, how I wish the horses would go more quickly. It seems to me years since we left Rome."

Miss Langdale had sent forward a messenger to make enquiries respecting the health of Mrs. Langdale of the Grange. She feared greatly, in Florence's excited state, the effect of any sudden shock. At the place where they were to leave the train, she saw, on the platform, her own servant awaiting her. His face was gravely ominous.

She motioned hastily to the man to keep back, and hurried Florence into the carriage sent from Langdale Hall to meet them. The luggage was rapidly transferred; with haste which satisfied even Florence's impatience : the necessary arrangements were completed, and Miss Langdale, after a brief conversation with her messenger, got into the carriage.

"Home," she said at once and very decidedly. Then throwing her arms round Florence, who began to persuade her to allow her to stop at the entrance to Godley, she said, vainly trying to repress her tears, "You must come to the Hall *first,* my child. It will not cause hurtful delay. I entreat you, Florence, to be ruled by me this once."

The sad solemnity of her manner and her tears, rare evidences of emotion on her part, awed Florence into silence, until the carriage drew up at the gates of the Hall. "Now let me go," she said, springing out wildly, "let me walk— it will disturb them less—I want to go straight up to my mother's room."

Something in Miss Langdale's compassionate glance, in the fond pressure of her arm, terrified Florence. She stopped and looked up in her face.

"I will not keep you in suspense," Maud said, tenderly ; "all our haste, my darling, has been in vain; your mother died before we left Italy. Come to my heart; you are indeed my child now."

Florence uttered a cry, and fell upon her neck. The strong woman put aside the domestics with a sign, and, lifting the slender girl in her arms, carried her to her room: Old Phillips, who had known his mistress from a child, thought that, mingled with her deep and genuine compassion, there was a suppressed ring of triumph in her voice, as she called Florence her own child. Marina, the waif and stray, who had troubled the proud woman's happiness, stood in her path no longer.

CHAPTER II.

THE old rooms at Godley Grange, though once more thrown open to the light of day, were hushed in solemn silence; and the light footsteps of the young girls were stayed as they passed their mother's door, as though a sound might still disturb her. It was a long time before they realised the fact that the object of so much tender care had been for ever taken from them.

As often happens in cases of long, wearing illness, the end at the last, though preceded by severe suffering, seemed to come suddenly. Mrs. Langdale had so often rallied, after alarming illnesses, that her children did not, till the last, give up the hope of seeing her once more revive.

Her husband had been less hopeful. From the moment when she was taken seriously ill Mr. Langdale despaired of her recovery. She had been sinking, he said, slowly but surely ever since "the little one" deserted her. That was the beginning of the end.

The bereaved husband's heart seemed turned to stone by this calamity, long as it had been expected. He went about, alone and tearless, shunning the sympathy even of his children. For the first time in their lives the pretty twin girls, who had been the objects of his tender care and affection since their infancy, felt afraid of their father; his grief was so stern and silent.

Gertrude had arrived in time to receive her mother's blessing for herself and her little son, whom she brought with her from her usually happy German home. The Count left her to comfort her sisters whilst he visited some relatives in a distant county.

It was in vain that she strove to win back her father's entire confidence. In his heart of hearts he blamed her for having quitted her suffering parent, although he had sanctioned her marriage. He did not, however, view her conduct in the same light as Florence's transgressions. Her name was never mentioned at home in his presence, and, the moment he heard from Dr. Forsyth that she had returned to the Hall, he gave orders that she was not, on any pretence to be admitted at the Grange.

Meredith tearfully confessed, after strict examination, that she had written to Miss Florence ; and narrowly escaped sentence of dismissal from the establishment. Nothing but her devoted attention to the invalid saved her from this punishment, though it should have borne with it its excuse. Mr. Langdale on this point was peremptory. No inmate of his house should hold any communication with the occupants of the Hall. Florence had ceased to belong to the family since Miss Langdale's adoption of her.

Dr. Forsyth, always Florence's friend, argued with the angry father in vain. "A positive case of monomania, madam," he said to Miss Langdale, after visiting Florence, who was confined to her bed by severe illness. "Frank Langdale is not sane, I assure you, if you approach him from that direction. He idolised his poor wife. Even his children were as nothing compared to her. That sweet creature, the Countess, who sacrificed years of happiness waiting upon her mother until her sisters grew up, is sadly out of favour. She ought, I suppose, to have grown old, or died, in harness. Mrs. Langdale was as well as usual until the severe frost set in after Christmas. Miss Frances and her twin sisters nursed her devotedly, with good Mrs. Meredith's experienced aid. But you may as well talk to a stone as argue with Frank, when his mind is once made up. He was always the most obstinate man of my acquaintance; and this last affliction, instead of softening, seems to have made him as hard as iron. Do not, on any account, suffer Miss Florence to visit the Grange against his orders. It is impossible to say what cruel accusations he might bring against her.

"Florence is at present too weak to go anywhere," said Miss Langdale, anxiously. "I scarcely know what course she will pursue, if health and strength return. I am afraid, Doctor, she is a thorough Langdale, and has her full share of the family wilfulness."

"Well, she is safe, at all events, just now, and we must try to keep her quiet. I am by no means sure that you will not have to take her away again. Not so far as Rome. That would revive disagreeable associations, and she is not strong enough. How would it suit you to pay a visit to Miss Ellinor, at her place in the North Riding? That might revive our patient, and she could be as retired and quiet as she liked. Sea air would be the best tonic for her!"

Miss Langdale paused for a moment. "I will tell you on your next visit what I think of your plan. It is certainly well worth considération. Ellinor and Florence are great friends, and her gentle disposition makes her a sympathetic companion in sorrow. I am sometimes too abrupt, and, just now Florence is, perhaps, less inclined to confide in me, as she knows that I was not her mother's friend. Still, I am sure she loves me, and I shall bide my time. That hard, cold, domestic tyrant is playing my game for me."

Dr. Forsyth took his leave and drove home thoughtfully. He was sincerely attached to Florence. Her girlish confidence had touched his heart, and he would have given the world to reconcile her with her family; but, at the next attempt he made to approach the subject, Mr. Langdale cut him short abruptly, declining to hear a word he had to

say. "Florence has chosen her own lot ; let her abide by
it. It is too late to repair the wrong she has done me
and my children. Let me hear no more about her unavailing,
tardy, sorrow."

Even Meredith dared not approach her darling, though
she sent many a stealthy message through the keeper's wife.
Weak in health, half broken-hearted, Florence was compelled
to yield to the sentence of exclusion passed against her.
Exaggerated reports, if indeed such could be, of her father's
anger, reawakened her fear of his severity. When she became well enough to leave the house, she shrank from en-
countering him; and confined her walks entirely to Miss
Langdale's grounds, where there was no danger of meeting
any inmate of the Grange. In her nervous misery Florence
fancied that all were leagued against her, and that her sorrowing sisters, as well as her indignant father, reproached
her as being the cause of their beloved mother's last illness.

In the absence of family affection, and tortured by re-
morse, Florence turned to Miss Langdale for comfort. The
slight coldness which had existed since their return, vanished in a moment when the forlorn girl appealed to Maud
for sympathy. The flood-gates of strong passion at once
gave way, and the proud woman's earnest love was poured
out like a torrent. Her very nature seemed changed, and
no mother could have been more gentle in her ministrations
than Maud Langdale became, as the sick and sorrowful
outcast threw herself upon her compassionate affection.

No one who had known Miss Langdale in her unloving,
unloved state, would have recognised her now. Her very
features seemed altered by the new, womanly expression
which beamed from them. No longer selfish nor exacting :
she consulted Florence on all subjects, and strove to interest
her in all her pursuits and employments. On no occasion

did she allow a wish of her own to interfere with her young favourite's happiness and welfare. She would even have conciliated Frank Langdale, had it been possible, when she saw that, do what she would, Florence's bright smiles were gone, and her health impaired; but the Master of the Grange sternly repulsed her overtures of friendship.

The seeds he had sown must be reaped; and its fruit was bitterness, even to herself, though she had won the battle. As she saw the low-spirited, pale girl musing languidly on the terrace, or among the dark old Langdale trees, never quitting the precincts of the mansion, dearly as she loved her, Maud would have given the world to see her once more at play by the lake side with her white frocked sisters, or buried among reeds and flags; with her bright shy eyes uplifted in wonder at the solitary kinswoman who was trying to beguile her away.

Maud wrote to Ellinor, who was now residing on her own property on the sea coast, proposing a visit from herself and Florence, and received a most warm and kindly response. Ellinor had defended Florence warmly at the Grange, when, as Gertrude's bridesmaid, she had been staying with the family, after Miss Langdale's departure. She was, however, too imperfectly acquainted with the exact mode of Florence's introduction at the Hall, to explain the circumstance satisfactorily. Phillips had obeyed his mistress's orders, and never divulged the story of his conducting the young heiress to Miss Langdale.

Ellinor warmly entreated her sister to come at once to her house, where she promised Florence, for the present, perfect retirement. It was even possible that a meeting might be arranged, later, between her and Gertrude; as the young countess had promised to visit her before leaving England, and Mr. Langdale's restrictions might not

affect the proceedings of his married daughter, when not
under his roof.

Comforted by this prospect, Florence readily accepted
Ellinor's invitation. They had been excellent friends
during Miss Langdale's illness; and any change must be a
relief from a place, where at every turn she was reminded that she was an exile from home—where she dared
not visit her mother's grave, nor pray in the same church
with her sisters, for the fear of meeting her father's reproach-
ful glance.

CHAPTER III.

THE young Countess had formed a strong friendship for,
and never ceased to take an interest in, Bertina Noel, since
their first meeting; and one of the first times of leaving the
house, after her mother's death, and the ensuing period of
strict seclusion, Gertrude asked her brother to accompany
her to the Eagle's Gorge.

Fritz accepted his sister's proposal gladly. Much as he
loved his suffering mother, he was very weary of inaction,
and of solitary rambles in a district which he had always
disliked. There were also reasons, which he confessed to no
one, which made Gertrude's suggestion peculiarly accepta-
ble.

The great Mill was at work, but, nevertheless, the
brother and sister were doomed to be disappointed. Miss
Noel, they were informed, had temporarily given up her
situation on account of her mother's illness. She was, and
had been for some time, living at home.

The warm sympathies of her visitors were still further

enlisted in Bertina's behalf by the knowledge that she was likely soon to suffer the bereavement they had just sustained. Mrs. Noel's sudden illness, they were informed, was of a nature that admitted no hope of recovery.

It was the same lovely season as when Fritz had first visited the beautiful Gorge. He did not tell his sister how often, during his visits to the Grange, he had trodden that narrow pathway, since then, on every conceivable pretext. The stone house, with its square courtyard and dial, with the clustering hawthorn bushes and dogwood, was basking in the sunshine, innumerable violets sent up perfume from their hidden beds among dark leaves, pale primroses strewed the grass, and the pigeons flew in and out of the dove-cot, but no light foot trod the path before him. He had fancied as he walked along, that Bertina's bright scarlet shawl and black skirt must be visible at the next turn.

Gertrude went in softly at the open house door, leaving her brother in the courtyard. She was afraid to ring, for fear of disturbing the invalid, and yet she could not bear to go away without making some enquiry. An elderly woman servant came out of the offices on hearing her footstep, and said she would go up and sit with Mrs. Noel, while her daughter came down to the visitors.

A silence, as of death, lay on the little sunny room looking into the courtyard. Gertrude felt oppressed with the stillness, which reminded her of her own home, when the deep shadow lay upon it which was gathering here. She went to the window and set it open, calling softly to her brother. They were talking together in low tones at the casement when Bertina came down.

She looked taller and slighter than when Fritz first followed her through the gorge, and her face bore marks of

16

care and watching, but a bright blush banished them as she welcomed the brother and sister.

Fritz must come in, she said, and rest. For the present she was quite at liberty and very glad to see them. Mrs. Noel knew that they were below; and, with her usual hospitality and housewifely care, had ordered refreshments for them. Presently she would like to see the Countess, if she would not mind going upstairs.

Gertrude acceded cheerfully, and an hour passed during which the young people partially forgot their sorrows, and Bertina learnt what a happy, though far distant home, her friend possessed. There were wonderful things to be related of little Count Fritz who was said to be the image of his uncle; some day the proud young mother promised to bring him over to see Bertina, or else she must visit them at the Grange.

After they had partaken of a simple rural repast, Gertrude was summoned upstairs. Bertina and Fritz went out among the hawthorn trees, and gathered violets for the Countess to take home with her. Nowhere was there such a profusion of wild flowers as grew round the old-fashioned Dower-house in the Eagle's Gorge.

Mrs. Noel was sitting up in bed, propped by pillows, looking anxiously towards the door, when Gertrude entered. She signed to her to sit down by the side of the bed, and took her hand silently but gratefully. Gertrude asked some kind questions about her state of health, but the sick woman waved them off impatiently.

"No matter about that," she said, at last; "I know that I am dying. Bertina does not believe it, but I feel that my hour is very near at hand. Ah me, I did not think that I should take it quietly. I was impatient enough once, and full of activity, but that is all over."

She sighed, as though the loss of strength were worse than death itself. Gertrude strove to comfort her.

"Yes, that is all quite right, Madam. It is what my good child says to me and the clergyman, but I like to hear it from you. Never mind me, I am not worth thinking about. It is Bertina I want to speak of. Anxieties trouble me which I dare not confide to her, though she is my right hand, my mainstay. May I speak of them to you?"

Her eyes, still beautiful, brightened, and the hectic colour flooded her cheeks. Mrs. Noel was still very handsome; and the delicate attention paid to her invalid costume and surroundings, embellished her transparent complexion, and regular, though wasted, features. The room, like all in the old house, was very picturesque, with flowers creeping in at the low casements, carved ceiling, and ancient furniture of dark oak. In the softened light the dying woman looked younger and fairer than of yore.

"I must speak," she said impetuously, when Gertrude, alarmed at her agitation, strove to quiet her. "I have never told Bertina what a shock I got one day, when she was working at the Mill. I believe it brought on my illness. A man came to the door and enquired for Bertina, and after those poor children who were nearly drowned in the flood, after the waterspout. I am not brave like Bertina, though I used to be rash enough—but my nerves are shattered. I did not go to the door myself. I let the servant speak to him, and after a bit he went away."

She turned nervously on her pillows. "You'll excuse me, Madam, I am not a lady born, like my poor child. She is a Noel all over, all but their badness. I don't know how to tell my story—Bertina would make you understand. I did not go out; but I looked from my little window over the porch, to see the stranger go away. This is a lonesome place, and I am always afraid of strangers lurking about; especially when Bertina is away. The man looked like an old soldier. He was wrapped in a cloak, for the day was cold and stormy. As I stood at the window he stopped and turned round, looking back at the house; and I believe he saw me. Such a glare of hatred shone in his eyes as I never saw in any human face before, but one—I should say. I shrank back, and, when the man was gone, I bolted and made fast every door and window.

"When Bertina came home and found the house shut up, and me still scared and pale, she asked the reason, and I said a strange man had been peering about, asking after her and the children. I did not like to say more than that I disliked his appearance; and, indeed, the likeness I had traced seemed, when I thought about it, mere fancy. My daughter said it was a strange old man who had risked his life to bring back those poor babes, over the Calder, to their mother. But, when she added that he came from Noel Hall, my heart died away within me.

"I went to the place, but I saw nothing of him; and after all I began to think it was all nonsense, when one day Mr. Haywarden, the lawyer from Hazeldon, rode over to see me. He does call sometimes, and it was owing to his friendship and honesty that I got my rights, as Cuthbert's lawful wife and widow."

As Mrs. Noel pronounced the name of her husband, the light faded in her dark eyes, and the colour left her cheek. Gertrude hastily poured out from a bottle on the table some stimulating cordial, which revived her. Presently she went on speaking.

"The good lawyer talked at first, as usual, about anything that came to hand, admiring this old place as he always does. From that he went on to tell me what sums Mrs.

Langdale was laying out at Noel Hall. Then he asked me
some sly questions. My heart misgave me sadly, when I
saw that he was trying to find out whether, since the date
of his supposed death, I had heard any tidings of my husband.

"The old man at the Hall, he said, professed to have
seen him in the Colonies, among the gold-diggers, and such
like scum of the earth and God-forgetting sinners. There
was some link between them, but he believed the old soldier
was wrong in his head, at times, from fits, and not to be
trusted as to memory.

"Mr. Haywarden looked hard at me, but I never spoke a
word. If my husband were still living, he went on, it
would raise a question about the sale of Noel Hall, and
many other matters relating to the property. Surely if he
were still above ground, the person whom he would communicate with first, would be his wife?

"*That angered me*, and I spoke out. Bertina would have
quieted me, but she was not present; and I have never told
her one word about the lawyer's visit, except that he paid
me my money as usual. I said that the last person Cuthbert ever consulted or considered was his wife, and that,
living or dead, I never wished to hear his name again.
After that Mr. Haywarden went away.

"Of course I said nothing of my silly fright about the
old soldier at the Hall, and the look that scared me—just
like the one my bad husband cast at me, when he said he
hated my fatal beauty :—it had been his ruin. It was a
notice, a warning of coming evil. The man *had* seen Cuthbert, and knew how he hated me. I did not for one moment imagine that old vagrant was my handsome, extravagant husband, Cuthbert Noel, but he came as his emissary
to spy upon me."

"Indeed you are altogether mistaken," said Gertrude. "The old General at the Hall, as he is called, is quite well known to me. He was very kind always to me and to my sisters. I do not think that anyone bears him ill-will. Even Miss Langdale, who once entertained a strong prejudice against him, now suffers him to be her tenant. He is a great favourite with my father."

"I am not afraid of *him*," said Mrs. Noel, in a feebler tone. "It is her father, whose influence I dread over Bertina. She has always loved him, and refused to believe that he was as worthless as I, to my cost, knew him to be. This is the only point on which we ever disagreed."

"Surely you would not wish your child to think ill of her father," said Gertrude. "He may be much changed, if he still lives. Death settles all scores, and sanctifies even the erring. Leave all in God's hand. Your husband may yet be your daughter's best protector."

"You know not what you say," said Mrs. Noel, gloomily. "Where is Bertina? I am never easy when she is out of my sight."

"I left her with my brother," said Gertrude. "He is walking with her in the copse. I can see them plainly."

"Go to them at once," said the mother. "Don't stay, never mind me. It was just so—just such as he is, that blighted all my happiness in my mad youth. It is true Bertina is a lady, a Noel, but that will only increase her unhappiness. I was nothing better than a poor mill girl when Cuthbert's roving eye lighted on me, and I have more reason than he ever had to curse my fatal beauty. Your brother is, perhaps, not like him; you at least do not think so, but I can tell you Cuthbert was lovable enough then— to my endless misfortune. Tell your good father to look after my poor lassie when I am in the grave. It will not be long ere his care is needed."

Gertrude solemnly promised to bespeak Mr. Langdale's protection for the forlorn girl, who would, indeed, she foresaw, soon be, like herself, motherless. Mrs. Noel pressed her hand silently, and she departed. Bertina with a flushed cheek was waiting for her at the house-door; Fritz in the court-yard. Bertina after a hurried leave-taking, ran up stairs at once to her mother's room.

CHAPTER II.

CUTHBERT NOEL'S unacknowledged wife, and reputed widow, was more honoured in death than in life. A long procession wound through the Eagle's Gorge, on the day of the funeral, and her weeping daughter was supported on the arm of the proprietor of the great Mill where she had held a responsible position. Bertina was universally respected, and, though all the assistants at the mournful ceremony were on foot, she felt herself comforted by the sympathy of the young girls whose labour she had superintended; and by the respectful attendance of so many of her own people during the solemn hour at her mother's funeral.

Once only she looked up, and put back her crape veil, as a response, loudly and fervently uttered, struck her ear. The accent was different to that of the worthy Yorkshire folk, and instinctively moved her, but the crowd closed up thickly between her and the speaker; tears filled her eyes, and she heard and saw nothing but the sad paraphernalia of death.

By her own wish, Bertina returned alone to the old

Dower House, refusing the companionship and hospitality proffered by many of her friends. She let herself in, quite calmly, and, with the aid of the old servant who had nursed her mother, set everything in order. It was true that the small stone house looked sadly desolate, but it was *home*, and Bertina had resolved to stay there.

She fed the pigeons and poultry, her mother's favourites, but of late her own especial charge. As she stood thus occupied, in front of the lonely building, she saw a man earnestly regarding her, from the depth of the thicket. Bertina was not timid like her mother, but, at the present moment, she shrank from observation; and was about to re-enter the house, when she heard her own name slowly pronounced in the same deep tones that had attracted her notice in the churchyard.

"Bertina Noel," said the man, approaching her, while she involuntarily trembled and stood still. "Will you give a crust of bread, and a glass of water, to one who asks for them in your father's name."

"Assuredly," said the girl, while the tears which lay near the surface welled up again. "Come in if you like it, and take some refreshment, or shall I bring it to you in the courtyard?"

She signed to the wayfarer to sit down on an old stone bench near the house; and, going indoors, quickly, drew him a jug of sparkling water, and brought it out with half a loaf of home-made bread.

"I have taken you at your word, you see, master, but you shall have better fare if you like," the girl said through her tears. "No one shall be sent away from our gate to-day; especially one who came from far like you, to see my poor mother laid in her grave. I heard your voice in the churchyard, and it was you who saved the lives of those

poor little children. Tell me, did you know my mother?
You spoke but now of my father. What is your name?"

The man took the jug from her, and drank a deep draught
of the sparkling water; then he broke the bread in half,
and sitting down on the stone bench, eat his crust contentedly. "There's no liquor I like better than water now,
young mistress, though I did not always think so," he said,
answering her first question. "They've not spoilt your
well, either, with their milling and cloth dye, like the beck
that runs past Noel Hall. I saw ye there not long ago.
What did ye think of the old place?"

Bertina's eyes again filled with tears.

"I would rather not talk about it to-day. Though I have
nothing to do with Noel Hall, my father, and grandfather, and their parents before them, dwelt there. It is
very sad to see it in the hands of strangers."

"Yes, yes, and all because your father never could remember the value of money. Why, when we were at the
diggings together, it slipped through his fingers like water.
Cuthbert was the most unthrifty among us."

"I would rather not hear anything against my father,"
said Bertina, while the proud spirit of the Noels flashed
in her dark eyes. "I am his only child, and no one, not
even my mother, who was quick-tempered, and had suffered
sorely, ever blamed him to me."

"That's right, my girl, don't be afraid. *I* won't go
against you," said the General. "I'm a great upholder of
discipline in all states of life, and especially in families.
Cuthbert and I were good friends out yonder, and he often
thought of his little daughter, I can tell you. Your poor
mother had some reason to consider herself aggrieved, but
then again, Cuthbert lost caste by marrying her. They
were both sufferers."

Bertina's countenance had resumed its usually gentle expression. "You seem to know more than others about my father," she said. "Why did you not tell me this sooner? I am glad he thought of me sometimes."

"I did come to the gate once, but you were not at home, and, by the blink of the mistress's eyes, bonnie as they were once, I guessed I should get an unpleasant reception. So I bided my time. Still I wished to pay respect to the mortal remains of Cuthbert's wife, so I stood in a corner of the churchyard, and said my amen to the prayers. That couldn't harm her. And now, young mistress, remember, if you want a friend in need, there's one near you."

He rose to depart. Bertina felt a sort of shy reluctance to lose his company. "You are not rested," she said. "Shall I fetch you any more refreshment?"

"No, no, I'll not trespass on your kindness," the man said, touching reverentially the hand she held out to him. "You've not soiled and seamed your pretty fingers, young mistress, with hard work, though I've heard you maintained your poor mother. Well, honest labour is no defilement, even for a Noel. Good day. God bless you."

Bertina watched him cross the courtyard with wistful eyes. His presence seemed a kind of protection to the lonely girl, and she remembered with pleasure during the long solitary evening, his promise to befriend her if she needed assistance. Should such necessity arise, she resolved that she would go over, and enlist in her behalf the services of her father's friend, the occupant of the Gateway Tower at Noel Hall.

There were indeed reasons why the solitary girl, dwelling at the old stone house in the Gorge, might reasonably rejoice in having found an honest, though humble, protector. Ber-

tina had many admirers; some among the rough hands at
the Mill, and others higher in station. Hitherto her sedate
conduct, and her mother's watchful guardianship, had kept
them all at a distance; but it was a difficult matter for a
young girl to live entirely alone, without giving occasion for
scandal.

There were, too, other perils, of which Bertina was
vaguely conscious; but scarcely admitted as yet even to
her own heart. Ever since their first meeting, when he
had followed her through the Eagle's Gorge, Fritz Langdale had awakened an interest for himself in the girl's previously untouched heart. No word of love had been spoken,
but every flower he had gathered for her on his last visit,
each kind word spoken, were treasured in her faithful heart.

Her mother's last words had contained a warning against
listening to the love-pleadings of men above her present
station—a warning founded on bitter experience;—and Bertina, though she knew her mother's failings in judgment
and temper, dearly loved her expiring parent.

Mrs. Noel had endeavoured to persuade her daughter to
look with favour on a young man in the neighbourhood,
whose honest, industrious habits had placed him in a position to maintain a wife, and who earnestly sought Bertina's favour, but the girl's soul revolted against the match.
Though not proud, Bertina had the spirit of an ancient
race. She was a thorough lady, and she could not tolerate
unrefined tastes and habits. While occupying the position
of superintendent of the labour of the girls at the Mill, she
had always been kind and gracious; but she kept herself
aloof from all society, thus maintaining authority, and win-
ning respect from all classes. No one called her anything
but Miss Noel; and, in Mr. Langdale's family, where she occasionally visited, after Gertrude became interested in her,

Bertina was treated as a lady. It did not follow from this, however, that the overlooker at the Mill would be welcomed into the family as a daughter.

Neither was it certain, if she trusted to her mother's experience, that Fritz's admiration was more than a passing feeling. It was rumoured that an attachment, if not an engagement, existed between him and his cousin, Miss Ellinor Langdale, in whose company Bertina had once seen him. On that day, she could not forget it, Fritz had paid her no attention, and the young lady from the Hall had not thought proper to notice her.

It had been the same when, on a subsequent occasion, Bertina had met the younger Miss Langdale at the Grange. Ellinor scarcely spoke to her, and evidently considered her as belonging to an inferior class. She always felt humiliated after any intercourse with her rival.

Ellinor's sympathies, though gentle and womanly, had always been narrow. Gertrude's interest in the beautiful girl whom they had seen at the Mill, was quite incomprehensible to her friend. Neither did Fritz's wandering attention, and furtive glances, dispose her to overlook Bertina's inferiority of station. She felt somewhat offended by her being invited to the Grange, when she herself was staying there.

Any rustic beauty would have been more kindly regarded by Ellinor Langdale. She hated trade and its associations— the mills and machinery which defaced the hills and dales, and discoloured the glancing waters of her lovely native county; the loud-voiced mill girls, and the prosperous owners of the great works in the neighbourhood.

Neither Miss Langdale nor her sister, who had been brought to regard many of her prejudices as sacred, acknowledged the validity of Cuthbert Noel's secret marriage.

Bertina was regarded as an intruder, even upon the outskirts of the aristocracy of the county. Ellinor Langdale never once called Miss Noel by her ancient name.

Instinct taught her that, in spite of her contempt, Bertina was a very dangerous rival. Mr. Langdale and Mr. Haywarden had always, on good legal grounds, treated Mrs. Noel as Cuthbert's widow; and her daughter received at their hands tokens of marked respect. Nothing pleased the master of the Grange better than to notice the friendship springing up between his own daughters and the only child of his ill-starred friend.

Fritz was very little at home, and studiously cautious in his behaviour; only the eyes of a loving, jealous woman detected his partiality for the beautiful daughter of the ruined Noels—he did not own it even to himself.

At Gertrude's marriage, Bertina had been invited to be one of the bridesmaids, but she modestly and firmly declined the honour; and was not even present at the ceremony, saying that it would cause jealousy, and interfere with her duties. If she had accepted the invitation, very probably Ellinor Langdale would have found some excuse for refusing to be present at the wedding.

Bertina's reluctance to put herself forward in any manner, increased the respect and admiration entertained for her by Mr. Langdale and his family. Instead of her present voluntary isolation she might, had she so willed it, have gone away from the dull empty house to the Grange, as soon as she was released from the care of attending upon her mother.

CHAPTER III.

WITHOUT consulting Florence, Miss Langdale bent her proud spirit to make an effort to appease her cousin, before she took his daughter away from the neighbourhood. Frances, now the active managing mistress of her father's house, was surprised, in the midst of her domestic avocations, one morning, by a message from the Lady of the Hall, who wished to speak with her.

Frances was sorely perplexed by this request. To admit as a visitor, and without her father's permission, the proud relation who had never vouchsafed to pay the slightest courtesy to her dead mother; was more than she dared to do. After a moment's consideration, Frances sent word that she would come down to the gate and speak to Miss Langdale. She ascertained previously that her sister, with whom all communication was positively forbidden, was not in the carriage.

Miss Langdale was too impatient to remain seated. Frances found her walking up and down the old Roman road into which the avenue, leading from Godley Grange, opened. A very cold salutation was exchanged; the fair Saxon complexion of the young girl flushed proudly.

Frances was, of course, attired in the deepest mourning. Miss Langdale also wore black, unrelieved by colour. She did so from the first moment after her arrival at home, in compliment to Florence. Her costume, though somewhat stiff in fashion, became her well; and her manner was softer than formerly.

The old Langdale trees threw their shadow over the handsome carriage and spirited horses. They seemed chafing at the unwonted delay at an unusual halting place, tossing their manes and champing their bits, and throwing foam on the embossed harness. Miss Langdale, who was very careful of her beautiful Neapolitan greys, desired the coachman, who was also imported from southern Italy, to drive them up and down.

"You are," she said, "my cousin's eldest unmarried daughter. I should like to congratulate him on having so fair a mistress at the old Grange."

The blue eyes of the young girl filled with tears. "My father," she said gravely, "would ill bear congratulation at this time, on any subject. We have so lately lost our dear mother, that *strangers* cannot be admitted to our house of mourning."

She laid a strong emphasis on the word strangers. Miss Langdale coloured.

"It is scarcely courteous to use that term to a relative, though circumstances have kept us apart. I would have it otherwise now."

"Pardon me, Madam," said Frances, with grave dignity; "it is impossible that those who did not think our sweet mother's friendship worth enjoying, should be the friends of her daughter. If this is all, suffer me to leave you."

"Not yet—not yet," said Maud, impatiently. "If I could see your father, I would convince him how much I am in earnest. We were good friends formerly."

"That must have been a long time ago," said Frances, while the waving boughs threw flickering shadows over her fair, calm brow; "long before my recollection. Since we settled at Godley Grange, we have never seen any sign of kindly recollection on the part of the Lady of Langdale Hall."

"Foolish child," exclaimed Maud. "It ought to be enough when I, who am old enough to be your mother, tell you that I regret the past—that I would willingly allow it to be cancelled—forgotten—nay, more, that I am sorry to have offended you? What more would you have? Talk of the Langdale pride and temper—truly you have enough of both."

"I have at least sufficient self-respect to decline listening further," said Frances, stepping within the gate. "Miss Langdale, it is of no use to make overtures to my father through us. We are our mother's daughters, and cannot plead the cause of one who slighted her."

"Right, Frances," said a voice behind her, in stern, quick accents. "Marina's girls know how to keep in honour her blessed memory—all but one—and she is no longer my daughter. Suffer me to remind you, Madam, that you forget yourself, in thus lowering your dignity to me and mine. It is too late to renew our ancient friendship."

Miss Langdale had turned as pale as death at sight of her cousin. For more than twenty years she had not spoken with him—years of unkindness and neglect—her voice failed her now. She remembered Frank Langdale as 'her friend in youth, as her father's favourite nephew—other scenes, other thoughts, arose within her at the sound of his voice, at sight of his dark frowning brow.

"Cannot you forgive an angry woman? Does nothing plead for me in your heart?" she said, while tears rushed to her proud eyes, and streamed down her cheeks. I am much altered, and behind, around you, I see forms which I shall never behold in life again. My dead father and mother —others, friends of both—long dead but not forgotten. I own I have been wrong. Will you not forgive me?"

"No," said Mr. Langdale. "At your side I see another vision, my dear, lost wife, whom you persecuted into her grave. She had one pet lamb, you saw and coveted it, and

never rested till it strayed away from the flock. The mother never recovered from the shock. I saw it strike her—I
knew it was a death blow.—Marina never confessed it. She
would advocate forgiveness if she lived now—but she is dead,
and, with her, the softest part of my nature perished. I will
pray to God to forgive you—at present, I cannot."

He took his daughter's hand and turned away. Miss
Langdale's servant, standing at some distance, beyond ear-
shot, at a sign from his mistress went to the coachman,
who had stopped his horses under the trees. Frances was
weeping. Her feelings were touched more than her father's
by Miss Langdale's confession of error.

"It was for the sake of Florence that I came here——"
said Miss Langdale. "If you cannot and will not pardon me,
forgive your innocent daughter. She is very tender hearted,
not such a stony hearted creature as I have been—you once
knew me far otherwise—but, no matter :—Florence cannot
endure your displeasure."

"Then she should have shunned to awaken it," said Mr.
Langdale, pausing and confronting his enemy. "Florence is
like many another woman, too great a coward to bear the
storm she has herself provoked. She knew the risk she ran,
and willingly incurred it. Florence chose her own lot, and
must abide by it."

He walked on, drawing his daughter's arm within his
own ; while Maud, utterly defeated and shamed, got into the
carriage in silence, and drove away. Frances said softly,
after her departure, "Father, shall you be angry with me if
I say that I think Miss Langdale was really penitent, and
that I fancy our darling mother would have asked you to
forgive your cousin,"—she hesitated, then added, "and
Florence."

"Possibly," said her father, drily. "Your mother was

17

and is, an angel ! Scarcely more so in my thoughts now, than while she dwelt with us here; but I, Frances, am a man, and till earth's shadows and lights begin to fade, and all its glories here grow dim, I cannot forgive Maud Langdale. You know not what you ask, when you entreat me, in your mother's name, to pardon her murderess. That woman as surely killed her, when she stole away her child as if she had struck a dagger to her heart."

Mr. Langdale turned away from his daughter and entered the house alone. He went straight to his study, the gloomy room looking towards the avenue, where Mr. Haywarden had first made known Miss Langdale's views regarding Florence, and shut himself up there for the rest of the day.

CHAPTER VI.

FRITZ LANGDALE, though he had been very severe at first, had long since forgiven "the little one." He often said that the destruction of his hopes of the inheritance of Miss Langdale had made a man of him at once, and been the best thing that could possibly have happened to him.

He no longer felt angry even with Miss Langdale, and, when Frances repeated to him and Gertrude what had passed at the gate of the Grange, Fritz boldly declared that, in his opinion, his father carried resentment much too far.

Gertrude was inclined to take the same view with her brother, and her heart yearned towards Florence. Home influences and prejudices had less weight with them both than with their younger sisters. Frances, the home-bred, home-loving girl, stood up bravely for her father. It mattered little perhaps now, she said, to the absent ones, whether or

not the mistress of Langdale Hall had deigned to notice
them hitherto, but, for herself and the twins, it had been, and
still was, a serious disadvantage. She agreed with her
father, that these tardy overtures, made so soon after their
mother's death, added insult to injury.

It was the first time since Florence's transgression that
there had been any serious disagreement in the family :
Fritz and Gertrude steadily maintaining, that the mistress
of Langdale Hall had a perfect right to dispose as she
liked of the life interest in her property, and that, since
she had done so in favour of their own sister, ill will should
not be kept up ; also that Florence had been sufficiently
punished and ought now to be forgiven : whilst Mr. Langdale's three younger daughters considered, as he did, that the
offences against him, and their mother's memory, could not
be overlooked.

Mr. Langdale took no part whatever in the discussion.
The subject was not even named in his presence; and, during
the remainder of their stay at Godley Grange, his eldest son
and daughter respected his authority and wishes too much
to act contrary to either. Neither did he oppose Gertrude's
desire to visit Ellinor Langdale, or enquire whether she had
other guests. So long as no inmate of the Grange held
any communication with the inmates of the Hall, he appeared
to be satisfied. Day by day he became more immersed in
business ; or, when at home, the master of the house withdrew into greater seclusion ; not only hardening himself,
against those whom he regarded as his and Marina's enemies,
but shutting himself up from the love of those who shared
his every feeling.

Perhaps, in his heart of hearts, the man, angry as he was,
sympathised more with those who were about to transgress
his orders, than with those who obeyed them most scrupu-

lously. Though he would not for the world have sanctioned
the proceeding ;—though he carefully avoided the utterance
of one word of kindness, for which Gertrude's soft eyes
pleaded when she bade him farewell,—Mr. Langdale knew
perfectly that she would soon be under the same roof with
her sister ; and, over and over again, after she left him, he
saw in imagination, involuntarily, the meeting between her
and the little one.

It would have taken an almost unbearable load off his
heart to have said, " Let all be forgotten and forgiven," but
he would not. The time was not yet come. It seemed to
him an outrage to the memory of his dead wife, to forgive
those whom he persisted in believing to be her mortal foes :—
and yet, his loved Marina, he well knew, had never ceased
to plead for them. Even her loving Christian charity, like
the other good qualities on which he ceaselessly pondered,
increased the mourning husband's bitterness against all who
had not valued, as he did, this lost angel. Yet still, ever
and anon, sorely against his will, there flitted past the
shadowy couch, by which he watched in his dreams, the pale,
pensive, slender, face and form of the little one.

This phantom-like vision of the night was not the rebellious child, Florence, but a grave maiden, with sad, reproach-
ful, tender glances, which he dared scarcely meet. Out of
those dark orbs seemed to gleam the soft loving soul which
had lighted up her mother's sweet countenance. Never
before had he seen any likeness between the little daughter
born in Italy, and his fair wife ; but now the vision which
haunted his sick brain, partook of the characteristic features
of Marina and her youngest born.

Annie and May no longer dared to go to their father, as
of yore, in all their troubles. A dark inscrutable woe
seemed to have drunk up all the loving kindness of his

nature. Now, for the first time, these young girls, who had been long debarred from a mother's care, felt themselves indeed motherless. Frances, with the duties of mistress of the establishment freshly laid upon her, seemed suddenly to become a grave woman, raised out of their sphere. They missed, inexpressibly, the twilight hour, when, returning from their walks, they gathered round the bright fire in the invalid's apartment ;. her participation in all their joys and sorrows, her keen sense of humour, and ready never failing sympathy. Full of love, brimming over with regret, the twins no longer ventured to go to their once kind father, and weep out their sorrow in his arms.

Mr. Langdale had never courted society, and, at this time of sorrowful seclusion, none of his family had the heart to seek for any companionship outside the Grange; but still, after the young Countess had left them, and Fritz had been summoned away to his professional duties at Sheffield, the three girls found the old mansion, for the first time in their young lives, inexpressibly dreary. They had no intimate friends in the neighbourhood, who might, even at this sad season, have drawn them away from their own thoughts.

Dr. Forsyth and Mr. Haywarden were now received coldly by Mr. Langdale, who regarded them both as partisans of Miss Langdale and Florence. Dissatisfied with himself, and morbidly sensitive, the master of the Grange believed that every one blamed his conduct; and, indeed, the good doctor and lawyer, had tried more than once to bring their old friend into a more rational and kindly state of mind. The consequence had been, that they both felt themselves to be no longer welcome visitors at the Grange.

For his care of Mrs. Langdale's health, her husband could not fail to be grateful to her skilful and attentive physician, but the family no longer needed his care professionally ; and,

to say the truth, with its invalid mistress and Florence, Dr.
Forsyth's attractions to the Grange had flown. He had
never been cordial with its master since the failure of his
first attempt to bring back the outcast, and he considered
Mr. Langdale prejudiced and vindictive.

Perhaps the greatest alleviation of the dulness of the
old Grange, was when Bertina Noel was a visitor there.
Gertrude had faithfully performed the dying mother's commission, and Mr. Langdale, whom she had appointed, by
will, guardian to her daughter, scrupulously performed that
duty. Though Bertina still resided in the old Dower House,
she had relinquished her post at the Mill, and spent much
of her time with the motherless girls at Godley Grange.

Her own similar bereavement, and deep mourning, set her,
in a peculiar manner, in a position to sympathise with and
comfort these mourners. The entire seclusion of the place
suited her well, and she was able, in some measure, to enliven the old house. Mr. Langdale's stern face would soften
a little, at sight of his erring friend Cuthbert Noel's beautiful daughter ; and Bertina knew and felt, deep in her
heart's core, that he, of all men living, had thought and
spoken most kindly about her unknown parent.

No one at Godley Grange doubted the fact, that her
mother, though of lowly birth, was Cuthbert Noel's widowed
wife. Mr. Langdale said so, and his will was law—his
word never disputed,—except by one rebellious daughter.
His liberal ideas on all subjects prevented Bertina's honest,
active industry, exerted in support of her widowed mother,
from being regarded as a reproach. She was always treated
at Godley Grange with as much respect as any daughter of
the once haughty Noels would have desired.

Bertina's society was all the more welcome to her guardian
because it awakened no associations with, or remembrance

of, his absent daughter. Florence had left the Grange before Miss Noel's first visit there, and, although Gertrude had often spoken of her youngest sister, and Fritz had confided to her his sentiments, Bertina knew that the subject was prohibited in Mr. Langdale's presence. The clever, dark-haired, representative of the Noels seemed, in some way, to take the place of the little one in her old home.

Annie and May, affectionate, loving girls of nineteen, were not talented or accomplished. Frances, absorbed in household duties, gave every leisure moment to her easel, finding in her studio the nearest approach to happiness. Bertina was always ready to assist her host, to look over accounts and write letters, foreign or English, for the often overworked man of business. Oppressed by morbid thoughts, Mr. Langdale often felt the powers of his mind on the verge of failing him; at such times the clear sense, and strong young faculties, of one who had been accustomed, from earliest girlhood, to business habits were peculiarly useful.

One day when they were sitting alone in Mr. Langdale's study, after Bertina had looked over some complicated statements, the master of the Grange laid his hand kindly on hers, and said :—

" Ah, my dear, if your father had possessed such a head for accounts as you have, what a different position you might occupy now. If ever, as I have reason to believe may be the case, the family affairs of the Noels are re-established, they will be better managed than formerly."

Bertina's eyes filled with tears. " Would that my dear father were alive to benefit by whatever talents God has given me," she said; " of what use is it to me, that the fortunes of our race should change, when there is only one solitary girl to be enriched."

An unwonted smile softened her host's austere features.

" A time may come, Bertina, when you will feel less indifferent in this matter. Meanwhile, remember, your presence is very welcome in this mournful house. On your account, as well as because you are my old friend's daughter, I rejoice in seeing you here."

" Children, when they are happily married, do not belong to the home," said Bertina, blushing. " Madame la Comtesse, our darling Gertrude, is gone back to her German family. Your son will soon take to himself a wife, and make another nest. When that is done, let me be a daughter to you. I do think that Frances, May, and Annie, love to see me here."

" Who told you that Fritz was going to be married ?" said his father, sharply. " I do not believe it. I have never seen him pay attention to any lady except his sisters."

" I heard the report long ago, when I first knew your son," said Bertina, re-arranging the papers, nervously. " But, if it has not reached you, it may be untrue. I would rather not say more."

" No, no, let it die away," said Mr. Langdale, impatiently. " I do not believe a word of it. Fritz would have told me, if there had been on his part any serious intentions. I know to whom you allude, and I believe if Fritz brought forward any pretentions they would be favourably viewed ; but I am sure he has never thought of proposing in that quarter. It would grieve me inexpressibly. I have quite other prospects in view, which would not be distasteful, I am certain, to my son."

Bertina, having satisfied herself, apparently, that the parcels of papers were safely secured, laid them down again, and rose to leave the room.

As she did so Mr. Langdale also rose; and, with old-fashioned courtesy, opened the door for the young descendant of the ruined Noels to pass through.

" Do not give ear to idle gossip," he said; " Fritz is either heart-free, as he would phrase it in his German idiom, or he has placed his affections in keeping which would suit me better than even a half-sister of Maud Langdale's. And now I release you, and I thank you for helping me. Depend upon it, happen what may, since you can bear the desolation of Godley Grange, you shall always have the place of a tenderly-loved daughter and sister beside its hearth. Come here, as often as you can, to cheer us."

Bertina did not look up in his face; but, as she left the dark room, a ray of sunshine, such as seldom lighted up its depths, seemed to pass from it with her presence.

PART THE SEVENTH.

MARINA.

A chain is passed from heart to heart,
   Wrought of bright but treacherous things,
For the red gold and jewels' dazzling light
   Hides from us how fast it clings !
As we merrily fling it from hand to hand,
   Each part is so finely moulded,
That we guess not how heavily falls the weight
   Of those bright links all unfolded.

The flowers we gathered by copse and brook,
   When summer and life were young,
And soft words said on a moonlight eve—
   Of these the first links were strung :—
But the fairy-like texture grew firm and strong
   As a deeper tint, and a twisted thread,
Showed where jealousy mingled its tangled yarn
   But fled from the strife discomfited.

R. M. K.

CHAPTER I.

THE contrast between Ellinor's sea-beaten property in the North Riding, and the wooded houghs and cloughs of Langdale was very striking. Florence derived benefit in health from the change, wandering at will on the sandy beach, and looking out at the waves rolling madly into the bay; or, even in the calmest weather, at the long line of silvery foam, marking the dangerous breakers, where the thin, black ridge of rock, called Filey Brig, ran out far into the water.

Often and often, Florence would watch the struggles of the fishing smacks, or northern traders, and collier brigs, striving to round the point; and think of the day, long past, when the mother, for whom she now was mourning, had been cast a helpless child on that cruel reef.

Mrs. Langdale's father, an Indian officer, had, on his deathbed, sent his little daughter to England. Her mother had not survived her birth; and the distant relatives, to whose charge the orphan was committed, gladly made over their responsibility to Lady Barbara Noel, who had taken a fancy to the child rescued by her son from a watery grave.

The name of Marina, bestowed while the infant was quite unknown to them, had superseded her baptismal appellation, and the little maiden grew up, in the stately abode of the Noels, happily enough, until the death of Lady Barbara, and the utter ruin of her extravagant son, threw the adopted one, once more, on the mercy of strangers. Marina's sweet disposition, had, fortunately, won friends for her, and, in the protection and care of Mrs. Langdale, of Godley Grange, she remained until her death. The discovery of a mutual attachment between Frank Langdale and Marina established her in a home of her own ;—migratory, indeed, as she accompanied him to Germany ;—where he acted as commissioner for the house of business in which he was now a partner ; travelling, in the interests of the firm, over most parts of Northern Europe.

Northward, on the far side of Filey Brig, a dark line on the cliff commemorated Cuthbert Noel's gallant deed. Florence burst into tears when she heard that the buildings, just visible from her favourite post of observation, were named Marina. These were all new. Not as at Scarborough and Filey, divided into old and young. The little cottage, or pavilion, where Lady Barbara formerly passed a week, occasionally, in summer—and where she happened to be staying, with her son, when a sudden tempest wrecked the Lubeck trading vessel—had been washed away in one of the incursions often made by the sea upon that coast.

Marina, the new Watering-Place, consisted of a great hotel and a few shops now in progress ; with sites for a Church, and several detached villas. On paper it presented a flourishing appearance ; and, at a distance, the unfinished buildings on the cliff were not unpicturesque ; though, as yet, all was incomplete. It was said that the prospects of the new Bathing-place were most promising, and that the speculation was likely to be very successful.

Mr. Haywarden, who had always befriended Mrs. Noel,

now watched over the interests of her daughter. This detached portion of Cuthbert Noel's property, as well as the old house in the Eagle's Gorge, had not been sold. At the time of the dismemberment of the possessions of the family, the little strip on the coast was regarded as valueless: now it was possible that it might yield a large return for the money expended upon it.

For persons desiring more retirement than might be found at Scarborough, Marina possessed attractions; and the taste with which the winding roads and embryo plantations and gardens were arranged, on this wild coast, was very remarkable. Already, dots and streaks of verdure enlivened the cliff, marking the sites of the intended buildings. The soil was found to be very productive; and water, excellent and abundant, was supplied from a spring high up in the cliff, and gathered in a reservoir, which was to supply the houses. Valuable trees and shrubs had been planted, in expectation of the villas and terraces, which, ere long, they would embellish.

Ellinor Langdale's house was situated in a hollow of the moor, with yet higher ground behind the mansion, which commanded a view of the whole sweep of Filey Bay. The new town was not seen from the windows; but a knoll in the grounds, where a flag-staff had been erected by her grandfather, an old naval officer, afforded a prospect of the rising walls and shrubberies of Marina. Florence often went there. The very name of the place endeared it to her, and she sometimes thought that she would rather live on that wild sea-washed coast, and spend her life in rescuing shipwrecked mariners, than be the Mistress of Langdale Hall.

All the youthful romance which had hung over the park, into which she dared not penetrate—the Hall at whose dark tower and frowning battlements she had gazed through childish tears, wistfully—had long since vanished. The lowly Grange, whence she was for ever banished—her own old nursery and pets—her angry father and her alienated sisters—were now objects of Florence's brooding, morbid, fancies and desires. And yet the girl's nature was not envious or discontented. She had been warped from her natural duties and affections; and, now, those she had wilfully assumed sat heavily on her shoulders. Only the deep and true attachment, nourished by a thousand favours and instances of kind consideration, on the part of Miss Langdale, which bound Florence to her benefactress, prevented her going back, at all risks and hazards, to her own early home, and craving forgiveness.

Perhaps had she done so in the first moments of softening grief, after Mrs. Langdale's death, all might have been condoned; but, if there was such an hour, it had gone by before Florence's return to England. Mr. Langdale's heart turned to stone against her, when he arose from the first terrible prostration of grief which laid even him, the strong man, low in the dust; as he gazed on the form, soon to be taken from him, of the meek sufferer whom he had adored and tended. The time passed on, bringing no more soft moments.

Miss Langdale said very little to Florence of her reception at the Grange; but the girl knew that she had lowered her pride for her sake, and that the humiliation had been of no avail. She did not again propose to seek for pardon. The insult to her kind benefactress wounded her deeply. She knew well that nothing but Maud's deep love, and unwillingness to see her suffer, had induced her to make this unsuccessful attempt to pave the way for a reconciliation with her family.

Henceforward she determined to consider herself the daughter of the Lady of Langdale Hall. Florence told Maud, with streaming tears, that she had no other parent, she belonged entirely to her, and the acknowledgment was repaid by the most fervent gratitude; but the ties of nature were too strong to be broken even by the rude strain laid upon them. Though banished, almost heart-broken, Florence Langdale, the Heiress of the Hall, was her father's daughter still; and her heart turned back yearningly to her sisters, and her forsaken home.

Around Ellinor's mansion were thick coverts, carefully screened from the north and east winds, and intersected with sheltered walks. Miss Langdale, in another person's house, was not arbitrary, and the last few years had softened her temper and enlarged her views. She took great interest in Ellinor's new home, and, while Florence wandered on the shore, the two sisters might be seen walking together affectionately, about the farm and gardens. Everything was in admirable order. Ellinor was a gentle but judicious mistress; her servants loved her and served her well, though her will was not absolute law. To the poor fishermen, in stormy winters, she was a generous benefactress; and all the neighbourhood had reason to rejoice that the pleasant house under the moor was inhabited by its lawful mistress. Every day the associations with Langdale became weaker, while the ties which bound her to her own home and people acquired greater force.

18

CHAPTER II.

ON the shore of the German ocean the long parted sisters met, as though in another hemisphere. By common consent, not a word was said on the subject of Florence's departure from the Grange ; little Fritz was a medium for all sorts of caresses and interchanges of affection, and the new scenery and circumstances around them, as well as the description of Gertrude's happy home, afforded inexhaustible subjects for conversation.

It seemed to the young Countess almost as if she were in a dream, when she found herself actually dwelling in the same house with Miss Langdale, the formidable mistress of the Hall, that gloomy shadow which had clouded her childhood. The real woman was an agreeable, nay, even a lovable person, when seen in company with her adopted daughter and the gentle mistress of the mansion on the borders of the moor

Fritz Langdale had been invited to accompany his sister and nephew, but he was detained on business for a week at Sheffield, surveying a new line of railway. Gertrude and Florence had resumed their old habits of sisterly affection, when he found time to join them. A few days only were to elapse before he escorted Gertrude and her little son, to the port whence they were to embark for Germany.

Ellinor Langdale was less tranquil than usual, on the morning when the young civil engineer had written to say that he could get leave of absence. She half repented having given the invitation, though, in truth, it could scarcely, without absolute discourtesy, have been avoided. The presence of Miss Langdale, and of Frank's sisters, removed any objection as to the propriety of her receiving her cousin under her roof. It was, nevertheless, to herself more than doubtful whether this exercise of hospitality was in all respects judicious. When the note, accepting his proffered visit, was past recovery, she would have given the world to recall it.

The deed being done and past revocation, Ellinor's spirits gradually regained their usual tone. She received Fritz with graceful, though not entirely unembarrassed, courtesy; and strove in every way to make the house pleasant to him. Fritz did not seem at all to mind having no male companions. He had always liked his fair cousin, and he admired her more than ever in her own home.

He got on very well with Miss Langdale, though they both felt rather awkward at first meeting each other. The little episode in the aisle of Langdale church, when the great lady had swept past him so disdainfully, had long been forgotten and forgiven; and Fritz had never put himself in her way again. Her preference of Florence was not regarded with rancour, now that life was full of interests and occupations which led his thoughts far beyond local pride and prejudices.

Fritz had just accepted a flattering offer of an opportunity for studying on the continent a new system of engineering. He had great abilities, which promised to lead to honourable distinction. The world lay before him, and his path was chosen; one that would carry him to many of its pleasantest places, and even now made him perfectly independent.

All his plans and projects were frankly and freely discussed. Fritz made little or no distinction between his sisters and his cousins. Miss Langdale's strong common

18—2

sense made her conversation peculiarly agreeable to her young relative, and day by day she showed for him a more strongly marked partiality.

Perhaps, in this small coterie of ladies, it would have been unnatural not to find some web of fancy spun for the future ; but, if it were so, no one was rash enough to speak of it. More than once Miss Langdale turned aside in her customary walk through the park, leaving her half-sister to do the honours of the grounds to her last arrived visitor. Gertrude and Florence were only too glad to find an excuse for long *tête-à-tête* walks on the beach.

Inland a wild wide waste of rolling upland, flushed purple by the summer sun, stretched miles and miles away. The heath was all a-glow, clothing, what at another time of the year was dark of hue and desolate enough, with wonderful beauty. Fritz loved the moor even better than the sea ; and often persuaded his fair hostess to leave the sheltered wood walks, for the tracks among gorse and heather which wound upward, from the grounds to the summit of the adjacent heights.

More than once, when they encountered some rustic neighbour, the fervency of the blessing uttered would make Ellinor blush and even tremble ; but Fritz understood little of the Yorkshire dialect, and, *insouciant* by nature, enjoyed these lonely romantic rambles with his fair cousin, without troubling himself, in the smallest degree, respecting the comments they might call forth.

He regarded Ellinor almost in the light of a sister, only that it was more pleasant to be with her, than even with Gertrude ; whom, as well as himself, she closely resembled in person and feature. As for the little one, he often said jestingly, with her foreign eyes and complexion and manners, since she had revisited the land of her birth, she was

the greatest stranger of the party. More than the appointed
week slipped away, before any one of the party assembled
at Moriscombe thought it necessary to broach the subject of
their approaching separation. No one seemed disposed to
break up that pleasant reunion.

One summer evening, after a party of Ellinor's country
neighbours had dispersed, the young mistress of Moriscombe
and Fritz Langdale strolled out through the small gate that
opened right upon the moorland, and ascended the hill
behind the house. The sun was setting over the down,
but its rays were thrown afar, across the waves, as though
the light lingered more lovingly there than on the land.
The wide sweep of coast from Flamborough Head to the
heights crowned by Scarborough Castle, was distinctly visible ;—a quivering ridge of foam, tipped with fire, half hid
the narrow file of rocks, running out near the little town
that takes its name from that sharp dangerous ridge, which
on the inner side forms a natural breakwater, within whose
shelter a little fleet of coasting vessels lay snugly at anchor.
The lighthouse on the point, where the warning beacon was
just kindled, sending down its own red reflection into the
water, stood out boldly—a tower of strength—against a
white bank of fog, which lay curled up like some monster of
the deep. The capricious rays of declining light darted
from headland to headland of the wave-washed cliffs, giving
yet more eccentric forms to the excavations rent in those
mighty natural sea walls, by that turbulent encroaching
ocean. Entranced by the beautiful sunset, Ellinor and
Fritz walked on and on ; intending to return by a path across
the moor, which wound down into the combe. They were
talking pleasantly on various matters, and time passed
quickly. At last Ellinor stopped, in some perplexity.

" I am sadly afraid I have taken the wrong path," she

said; " how strangely dark it has become, since we turned
our backs on the sea.   It must be later than I fancied."

Fritz looked at his watch.   " Who would have supposed
that we parted with your friends two hours ago?" he said,
laughing; " but so it is, and though I should be sorry to be
rude to your guests, I must own time seems to have flown
much more rapidly, since we lost their company.   Do you
really think we have lost our way?   That would be a
charming adventure."

Ellinor looked grave.   They were no longer on the cliff,
but in a vast tract of undulating heath, intersected by tiny
sheep-tracks, and without any striking landmarks,—one
heathery hillock painfully resembling another.   Fritz had
relied implicitly on his companion's professed knowledge
of the road, and had wandered on, since they quitted the
regular path, trusting entirely to her guidance.

" Stay here, while I run up to the top of that ridge of
ground.   I shall be able to make out our bearings, perhaps,
better from thence," said Fritz ; " you are tired, let me find
a seat for you."

" No, no," said Ellinor, nervously, " I entreat you not to
leave me.   Let us at any rate keep together."

Her voice shook, and she silently accepted his arm.   They
walked on for a short distance, until the false track they
had pursued ended in a morass, over which damp, white fog-
wreaths were hovering.

Weary and terrified, Ellinor burst into tears.   Fritz felt
a little impatient.   The situation was becoming, to say the
least of it, unpleasant, and his companion did not appear
inclined to make the best of it.   His sisters would have
made a joke of the dilemma.   He was half inclined to wish
that he had Miss Langdale leaning on his arm ; or any
stronger minded female than the pretty mistress of the
sunny mansion under the moor.

"We have nothing to do but to retrace our steps," he said, ignoring the tears, and feeling excessively embarrassed. " You will have a long, toilsome walk home, I am afraid, but there seems no help for it. I do not suppose there is any other place of shelter."

Ellinor tried to regain her composure. Something in the dry tone of her cousin's voice made her guess that he was displeased. " It is entirely my own fault," she said, gently. " I misled you, and quite forgot that I had only taken this long round once before in broad daylight. I am almost a stranger myself in this country, and, until you came, I seldom ventured far."

Her soft voice and candid admission appeased Fritz, and he devoted himself to taking care of her, and enlivening the way by conversation. Unluckily the topic chosen was not altogether fortunate, nor could he have explained to himself or his companion, the mysterious connection of ideas which had suggested the subject to his mind, when at a loss how to reassure and entertain her.

" Miss Noel is staying with my young sisters at Godley," he said, abruptly. " Frances tells me that she is in great favour with my father, and that they are all fond of her. I am glad the poor girls have a little pleasant society."

" Miss Noel ?" said Ellinor, coldly, removing her arm that she might wrap her plaid round her. " Do you mean the young person with whom your sister became acquainted, at the Mill in the Eagle's Gorge ? The overlooker of the girls, in the room where there was such a bewildering noise of machinery, that I could go no farther than the door ? Does she really persist in calling herself Noel ? Is *she* staying at Godley with your sisters ?"

Fritz walked on sturdily by her side without again offering his arm.

"Yes, I mean Cuthbert Noel's daughter : a far better woman than her father was a man, and more of a lady than he was a gentleman. Miss Bertina Noel is an intimate friend of my sisters. My father is her guardian. Did you not know it ? I thought you had met at the Grange."

"Once only," said Ellinor, recovering from her vexation and surprise, and speaking more in her natural tone. " I liked best to visit your sisters when they were alone. It was quite by chance that I met the young lady in question. I am not sure that I even heard her name. None of Mr. Noel's family acknowledged his low marriage. I did not know that its validity had been proved."

"My father and Mr. Haywarden never entertained a doubt about it; after Mrs. Noel returned to Hazeldon, and produced the legal documents connected with the marriage ceremony, performed privately between herself and Cuthbert Noel. I believe he sent them to her in a tardy fit of death-bed repentance. They were, at all events, sufficient to establish the claims of his widow to some small remnant of his wrecked fortunes, and Bertina inherits her mother's rights."

"That is very fortunate for her," said Ellinor, icily. "I hope that she will be able to give up her very disagreeable employment. It was certainly difficult to recognise a daughter of the Noels, among those loud-voiced vulgar girls at the Mill—her companions, before your kind sisters noticed her."

"I cannot take your view of this matter," said Fritz, unceremoniously. "My father is a working man, I myself have entered an arduous profession, which I mean to follow assiduously. No honest employment is in our eyes derogatory. Miss Noel, I trust, may be relieved from the necessity of pursuing a toil, which, to a person of her sense and refinement, must often have been highly distasteful ; but, in our estimation, she is none the less honourable and admirable for having trod steadfastly the thorny path of filial duty, to the end."

A sharp cry of Ellinor's cut short Fritz's declamation. In the increasing darkness she had stumbled over an obtrusive root of heath, and nearly fallen. Fritz drew her arm kindly, but firmly, within his own.

"Do not let us quarrel over these social questions," he said. "It is like the old story of the shield, respecting which two knights fought to the death, instead of trying to look at it fairly, and from the same direction. We have been brought up differently, you, in the midst of our haughty, English landed gentry—I, among German democrats. I am a child of the people—you are a born aristocrat."

"You are just as much a Langdale as I am," said Ellinor. "Are we not cousins, and only once removed from the first degree."

"I am proud of that honour," said Fritz, kindly, but not tenderly, pressing the small white hand that trembled in his own. "But now, how are we to get out of the scrape we are in. All these hillocks seem like twin brothers, and that fog from the Marsh is following us up fast. You must let me leave you, to see if there is any outlet from our present difficulties."

Ellinor released his arm, and Fritz, after bidding her remain perfectly still, sprang up an elevation which promised a somewhat wider view than the perplexing hillocks. But the prospect only commanded wave upon wave of apparently endless undulations of heather, from which the crimson glow had quite departed. Dark and sad lay the lonely moorland, under a gloomy canopy of cloud, between which and the earth the fog hung out its threatening banners. Fritz hurried back to his companion, in considerable alarm and perplexity.

Ellinor had not moved since he left her. She stood pale and cold, a statue on the stony waste. During the few minutes which elapsed she passed through a crisis of her woman's life. She felt that the accident which had placed her and the man she loved, in peril together on the wild moorland, had not drawn their hearts nearer. They were cousins, friends it might be, but, on his part, nothing more.

Never in her whole life had she felt so bitterly alone, as while she stood waiting for him ;—and yet Fritz's rapid return gave Ellinor little comfort. She heard his voice calling to her, but she could not answer. Better for him to leave her to die here of cold and weariness, she thought to herself, than come back with a light laugh on his lips.

Fritz, however, was in no jesting humour. No doubt he could easily enough have found his way to some shelter, but with Miss Langdale it was different. Ellinor was not at all accustomed to long, rough walks ; she was already wearied ; and, in the increasing gloom, he dared not go far away from her in search of a wider prospect. They might, for aught he, a perfect stranger, knew, be miles away from her home ; and he was by no means certain that, under her guidance, they had taken the right direction.

"Go on," Ellinor said, almost pettishly, after they had walked some distance nearly in silence. "Leave me, I cannot keep up with you. You will come to some road or cottage, or meet some wayfarer who will instruct you as to the way back to Moriscombe. My sister will send the carriage for me."

Fritz slackened his pace considerably. "Come weal or woe, my sweet cousin, we will share it together. Hark ! surely I hear voices in the distance."

CHAPTER III.

THE travellers belated on the moor were, like Fritz and Ellinor, male and female. Through the driving mist the
voices sounded muffled and unreal, the approaching forms
loomed large and indistinct,—a tall man wrapped in a
large cloak, and a woman's figure similarly shrouded, the
face shadowed by a hat and closely veiled.

Fritz hailed them as they drew near. He was growing
very anxious to have his pale, shivering companion safely
housed. "Can you tell us the way to Moriscombe. We are
lost in the fog."

"Yes, yes, I'll set you right," was the reply, in loud,
hearty accents. "Lucky for you to have met me. Man
and boy, rain or shine, I know every step of these moors."

"This must be the Spirit of the Waste," Fritz whispered
to Ellinor; but she was too much terrified to smile, as his
sisters would have done. Her heart was dying within
her, of weariness, disappointment, and regret. She could
scarcely restrain her tears. Even the sight of these confident
strangers, so calmly threading their way through the mist,
failed to re-assure her. She looked at the veiled and now
silent woman, half inclined to believe that she was indeed
something weird and unearthly. Fritz, on the contrary, was
attracted towards her. Feminine sympathy, he thought,
might rouse his drooping companion. If the truth must be
told, the young man was somewhat weary of unavailing attempts to cheer her.

"This lady," he said, turning towards the silent figure,
now close beside him in the pathway, "is almost as much a
stranger in these wilds as myself. And yet I fancy we are
not very far from her home at Moriscombe."

No answer whatever was vouchsafed him. Perhaps the lady had lost her voice in the fog, for she said a very few words, in the lowest possible whisper, to her cavalier.

"Right—to be sure—you think of every one but yourself, my darling," he replied cheerfully, in the same mellow, cordial voice, which already had cheered the hearts of the desolate wanderers. "My daughter reminds me that our carriage is following us. She, and I too, prefer trusting to our own limbs and eyes in this fog; but our friend, a lawyer, by the way, who thinks what is paid for should be useful, has stuck to the carriage. If the lady is fatigued, we shall be happy to accommodate her with a seat in the barouche as far as the gates of Moriscombe. Nay, no thanks, it is right in our way. We passed the Lodge in coming from the Grand Hotel at Filey."

The offer was too kind to be rejected. Ellinor roused herself to thank the strangers, but the lady still remained perfectly silent. She rejected Fritz's outstretched hand, when some impediment in the rugged path made him involuntarily proffer assistance. Erect and unaided, the girl— he was certain she was young and beautiful—went proudly and securely on her way.

A faint rumble of wheels now announced the approach of the vehicle. The driver was proceeding with great caution, and the solitary inmate of the carriage had fallen asleep. Only a few words were uttered, as the tall gentleman in the cloak assisted Ellinor to mount the rattling step of the somewhat crazy fly, and the startled occupant of the barouche, scarcely awake, made room for her, silently, but politely.

The slender female form still went on along the track; a mute gesture having satisfied her companion that she, like himself, preferred walking. Fritz continued with them,

but, though the way was dark and intricate, he was not suffered to be of the smallest assistance to the lady. If need-
ful, she took her father's hand or arm ; and he evidently
understood and humoured the will, on her part, not to improve this chance acquaintance. In spite of her tacit inci-
vility, perhaps provoked by it, Fritz felt irresistibly attracted. He would have given worlds to see that veiled
face, to touch the gloved hand, to support the slight, graceful
form, on the rugged pathway. The words of her companion sounded indistinctly, as of one speaking in a dream,
—of what like would be her voice, her words, if he could
but persuade her to break silence.

All sorts of possible and impossible plans floated through
his brain, for the future. He must see her by daylight,
force her to speak to him, dispel the strange dislike and dis-
trust, which he had most unintentionally inspired. Meanwhile, mile after mile was trodden in darkness until the
trees of Moriscombe, almost the only verdant spot in the
district, now dripping with moisture, hung above them.

Fritz shook hands with the gentleman who had helped
him so cordially out of his difficulties, and longed to do the
same with the lady; but he dared not. A silent, stately
bow was all that was vouchsafed him, before she turned
from the gate to the spot at a little distance, where the carriage had drawn up, at the turn in the road leading to
Filey. Miss Ellinor, the woman at the Lodge said, had
gone home sadly tired : and Fritz, who felt himself to be ignominiously dismissed, had no choice but to follow her.

Ellinor Langdale, naturally diffident, felt much embarrassed at intruding upon the slumbers of the stranger in the
carriage. His manner, when roused thus suddenly, was
kind and gentlemanlike, and he strove to assist her as well

as the thick darkness permitted, removing the damp plaid she had worn about her shoulders, and substituting a macintosh of his own. When she began to thank him, he exclaimed, " Why, good gracious, whom have we here? Miss Ellinor Langdale. Don't you recollect your father's old friend, Mark Haywarden?"

It was now Ellinor's turn to be surprised, and she scolded her neighbour at Langdale for not coming to see her.

" Oh, business, business, my dear young lady. These are clients of mine. Came to look after this new watering-place. Investments. Ah, ah, you never had a head for moneymaking. Miss Langdale, your good sister, ought to take shares in our model Hotel, and Baths. I assure you it is a most promising speculation. Marina will be the glory of this fine coast. Capital air and water. In fact, everything that persons in health or sickness, could desire. That gentleman expects to make his fortune. And his daughter will be an heiress. Did you see her—no—well, that is a pity. She is very handsome."

A keen pang of jealousy shot through Ellinor's wounded heart ; but she was too proud to show it, or to ask questions about one whom she divined instinctively would be a rival. And yet could he be so frivolous, so lightly caught. A mere glimpse of a mysteriously shrouded form could not suffice to fetter him. She hated the veiled lady more than Bertina Noel. Not one of Fritz's attempted courtesies to the stranger had escaped Ellinor's notice. Jealous by nature, mortified by his coldness, she had seen the attraction exercised over her cousin by the silent girl who stepped so proudly along the path, scorning the aid she coveted.

Mr. Haywarden did not notice the weary girl's dejection. He thought that she was tired ; and, after a few kind sentences, the family lawyer fell back upon his investments and the flourishing prospects of his new client to amuse himself with, in recollection; perhaps he took another nap, while his companion looked out into the mist, and wondered how far behind them the walking party might be. When, after a time which seemed interminable, the carriage stopped at her own gate, Ellinor roused herself to be politely hospitable; and, in return for the great favour conferred upon herself, begged that Mr. Haywarden would bring his friend to Moriscombe; but he declined her offer of hospitality. His clients were only at Filey for a day or two, and he himself must return to Hazeldon at an early hour the next morning.

Ellinor retired at once to her own room, leaving Fritz to explain the cause of their detention, and her friends to place what interpretation they liked on her tearful aspect. She dismissed her attendant as soon as she was relieved of her dripping garments; and sat down by the fire, which in spite of the season was welcome at that moment, with her long light hair flowing loosely round her pale face, and her thoughts in troubled confusion. Never, till the moment· when he proposed to leave her on the heath, had she realised how dear Fritz was to her; and, now, the sorrowful conviction forced itself upon her that this love, the first and last she should ever entertain, was disregarded. The vainest woman on earth could not, after the adventure of that evening, believe herself the object of Fritz Langdale's affection. They were cousins, nothing more.

Whilst sorrowfully occupied with her own thoughts, Ellinor heard the door softly open; and Miss Langdale entered the room. A visit from her, at that hour, was so totally unexpected, that Ellinor had not even thought of prohibiting the intended act of sisterly kindness. She rose up to greet her, hastily, and in confusion.

"Do not disturb yourself, Ellinor," said Maud, taking a seat by the fire. "You look better now; but indeed, at first, I felt very anxious about you. Mr. Langdale, however, seems rather to have enjoyed the adventure. He is quite excited, and seems wonderfully happy."

Maud cast a penetrating glance at her young sister, but Ellinor's eyes refused to meet hers. They were fixed on the leaping flames and cracking logs, piled on the hearth.

"You are not used to hearing me retract my words, Ellinor," she continued gravely, "but I wish to unsay much that I have uttered. Fritz Langdale has won my heart: I hope he has succeeded in gaining yours. I cannot help thinking from your manner and his, to-night, that he has done so. If this is the case, my warmest wishes will be realised."

Ellinor turned quickly towards her. "This is indeed an unexpected change, Maud. Why did you, some years ago, set your face against my marrying any one? I should have fancied Mr. Langdale would have been the suitor most hostile to your wishes."

"It might have been so," said Maud thoughtfully. "But all that has passed away. My love for Florence has extinguished many bitter feelings, many long standing prejudices. I love her brother for her sake, and also for his own. He is a fine manly fellow. Ellinor, are you too proud to bid me love him for your sake also? You cannot, after your emotion to-night, deny that you are very dear to each other."

"I can, and I do deny it," said Ellinor, flushing crimson. "Mr. Langdale and I are nothing to each other. He thinks more of a girl he met upon the heath, than of me. He is a foolish, frivolous boy. Let us say no more about him."

Miss Langdale looked at her sister with astonishment.

"You are not yourself, to-night, Ellinor; I am sorry I have intruded upon you, but my motive was a good one. Florence will never be happy until this unfortunate misunderstanding with her family is at an end. It makes me miserable to see her wretched. Now it strikes me that, through your and her brother's attachment, a way may be opening for me to retrieve the mischief I have done. Frank Langdale will not accept any peace offering; but Fritz is less wilful. If my present arrangement of the succession to the Langdale property makes us all miserable, the sooner it is altered the better. As your husband, Fritz will be my natural heir."

Ellinor stamped her foot as impatiently as Maud, in her haughtiest mood, had ever done. "You will drive me wild," she said, impetuously. "There is no question of love or marriage between me and our cousin Frank Langdale's son. There never was—there never will be, such a connexion. Is not that sufficient? Ah, Maud, it is much easier to do fatal mischief than to remedy the evil. I am rich and independent. Most probably I shall never marry, though I would not, four years ago, bind myself to remain single for the sake of an inheritance. Leave your property to whom you like, so that it be not to me. I love this place. I wish for no other home. I shall never leave Moriscombe."

Miss Langdale rose, and bade her sister good night somewhat stiffly. Ellinor went as far as the door of the chamber with her, and suddenly threw herself on her sister's neck, weeping.

"Do not let us part in anger, Maud," she said. "I scarcely know myself, to-night. I am sure you mean kindly towards us all. I am worn out, and weary almost to death. Never let us allude to the subject on which you have spoken to me, again."

Maud Langdale returned her embrace warmly. She did

19

not return to the drawing room; where she heard Fritz laughing and talking with his sisters, evidently in high spirits. Every one in the establishment thought, like Miss Langdale, that he had wooed and won the heiress during the long, damp evening spent alone together, on the Moor. Ellinor's tears and Fritz's exuberant spirits led to the same conclusion; and he alone was utterly unconscious of the part, by common consent, assigned to him—that of a successful lover.

CHAPTER IV.

ELLINOR did not make her appearance at breakfast the next morning. She had not recovered from her fatigue, Miss Langdale informed her sister's guests, as she took her place at the head of the table, and poured out the tea, while Fritz, as usual, presided over the coffee. No one seemed to feel disposed to prolong what was usually the pleasantest repast at Moriscombe. Soon after ten o'clock the whole party had dispersed themselves abroad, each taking a different direction.

Fritz Langdale had an irresistible inclination, which he confided to no one, to walk to the watering-place on the coast, called Filey; which, as yet, he had only seen from a distance. It was one of those crisp, lovely mornings which often, by the seaside, follows a night laden with mists and vapours. Sky and sea, cliffs and pebbles, all seemed to have been washed clear of every stain. The air, brisk yet balmy, blew refreshingly in his face, straight across the ocean.

A rugged stair, in the face of the high down capping the

cliffs, afforded an opportunity of which Fritz availed himself, for scrambling down to the beach, strewn with immense boulders, against which the incoming tide was breaking fiercely. After a walk of four or five miles, a vale, which almost looked as if, in some previous age of the world, it might have been an estuary, opened up into the heart of the moor, with the scattered cottages and square-towered church of old Filey near its entrance. Further south a broad terrace, faced with granite, against which, in stormy weather, the sea dashed furiously, one or two cold-looking rows of handsome stone houses, and a pretentious hotel, constituted the modern watering-place.

An archæologist would certainly have made his way to the ancient church; and a lover of sea-weeds and fossils might have found curious specimens of the wonders of the coast in the quaint shops, belonging to the old regime, behind whose shabby, green glass windows, a very miscellaneous collection of treasures was exhibited. Fritz, however, turned his steps in the direction of the new town.

As he walked along, he pondered over what steps he should next pursue. He had not recognised Mr. Haywarden, and Ellinor, absorbed in her own feelings, had not mentioned the name of her companion in the carriage. Fritz, indeed, had scarcely seen her since they parted in the fog.

He was entirely ignorant respecting the name of the father and daughter, but he knew that the carriage belonged to the principal hotel at Filey; and, swayed by various motives, he had persuaded himself that it would be only common courtesy to thank these strangers, for the timely help they had afforded to himself and his weary companion. It was true that he had done this over and over again already, but still Fritz was of opinion that he ought to repeat his devoirs to the veiled lady and her father.

A waiter, belonging to the Royal Hotel, was rubbing his hands on the steps, looking after the omnibus which had just departed, when Fritz approached, and, by way of opening the conversation, asked for sherry and soda water. The man brought the desired refreshment to the coffee room, which happened to be empty, and, after the manner of his class, was quite ready to be communicative. Yes, they had heard how thick the fog was the night before,—one of their drivers had nearly lost his way on the moor, though a native of the district. A party staying in the house hired the carriage for the day :—" The gentleman, sir, just gone off to the station in the omnibus," he concluded, with a gracious wave of his hand in the direction of the vehicle just turning the corner of the street.

" The gentleman," Fritz repeated, mechanically. " What has become of the young lady ? Is she here still ?"

The waiter looked significant, especially when Fritz compensated him liberally for his trouble, and for the sherry and soda water.

" The lady—oh yes, sir, the *young lady* is with us still. She and her papa think of remaining some days. Most people are pleased with Filey at this season. The old gentleman—the party from the West Riding—professional, I fancy—much pleased too, but called away on business— perhaps coming back to spend Sunday with his friends. Two services—excellent preacher—curious monuments in the Church, sir. I don't know if you are a stranger—a great deal that is well worth seeing in our town and neighbourhood."

Fritz thanked him for his information; and, in return, communicated the fact that the party stopping at the inn had conferred a favour upon himself, and the lady at whose house he was staying, for which he desired to express his gratitude. Could he see the gentleman?

Enquiries were immediately made as to the exact whereabouts of the occupants of No. 6, and it was ascertained that the lady and her father had walked out in the direction of the Reef. The waiter adding, blandly, that it was the most interesting point of view along the coast.

There was tolerably good walking ground on the inner side of the long spit, or file, of sandstone capped with clay, worked into all sorts of fantastic shapes by the action of the water. Formerly, it was said, the cliff ran out to the end of the reef, warranting the name given to the place by Ptolemy, "The deep-havened Bay." Now, only this thin ridge of rock was left ; against which, as he leant for a moment, Fritz could feel the throb and shudder of the land, as the mighty waves threw themselves against it. The clay had almost all been washed away, excepting the coating on the summit ; only the horny tongue of sandstone remained,—barring the fury of the North Sea.

As he walked along, the young man involuntarily pictured to himself the tall slight figure, that had glided through the mist by his side the evening before, lightly surmounting the impediments of the stony track ; springing from stone to stone, or mirrored in the deep pellucid pools lying under the rocky wall, safe from the encroachments of the tide, into which he was sorely tempted to plunge, for a salt-water bath.

Then again, after the fashion of day dreams, the vision slightly altered its shape, and it was Bertina Noel's slender form, her black dress and scarlet shawl, that he was following through the Eagle's Gorge. Fritz started, when at a sudden turn, a sort of rustic grotto or alcove, partly natural, partly artificial, and open to the sea in front while the rock towered high at the back, came in view ; tenanted by one solitary female figure.

The waves rolled in, clear as crystal, to the margin of yellow sand, which as yet had never been overflowed. Just where they stopped, three or four boulders of rock had fallen from above, and marked the line which the mighty waters were bound, by a perpetual decree, to respect. On the largest of these stones a lady was sitting, reading. Her face was turned toward the sea and the light, away from Fritz, but he recognised the slight, tall figure of his companion in the mist. A violet-coloured veil fluttered in the wind, thrown back from her face, and the cloak had fallen unclasped from her small throat and falling shoulders.

Fritz took a few hasty steps forward; he was afraid the fair creature before him, if warned, would reassume her disguises; but the lady was so absorbed in her book, that she did not hear his footstep. The sea-weed strewn over the sand deadened the sound. Through the arch, seaward, the light fell full on her features, which were soft, regular, and beautiful,—on the dark hair, smoothly banded, and crossed over her brow with a narrow line of velvet of the same tint as the veil—the whole of the rest of her costume was black.

"Bertina!" exclaimed Fritz in amazement, while a deep throb of joy ran through his whole frame. "Is it possible that *you* were my companion in the mist, last night? And yet, I knew, I felt that it was so."

The lady started at his voice, and seemed half inclined to resume her disguise; but it was too late for concealment. She said coldly,—

"You had another companion yesterday evening, Mr. Langdale. Ours was but a chance meeting."

"No, I cannot accept your expression, Bertina," said the young man. "Nothing happens by chance; and your name was on my lips, a moment or two before I saw you."

Miss Noel flushed angrily. "I would rather not be

named before Miss Ellinor Langdale," she said, haughtily.
"Pardon me if I leave you. I have been here too long
already. My friends will be expecting me."

Fritz knelt on the low rock near her. " Do not leave me
till you have told me why you are here?—with whom? May
I not bring Gertrude to see you?"

"I would rather you did not mention to anyone that you
have seen me," said Bertina, uneasily. "There are circumstances which I cannot explain, which matter nothing to
anyone," she said bitterly. "It is sufficient that your father,
my guardian, approves of my proceedings. No one else"—
she hesitated, then added—"Few others, have any right to
question me."

Fritz drew back offended. A recollection of the tall
man in the cloak, whose aid had been accepted when his
own had been avoided, the night before, came back to him,
unpleasantly. "Forgive me," he said, rising; "I did not
mean to intrude upon your confidence. If there is any
secret in the matter I shall respect it, only do not let us part
in anger. Next week I leave England."

Bertina turned towards him quickly.

"Why should you go?" she said. "Would it not favour
your present happy prospects better, to remain in this
neighbourhood?"

Fritz looked at her with surprise. "To remain *here*," he
said. "Until within these last few minutes, I cannot say that
this barren sea-board, swept by keen north-easters, appeared
as tempting to me as to the Sea Kings, our progenitors.
No, Bertina—Miss Noel, I ought to say—I have other prospects—at this moment they do not look very brilliant, but
I trust they may mend—an ardent pursuit of my professional duties, a busy life, will, at all events, suit me better
than loitering on the sea coast of the North Riding. I
never care to see it again."

Bertina brightened visibly.

"You are right," she said, softly, "and I am glad you do not despise an industrious career. Now I must leave you, and return to"—again she hesitated—" to the Hotel."

"May I not go back with you? The beach affords but rough walking. Would you not like first to ascend this rocky wall—I know there are steps to the summit here-abouts—and see this bold coast, on which you wish me to build a hermitage, from headland to headland. The view must be splendid?"

"Provided you ask me no more questions," said Bertina, smiling for the first time. Fritz swore to be discreet, and was permitted, as a reward, to assist his fair companion over the stones, and up the rugged ladder cut in the rock, which led to the top of the reef. Below them thundered the waves of the North Sea, and the wind was so fierce, when they rose above shelter, that, but for Fritz's aid, Bertina could not have kept her footing on the narrow ledge. Dizzy with the whirling eddy of the waves, half blinded with their spray, the young girl, nevertheless, felt happier as she stood silent, supported by his friendly arm, than when she sat alone in the sheltered cove under the lee of the rocks.

There was no crimson flush now on land or sea. The morning sun, in bare reality, shone over a wild heap of heaving waters, and showed the fine bold cliffs, from the North Landing at Flamborough Castle to Scarborough. Except one wooded dell, in which Moriscombe lay shrouded, scarcely a tree was to be seen; the wooded ravine behind old Filey Town, ran up inland out of their view. Bare bluffs and moors, with a turbulent ocean, made up the picture before them.

Bertina turned away from it without reluctance. "Like yourself,' she said, dwelling upon the words which had given her pleasure; "I do not care to behold that cruel-looking coast often. It is grand, but forbidding. Let us go back to the beach."

Fritz accepted the implied permission to escort her; and aided Bertina in the descent of the rocky stair, and along the weed-strewn strip under the reef. As they went along, he told her that he had joined his sisters at Moriscombe, in order to escort the Countess on her journey; and of his own and Gertrude's happy reconciliation with Florence. He hoped that his father, also, in time would be appeased.

Some happy instinct prevented his mentioning Ellinor's name, but he said how unexceptionably agreeable Miss Langdale made herself, and how entirely she seemed to have laid aside former prejudices and animosities. Bertina listened with interest. When he paused, she said. "Your father may, eventually, be willing to forget and forgive the past; but the time is not come yet. He thinks that Miss Langdale's enmity was against the wife he has lost, whose image is ever present to his memory. You must wait."

"Well, I must bide my time," said Fritz, meaningly. "That will be my motto for many a long day, I suspect. Never mind, patience conquers many difficulties. If only there is the faintest glimmer of hope, I can wait."

He held out his hand to take leave. They had reached the steps leading up the sea wall which protected the terrace. No one was in sight, but the ordinary frequenters of the beach.

Bertina gave him her hand, "Patience and Perseverance," she said. "I have a right to recommend them, for I have practised both: and, in the end, in most cases, if not in ours, they lead to prosperous fortune."

She turned quickly away, but Fritz stood still, watching her as she ascended the steps; and his eyes followed her tall graceful form, till she entered the Hotel. It was a satisfaction to him to perceive that no one came to meet her. As long as she remained in sight Bertina was quite alone.

Fritz strode along quickly on his homeward way, pondering over the mystery. Who could Bertina's travelling companion be, for he knew another person was in the carriage? In age, in manner, in speech, the tall man in the dark cloak, dimly seen through the mist, might be, as he had averred, her father; but Bertina had no living parent. Fritz stood still, unconsciously, in the pathway, trying to come to the conclusion of these agitating doubts; but it was in vain that he tried to account for her presence with these, to him, unknown companions, at Filey.

The only satisfaction in the matter was, that he had perfect trust in Bertina; and her last words held out encouragement for perseverance, and hope in the future. His father approved of her conduct, and Fritz knew well that Mr. Langdale felt the deepest interest in his old friend's daughter. Perhaps some companion of the ruined exile had returned, gifted with paternal authority, to England; and, to such a person, the desolate girl might naturally cling with almost filial affection. Fritz recalled with pleasure the cordial tone and clasp of the hand, warm even to friendliness, with which Bertina's new protector had parted from him, the previous evening.

CHAPTER V.

MAUD LANGDALE was sorely disappointed by the failure of the only attempt at match-making she had ever commenced. Fritz's merry laugh and unsentimental demeanour were as discouraging as Ellinor's tears and indignation.

She wandered about in the plantations the next morning, after breakfast; feeling, like most strong-minded people, peculiarly discomfited when her will was thus baffled and set at nought; even Florence's society was distasteful to her for the moment, now that her latest scheme for restoring her tranquillity, had failed.

In the course of her aimless walk, Maud at last found herself in the knoll overlooking the coast, where a flag-staff had been erected, and a seat placed, commanding an extensive prospect. Tired of herself and of everything around her, Miss Langdale, remembering the circumstance, turned into the narrow winding walk, through hardy shrubs which led up to this post of observation, intending to rest there awhile before returning to the mansion.

All Maud's pride was up in arms, when, on turning the corner of the walk, she saw a stranger, quietly established in this private part of her sister's grounds. On the bench lay a large cloak, apparently just thrown off; while the individual to whom it belonged, was standing surveying the buildings on the cliff, through a glass which he had unstrapped from his shoulders.

Maud's step on the gravel announced her approach, and the gentleman turned round and confronted her. As she met his gaze, the angry address which the Lady of Langdale was about to utter, died unspoken on her lips. The strong woman stood still, and trembled.

The stranger took off his hat, courteously, and apologised for his intrusion. He had been told by a rustic, that the best view of the new Watering Place was to be obtained from that point; and, the hour being early, he had hoped to make his inspection without disturbing the family.

Maud listened as one in a dream. That voice sent her thoughts back many years, and yet it seemed to her as if its

mellow tones had rung in her ear not long since.   She
dared not rebuke the stranger.   The same strange dread
which had cowed her haughty spirit, when she strove to
beard in his den the vagrant who had presumed to shelter
himself at Noel Hall, again took possession of her faculties.
She was forced to seat herself silently on the beach.

"Are you interested in yonder, fair white houses on the
cliff?" said the stranger, politely offering his glass, which
Miss Langdale declined with a gesture.   "Suffer me to
alter the focus: your eyes are younger than mine," he
added, moving the slide of the telescope.   "Perhaps you
do not require it?   To me it is always delightful to see
tokens of human habitation in a wild scene like this.
Marina is a capital name."

Miss Langdale, who detested the new bathing place, did
not speak.

"You landed proprietors like to keep the pleasant
places on God's earth to yourselves, I fancy," said the
stranger, smiling.   "I am of a different way of thinking;
perhaps because, for a long time, I have been a wanderer,
without an acre of land I could honestly claim.   This is no
longer the case now.   I have the interest of a proprietor in
these rising villas—in that embryo church tower.   I am
particularly glad that the new town, in which I am so
much interested, forms so pretty an object from these
grounds."

Miss Langdale forced herself to speak.

"This place is not mine; but, if its mistress is of my
opinion, she will plant out yonder eyesore.   New buildings are seldom an improvement to a property."

"*Chacun à son gout*," said the stranger.   "Perhaps the
name, which seems to me well-chosen, does not strike you
as suitable.   You would not have called the new town
Marina?"

"No," said Maud, "I hate the name. It has to me very painful associations."

"That is unlucky," responded her tormentor. "I am fond of the sea, and I like to hear of a bold deed being kept in memory. I have heard that a child, named after the incident, Marina, was saved on this coast from drowning. Is my local tradition correct?"

"Yes," replied Miss Langdale, unwillingly, her words seeming to be dragged from her by force. "I have reason to remember that shipwreck. All the misfortunes of my life come from that source."

"Ah," said the stranger, drawing a deep breath, "I have touched unwittingly on a tender chord—forgive me !—my best friend in the world, Frank Langdale, on the contrary, has told me a thousand times that his life's happiness dates from that event."

Miss Langdale, whose eyes had been riveted to the ground, suddenly raised them. "You are a friend of Mr. Langdale of Godley Grange?" she said, more courteously. "Why did you not mention it sooner?"

"Because I was not sure that it would be a passport to your favour," said the unknown, fixing his dark eyes upon her. "If you so bitterly dislike the name of yon white-walled town, because it reminds you that Cuthbert Noel there did the one good deed of his bad life, in rescuing Frank Langdale's fair wife from an untimely grave, under those turbulent waters, I can scarcely reckon you among the number of her devoted husband's friends."

"Mr. Langdale is my first cousin," said Maud, haughtily. "Circumstances have caused temporary estrangement, but I respect him sincerely. I trust we may soon be on better terms. Meanwhile, as his friend, I am certain that Miss Ellinor Langdale, to whom this quarrel has not extended, will bid you welcome, if you wish to extend your walk as far as her house."

Her stately courtesy seemed not lost on the stranger. He thanked her warmly, but declined the invitation to the Hall, which was but at a short distance. All he had wished was to study the site of the new buildings from this elevated point.

"Time will reconcile you alike to the name and the place," he said. "Time does everything except alter one feature of your face. I wish I could say as much."

He turned to leave the knoll.

"Wait!" said Maud, in a trembling tone. "Have I seen and heard you speak before? Every word brings back the past. When, and where, have we met?"

"Nay, there are many reminiscences of our past lives which even a stranger can evoke;—like my careless mention of the name of yonder town," said the stranger. "I may have seen a picture of you in your gay youth, or even heard you described. I knew those who have loved you well, and are now themselves forgotten. And yet you *are* changed. Something is gone from you, Maud Langdale; what is it? I miss something that I fancied never would drop from you. What have you done with your pride? What has made you so womanly?"

"Love," said Maud, still speaking under the same strange feeling of compulsion. "A little child laid her hand on my arm trustingly, and I never could shake off the touch. A voice carolled words in my ear, and the wind blowing past me brings them back. If this had happened to me sooner, I might not be going to my grave unloving and unloved, as I am now."

"That is utterly false; no woman has been more loved, more wildly worshipped," said the stranger, drawing nearer to the now weeping woman. "But for a fatal tie—a most unhappy entanglement, which was his ruin—Cuthbert Noel would have won you for his wife. Children of your own would have laid clasping hands about your neck, little voices, in language sweeter than songs, would have called you, mother. But it was otherwise decreed. The death of Cuthbert Noel's low-born wife—for she was his wife—came too late to set him free. Had his sons lived, he might have acknowledged their mother sooner; but he never cared seriously for any woman but one. You best know, Maud Langdale, of what like she was, whom Cuthbert Noel loved to the last."

"Who are you?" said Maud suddenly, uncovering her face, and lifting tearful eyes to meet the stranger's. "If the grave had not years ago closed over Cuthbert Noel, I should think I heard his voice now. Are you a Noel?"

"I once was one of that ill-fated race; now I have no name, no family. Maud, you *have* seen, have spoken with me before, that is why the tone of my voice sounds familiarly. In Cuthbert's name, I asked you to let me shelter myself at Noel Hall, and you granted the permission kindly. Under my superintendence, the place has risen from its ruins. It is almost what it used to be in the life-time of Lady Barbara, only your smile has not shone upon it. Now do you recognize me?"

Maud sprang from her seat, her eyes flashed angrily with her wonted pride. "This insolence is not to be borne," she exclaimed, "do you dare to tell me that you are the forlorn vagrant, whom I tried in vain to eject from Noel Hall? Frank Langdale's insolent protégé! This is too much!"

All her recently acquired womanliness was gone. Maud was once more, Miss Langdale, of Langdale Hall. Nevertheless, the bright blush became her, and her dark eyes flashed with the fire of her youth. The stranger gazed long and steadfastly at her.

"You are a wonderful creature," he said at last, "I am glad you have not altogether laid down your pride; it makes you look like a handsome fury. Marina, poor Frank's lost angel, never was fit to be compared with you for beauty."

He turned round as he spoke, and strode away from the knoll. Maud watched his tall form with a sort of fascination; and, when the turn in the path hid it from her view, she changed her position that she might see it again. All the pride departed from her face; she bent her head low, till it rested on the hands clasped upon her knee, and wept bitterly.

Presently she started up, and going to the edge of the knoll, watched to see a tall form emerge from the Moriscombe trees, and cross the path, far down below her. "Did he think I had forgotten him?" she said softly, "who, but Cuthbert Noel himself, would have dared to look me in the face, and call me beautiful, after that degrading confession?"

She went back to the bench, when the man's figure was lost to sight, and sat down thoughtfully. Perhaps, of the whole strange scene just passed, her memory was most busy with the thought that the lover of her youth preferred her to Marina. A warm blush again suffused her regular features, and the head, slightly bent to one side, the wistful eyes, strangely resembled the picture hanging in the Hall at Langdale; only the abundant brown hair was no longer cropped short, like a boy's, and the stiff cloth habit had been long since, to please Florence, replaced by soft lustrous silk and costly lace.

PART THE EIGHTH.

DARKEST BEFORE THE DAWN.

In starry mansions, in realms of light,
  Where seraph harps are ringing;
Those visions fair that we lost on earth
  Glad hymns of joy are singing:
Their voices float on the cool night air,
  Their forms in the moonbeam hover,
And a brighter light on the earth is shed
  As they pass its surface over.

The grass is withered, the flowers lie dead,
  In that garden once so fair,—
But the pine boughs cross in the lowering sky,
  The yew casts its shadow there;
The graves of those whom I loved and lost
  Still hallow that holy ground;—
And *there*—if they linger yet on earth—
  May youth's bright hopes be found.

R. M. K.

CHAPTER I.

MR. LANGDALE was always an early riser, and, of
late, sleep had only for a few hours deadened
affliction. Since his wife's death, the master of
the Grange occupied the dressing-room, facing eastward
up the long avenue, and above his own study.

Curtains and window blinds were drawn aside that he
might welcome the first ray of morning, which often broke
upon a weary vigil. When inaction became intolerable,
Mr. Langdale would rise and dress himself, and devote the
early hours of summer daylight to study.

The sun shone so brightly one fine September morning,
that he was tempted—contrary to his usual custom—out of
doors; and his steps involuntarily led him in the direction
of Langdale churchyard. Marina was not buried in the
chancel; by her own wish she had been interred under a
group of trees, close to the pathway leading from the gate
nearest to the Grange. Her husband and children passed
the spot on their way to the sacred edifice.

It was still so early that the sunrays fell in long lines
athwart the sward, and the ground beneath the ancient yews
was in deep shadow. A few scarlet berries gleamed amidst
their dark foliage, and the low sunbeams lit up a wreath of

delicate white flowers, freshly hung on the cross at the head
of Mrs. Langdale's grave.

Her husband's grief was of too stern and reserved a nature to display itself in floral decorations, but Frances and
the twins loved to twine the emblems of summer, as they
had done those of spring, round the insensible marble.
Even Mr. Langdale would pause and pluck off a dead leaf,
or an unsightly stem, and gaze with satisfaction on those
mute tokens of regard and filial affection.

The flowers were always removed before they faded, and
a fresh garland placed in their stead the following Sunday
morning. It must, indeed, have been an inclement season
which prevented the young girls at the Grange from adorn-
ing the simple marble cross with its usual tribute of love.

On the previous evening, when, as usual, at the quiet sunset hour he visited the churchyard, Mr. Langdale had
noticed that there were no flowers on the grave. Now, as
he approached, athwart the green mound, he saw the shadow
of a female form, kneeling to affix a fresh wreath.

Frank Langdale stopped short under the yew trees,
breathing quickly. Across his mind, with the lightning
quickness with which affection paints such pictures, came
the recollection of his youngest daughter, whom he had not
seen for years, as she had looked, when he came to tell Marina of Miss Langdale's proposal, and found Florence lying
on the couch beside her. Could it, indeed, be "the little one"
whom he saw bending lowly over her mother's grave ?

 - Miss Langdale's absence from the Hall with her adopted
daughter, had not prepared him for this sight. He believed
them to be miles away, and yet, that slender black-robed
form, now prostrate in bitter grief, humbly kissing the
daisy-enamelled sod ; could be—was—none other than
Florence Langdale.

The humility of the mourner's attitude touched Mr. Langdale's hardened heart. Not a sob disturbed the solemn silence of the morning—the mournful tranquillity of that sacred place. The slight girlish figure lay prostrate on the turf, like a flower so rudely pulled that the stem had lost its strength.

Over the father's heart—like sweet refreshing waters—rushed a tide of memories connected with the wife he had lost, and her child. At that moment he scarcely recollected that Florence was his own daughter, nor her offence against himself. She was "the little one"—Marina's darling—once more.

He saw them in the invalid's room at the Grange. Florence still a child, low at her mother's knee, reading or listening; then again, he remembered her devoted attention to her suffering parent after she had rejected Miss Langdale's first overtures, and elected to remain at home. Words of love, spoken by his angel wife, floated in the air, were written on the grass—painted by the sunbeams, as they flickered through the boughs, and fell in bright waving lines and patches of radiance on Marina's grave.

Florence had lifted her head, but she had not risen from her knees. She was again busy with the garland on the cross, lovingly bending the wire, so as to encircle it closely. Among the rarer flowers of Ellinor's hothouse, were tufts of heath from the moor, which Florence had gathered on her last evening at Moriscombe, and brought home in the German basket, the only relic in her possession of her dead mother. It had contained her gifts to the cottager who had told her of Miss Langdale's illness, on that day when she first entered Langdale Hall.

Even this trifling emblem of the dead, at this moment of reawakened feeling, was not lost upon Mr. Langdale. He

remembered the little one's delight when she found her
mother's basket, which she had carelessly left behind her on
the grass at the river's brink, safe on the hall table, full of
beautiful fruits ; the proud generosity with which she distributed its contents, and the care lavished on the few choice
fern leaves and flowers which alone she appropriated. From
her earliest childhood, Flo was as generous as a princess.

Once more, bending lowly in prayer beside her mother's
grave, he saw Marina's little one ; despondent, fragile,
broken-spirited, kneeling on the dewy grass, alone, an outcast from family affection. Only at that untimely hour dared
she approach that hallowed spot !—only when her sorrow,
her repentance, could not disturb the privileged grief of her
father and sisters ; of those who had shared the last vigils,
and watched beside the dead form, of the mother who had
loved her best of all.

Mrs. Langdale's fatal illness had been brief, but, at the
last, she had bitterly regretted Florence's absence.   Her
blessing and forgiveness had been transmitted ; but no
one, save her husband, knew how warm the love and compassion had been with which, when she realised the approach
of death, she had mourned and moaned for the little one.
At the time this had increased his anger.   Now, like clouds
before sunshine, the darkness rolled away ;—the heart of
stone melted in the man's bosom, and became warm living
flesh.   All real, all imaginary offences vanished, as he
watched his child kneeling in tears beside Marina's tomb,
and he came suddenly out of the shadow of the yew trees
towards her.

Florence trembled and started up.   "Do not be angry
with me, father.   These are Ellinor's flowers," she said,
pointing out a label on which her name was written.   "She
asked me to hang the wreath on the cross, for her."

Mr. Langdale's heart reproached him when he saw how much she was terrified. He came close up to her, and took her hand. "Let it be a peace-offering, he said, gently. Henceforward I recognise you as ' the little one.' "

Florence threw herself into his arms. " Indeed, indeed, I never meant to leave you and mamma. I was told, quite suddenly, that Miss Langdale was dying, and I wanted to thank her for her great goodness to me, that was all. I meant to come home immediately—but then I was afraid. I thought you were so angry with me and with our cousin, and she was so ill and lonely. I can't think how it happened— but indeed, indeed, I did not willingly forsake my mother. Never, never, can I forgive myself for grieving her."

"Marina knew you better than I did," said her father. " She always took your part. I did not ; even now I can-not quite forgive you for making her suffer—but we will not speak of it again. *Here*, at all events, let there be peace between us. Come here as often as you like."

Florence thanked him warmly. "I shall not feel quite an outcast from home, if I may sometimes visit this spot unchidden. I came early that I might not intrude upon your grief. I will not trouble you longer."

She dried her tears and took up her basket, preparing to depart. Mr. Langdale lingered for a moment. "Are you happy, child ?" he said at last. "Is Miss Langdale kind to you, still ? If she changes, come back to us."

"Miss Langdale has been like a mother to me since I lost my own," said Florence, eagerly. "There has not been the shadow of an alteration. I believe it would kill her to part from me."

"Neither do I wish it," said Mr. Langdale, gravely. "It is too late. I have other children who have always been dutiful to me and to their angel mother ; but I did not mean to reproach you. Say nothing to my Cousin Maud of what has passed this morning," he added, in a harsher tone. I do not desire to make any outward difference, but, remember, there is peace *here*, at your mother's grave, and in my heart, towards *you*. Let this suffice for the present."

He turned quickly away, and left the churchyard. Stern grief and pride were busy at his heart. He could not forgive Maud Langdale, as he had done his daughter.

CHAPTER II.

AUTUMN had settled prematurely, as is the case in all manufacturing districts, on the winding valley of the Lang. The leaves, withered into a dull, dark brown, already carpeted the soil under the old trees; save when at sunset the last beams shone warmly on the woods, gilding them with a glory not their own. It was a dull foggy season, and the wind, when it shifted its course, only altered the direction from whence the mist and smoke wreaths swooped over the low lands near the river.

The old rooms at the Hall looked dark and dreary in the scanty daylight, which penetrated with difficulty through the small-paned mullioned casements. Florence wandered disconsolately from one sombre apartment to another, trying to find a painting light by which to complete the paintings and sketches begun in Italy. Tears filled her eyes when she first took them out of her portfolio.

It seemed to the forlorn girl as though she had left her life's happiness behind her in sunny, southern Europe. Since the day when the tidings of her mother's illness had reached her, Florence had known nothing but sorrow, relieved only, for a brief space, by her reconciliation with

Gertrude and Fritz, at Moriscombe. From the moment of their departure, impatience recommenced. It was in accordance with her adopted daughter's wishes, that Miss Langdale returned home.

Now that she was once more at the Hall, settled there apparently for life, Florence longed to be away from the place. The one brief interview beside her mother's grave with her surviving parent, did not tranquillise her. Mr. Langdale's cold permission that she should revisit that sacred spot, was far from satisfying the girl's yearning for affection. She still felt herself to be unloved, and she knew that her kind adopted mother, was still unforgiven.

If Mr. Langdale sometimes started when a shadow fell athwart the grass, or a footstep sounded on the gravel, he was speedily undeceived. A waving bough swayed by the strong wind across Marina's grave, or one of the school-children crossing the churchyard, was the cause of the slight disturbance of his melancholy musings. Florence, if she came there at all, took care not to encounter her father.

Though he would not have owned that he was disappointed, Mr. Langdale often wondered that the child, as he still considered her, did not avail herself of his permission to visit her mother's grave. He treasured up this omission among her other offences. The little one, after all, had forgotten her mother. No fresh wreath, instead of the one with which he desired them not to interfere too soon, was placed on the cross; until, when it was quite faded, the twins tenderly removed Ellinor's garland, and substituted fresh, late-blooming, flowers. It did not occur to any one but her father, that Florence should have renewed the offering, nor to think that she dared not do it. Behind the crimson curtains, which used to be put back completely, now only partially withdrawn, of Miss Langdale's large pew in the chancel, her sisters fancied that Florence must often be sitting; but, if so, she waited till every member of her family had left the church, before she moved.

Perhaps if these affectionate girls had seen the tall, slight, form that timidly followed them down the aisle, with a tread so unlike the bounding footsteps of the little one, they would have waited for her, and, even in defiance of parental authority, have found some mode of communication; but Florence shrank from the eyes of her sisters, almost as much as from meeting her father. She leant, heavily for one so young, on Miss Langdale's arm; and got into the carriage, which waited for them at the churchyard gate, without casting a glance either to the right or left.

There were not many Sundays, during that damp inclement autumn, when Florence could venture to church. Dr. Forsyth shook his head when he saw her growing thinner and thinner, paler and paler, week by week. He suggested to Miss Langdale that they should spend the approaching winter in Italy, but Florence refused to leave England.

Maud watched her with a mother's anxiety. Every possible means of giving her pleasure, and benefiting her delicate health was tried, and all in succession failed. Florence was too weak to walk, too nervous to ride, even the luxurious, well hung carriage, shook and fatigued her. She spent days and weeks without leaving the house.

One afternoon, when the sun shone warmly overhead, the mistress of Langdale proposed that they should visit Noel Hall. Florence assented with some animation, and they drove together to the summit of the hill. Far above, and out of the reach of the smoke, the large trees near the old Hall had not lost their leaves. A warm glowing hue pervaded their foliage, making the picturesque group on the hill top, look yet more massive. Over the walls of the mansion a scarlet-berried creeper stretched its vigorous growth, and, in the corner of the courtyard, were richly-glowing chrysanthemums and hollyhocks. There were no unruly children, no unlicensed curs, at play on the flag-stones, no women and girls drawing water at the well. All was solitary, well ordered, stateliness.

Over the portal were the deep cut letters, freshly pointed and cleared from weeds and lichens, of the presumptuous motto of the reckless, haughty Noels. Gleams of light shot from the painted windows, glooms of deep shadow fell over the pavement from dark stone statues of knights in armour at the angles of the walls, or ponderous bears and lions, carved in imitation of nature, grim and forbidding.

The curly-headed boy ran out at the sound of carriage-wheels. Miss Langdale and Florence alighted, passing under the arched gateway. Maud looked round; but there was no one sitting in the sunny corner of the courtyard, which had been the General's favourite station.

The old dame had shifted her quarters from the banqueting hall,—now restored to its ancient splendour, hung with arras and old family pictures,—and invited the ladies into a small oak-panelled room, where a cozy fire was burning, with Meg, the black cat, stretched on the rug; tired probably of her nightly maraudings, in Miss Langdale's game preserves.

"There, sit ye down, and I'll make ye some tea, Miss Florence—ye do look bad surely," she said, as the pale girl entered. "Ye'll excuse me, madam, but she do look as if she ought to be attended to first, and ye see I've known Miss Flo from a baby."

She bustled about, and soon poured out, from an old-fashioned tea-pot, a refreshing cup for the delicate girl. Miss Langdale said quietly,—

" Autumn is a trying season—Miss Florence will be better when we have clear frosty weather. The air here is purer than in the valley. If you like the change, Flo, we will come to Noel Hall for a little while."

" It be fresh enoo' up here, to be sure," said the dame. " It *do* blow of a night, I can tell ye, but the slates don't rattle off now same as they used to. All's right and tight. But it be mortal lonely, since all the folks be gone."

Meg yawned and got up, arching her back and bristling up her coat; but when Florence gently stroked her, the black cat purred, and rubbed herself against the young lady's soft mourning dress.

" What has become of the person who lodged in the Gateway Tower?" said Miss Langdale, breaking silence with an effort.

" Oh aye—the old General. He's cleared off at last," said the dame. " He's been gone a month or more. I don't think the place suited him so well, after it was put in order. He just liked picking up bits and pieces, and making the old things fit, in his own ramshackle way. When the workmen began at the Gateway Tower, he said it was high time he should flit; and there was no one cared to hinder him."

Florence looked bitterly vexed. " I thought I should have found my old friend here," she said; " but every thing and every one I loved as a child, seems to shun me. I would rather not go up the staircase of the Gateway Tower, if the General is not there to welcome me."

Maud acquiesced, as she did in all Florence's most wayward whims. " We will do just as you like best, my love. Perhaps the air on the hill-top is too keen for you. Did the man say nothing about returning?" she said, addressing the dame. " He told me that he did not ever wish to leave this place."

" He'd be back some time when he was least expected—

may be Christmas," replied the dame. " Just at present he was going on a visit to his daughter, down in Calder Vale. That's about all he said, Mistress Langdale ; and I mind it, because it puzzled me to hear he had kith and kin near at hand. He always seemed strange-like. Ned will go with ye if ye want the doors stirred, they are terrible hard to open, sometimes ; but the little chap, though he's small, is uncommon handy."

Miss Langdale, however, declined the lad's attendance. Her own spirits seemed to be as much damped as were those of Florence, and the short daylight of the autumn afternoon was closing in. It would not have flattered the clever architect, who had put forth his best abilities to restore Noel Hall, if he had seen how carelessly his work was scanned by the eyes he had intended to gratify.

After this drive Miss Langdale's Neapolitan horses remained in the stable. The Italian coachman was left to exhale his wrath against the climate of the foggy north, and perhaps the caprices of English ladies. Florence shrank from the keen winds on the hills, and the damp mist in the valley ; even when the sunshine was bright and clear she did not care to leave the house.

Once or twice only, she stole through the grounds by the private path, to the Church, watching before she emerged from the trees to see that the place was quite solitary. The last of these visits was paid on a gloomy November evening, with rain falling and the sward thoroughly wetted. Miss Langdale missed her young favourite, when the dark, short day came to a close ; and, in great alarm, instituted a search which ended in the rural Church-yard. Florence was discovered by Maud herself, totally insensible, lying on the damp grass, under the dripping trees, beside Marina's grave.

CHAPTER III.

ONE of those lovely, summer-like days of late autumn
shone over the land, which often gild the declining year.
The mist, like a filmy veil over a beautiful face, increased
the delicacy of the tints on the foliage that fringed the
sides of the clough, through which the Lang found its way.
The Yorkshire hills, seen through the glowing mirage,
seemed mountainous; the sunrays streaming down, across
dark soft piles of grey and purple clouds, into the rich
masses of woodland. Here and there, sharp lights caught
the scarpèd ravines where stone had been quarried, or
glittered in the stream; but, generally, the radiance was
sobered and saddened by the same transparent atmosphere
which hung above the beautiful valley.

From the Hall Terrace, the view was especially lovely.
Florence had yielded to persuasion, and lay on a sofa enjoying the soft sunshine. Maud Langdale, too impatient to
sit still, walked up and down; stopping frequently to speak
to the languid girl, or to order a domestic to make some
fresh arrangement for her comfort. That very morning
Dr. Forsyth had told her that, unless Florence could be
roused to take interest in life, he had the very worst apprehensions respecting her health.

Maud remembered the day when, with similar impatience,
she had awaited Mr. Haywarden's communications, and
rebelled in spirit against her cousin's decision. Now, her
granted wish had turned to a curse. Withered prematurely, pale, inanimate, she feared dying, lay the once fair,
now faded, broken-stalked lily she had culled; stealing the
tender blossom ruthlessly away from the humble home of

Frank and his Marina, that high peaked grey-roofed old house, just visible through the trees of the Park.

One of the few, sharp dazzling rays of light, which seemed to come direct from Heaven, uncontaminated by the mist and smoke wreaths that hung over the valley, struck upon a high window set deep in one of the peaked gables of Godley Grange, making the old house seem strangely near. In summer the building was not visible from Miss Langdale's terrace, though a portion of the garden, sloping towards the lake, was always plainly seen —that old fashioned parterre where Ellinor had watched, through tears, the little white frocked girls at work and play.

Now, the glass shone like a star through an opening in the nearly leafless trees : Florence's eyes were fixed upon it, with a sad, weary, longing expression. She had not spoken the last time Maud stopped by her side. Her old habit of reserve had crept upon her of late, and the sick girl's thoughts were away—it might be, in her old nursery, where that golden radiance glimmered on the diamond-paned lattice—or in the world of spirits, with her gentle mother.

Miss Langdale crossed the grass suddenly, and coming close to Florence, stood still, gazing out over the valley. This time the young girl looked up in her face affection-ately, saying, "We did not see any view more beautiful than this, in all our wanderings."

Maud stooped down, and kissed her. "None that had the same charm" she said. "After all those were strange lands. Here all we look on is our own."

A shade crossed Florence's face.

"I am not sure that I enjoy it more on that account," she said, mournfully. "Langdale Hall was like Paradise when its gates seemed for ever shut against me. Now that you say it is to be mine some day, I have discovered that property and riches bear with them a heavy penalty.

"Would you be happier, Florence, if the will were revoked that makes you my heiress?" said Miss Langdale, trembling. "Must I, after all, give you up? Can you find happiness and health nowhere but under those high-peaked gables, where yonder star of light seems beckoning? Have I read your dream rightly?"

Florence burst into tears, and threw her arms round Maud's neck,

"No, I do not wish to leave you. I have no mother but yourself," she said. "I do not think I should be happy now at the old Grange. My place is filled up."

Miss Langdale warmly returned her embrace. "I am glad you do not wish to leave me, Florence. Let us take that star as an emblem of hope. See how it lights up the old Grange. Perhaps it has penetrated within its walls, and brightened the darkness. Tell me, my darling, what it is you wish me to do?"

"There is nothing to be done," said Florence, gloomily. "When I am dead, tell my father, or let him be told, for I do not wish you to encounter fresh humiliation on my account—that I was glad to be taken out of the way. And. oh, let Fritz be, as we used to call him in jest, the heir of Langdale!"

The sunset light had faded from the windows of the Grange, but the evening star shone down through the Langdale trees, and cast glimmering light over the paved Roman road leading to Godley Grange, as a tall female, wrapped in a cloak, passed through the gate, and walked with a quick, firm step down the long avenue.

There was a light in a window on the ground-floor, usually at this hour. Mr. Langdale, of late, had given up spending the evening with his daughters; when tea was over, he retired to his study, where he often sat up, reading or writing, until after midnight.

The woman paused for a moment, and stood looking at this lighted window; then she pulled the bell at the entrance, not loudly but decidedly. A servant answered the appeal immediately, and went, at the request of the stranger, to enquire if Mr. Langdale would object to speaking with the person who waited outside, on urgent business. It was a matter, the woman directed the servant to tell her master, of life and death.

Mr. Langdale did not keep the petitioner waiting. He concluded that one of the not unfrequent accidents at the neighbouring coal-pits had occurred, and that the mother or sister of some sufferer, needed aid; and his heart, in cases of distress, was warm and soft. Nevertheless, when the servant introduced the tall female, who stood still and silent until the door was again closed, a sort of angry suspicion stole upon him.

"What is your business with me?" he said, somewhat coldly. "Do I know you, or any of your family? What is it you want?"

The woman stepped into the lamplight, threw up her veil, and dropped the heavy cloak. "You knew me once, Frank," she said. "I am your cousin Maud, and I have come to ask a favour. You hold life, and death, in your hands."

Mr. Langdale turned deadly pale.

In the still handsome, haughty face, on which the lamplight shone fully, tumultuous emotions were betrayed, but Miss Langdale's voice was firm. He was the most agitated of the two.

"My cousin," she said, "I have come to you as a suppliant. We have both erred, but mine was the greatest

21

transgression; and now, my punishment is more than I can bear. Grant me your forgiveness. Perhaps, if you do this, God also may pardon my sin, and not take the child, Florence, from us."

Mr. Langdale started. "What is it you say," he exclaimed. "Is Florence really, dangerously, ill?"

"I do not believe that she will ever recover unless you forgive us—her and me," said Maud, simply and sadly. "Her loving heart is almost broken, and she will not sever her lot from mine. Frank, you must forgive me, as well as the child."

She stood with her hands clasped, as though ready to sink down on her knees before him. "Florence is no longer my heiress. At her request, I have destroyed the will which made her heiress of Langdale; my savings are all she will consent to receive from me, but she loves me dearly, in spite of all my wickedness."

Mr. Langdale was much affected. "Did the child ask you to come to me, Maud?" he said, "or is this act of your own prompting. Florence should have had my pardon long ago, if she had pleaded for it half as humbly as you have done."

"Florence knows nothing of my visit to you to-night," said Miss Langdale. "I cannot see her waste away before my eyes, without an effort to save her. I would have died to give her pleasure, but she never asked me a favour, until this evening; and then it was coupled with the conviction that she would not live. She begged me to make Fritz the heir of Langdale, and I have done it. May we not be friends?"

Mr. Langdale took her offered hand. "Would that you had shown yourself in your true colours sooner, my cousin," he said, with a sigh. "Why have we been foes so long?"

"Because you wounded *my* pride more sorely than I have humiliated myself now, once before, when I was ill able to bear it," said Maud, fire flashing from her eyes. "Did it never strike you, Frank Langdale, that I was not a woman to forgive being slighted—having another preferred before me? If you did not guess it—if, blinded by your love for a fair girl, you did not even perceive it—learn my life-secret now—it is in some sort a palliation for my sin towards you and your wife. I cared more for you than I ever did for Cuthbert Noel, the unworthy lover of my girlhood. You rescued me from bitter shame. You pointed out to me that I was fitted for better things than to be the bride of a spendthrift, a ne'er-do-weel, like the last of the Noels; and I took your advice, and, in so doing, ran into a more destructive peril. I loved him with a girl's blindfold idolatry—*You* I worshipped, as women worship heroes, and with my eyes open, saw in you all that was most calculated to make a wife happy. You won my heart, and then you married another woman. Is it a marvel that I hated her?"

The blood rushed to Mr. Langdale's brow. "Do not name her!" he said, sternly. "I cannot bear it from your lips. And you call this an excuse. To me it seems an aggravation of your crime. But I do not believe it. Love works no evil to its object. You have blighted my whole life."

"Love turned to hatred, works woe," said Miss Langdale. "Woe, to the breast it enters, first of all! Frank, I am humbled now. I ask your forgiveness for myself, and for your innocent child, on my knees. It was I who lured her to Langdale; or rather, her own sweet impulse of womanly compassion and gratitude first led her there, and I drew the net tight, and kept her my prisoner. I loved her with a wild passion which disclaimed rules and regulations. I won her affection and pity, and I wound myself into her tender heart. The child cannot be happy, she says, unless you forgive me also."

Mr. Langdale prevented the gesture with which the passionate woman strove to humble herself yet more before him; and, sadly and sorrowfully, took her hand in his own. "It is enough, Maud," he said. "Take me at once to the little one."

CHAPTER IV.

FLORENCE had gone from the terrace to her own apartments, fatigued with the slight exertion which she had made to please Miss Langdale. The evening star shone down upon the tops of the trees in the clough, and glittered in the distance on the waters of the lake.

As she lay on the couch beneath the window, the young girl thought sadly of her old home, hidden among the trees of the valley. What was the meaning of this increasing weakness?—of the utter incapability which she had lately experienced to rouse herself to the slightest exertion—of the indifference to life's pleasures creeping fast upon her. Was it Death that was approaching? She shuddered at the dreary prospect.

And yet, if this isolation were protracted, what was life worth? With the impatience of youth—the fretfulness of ill-health—Florence tried to persuade herself that she was ready to leave a world which had disappointed her so sadly. Death to the very young seems nearer—is scarcely so terrible when vaguely apprehended, as in the active career of middle age; but, now, when for the first time Flo tried to face the dark menacing spectre, tears of self-pity filled her eyes at her own early doom.

Her attendant had been forbidden to light candles, or to close the window. Excepting that faint ray, quivering

over the trees and water, all was darkly, solemnly still.
Florence shivered as the evening air stole in through the
casement. She tried to draw it close, but her weak hand
failed her ; so she lay quiet, half crying, longing for light, for
some human companionship—wishing that loving arms were
round her—thinking of her home.

It was a relief when at last the door was gently opened
though only by a servant—the pretty maiden who had
waited upon Florence since her arrival at Langdale now
bustled about the room, lighting it up cheerfully, closing the
casement, and kindling the wood fire piled upon dogs in the
large open grate. The flames lit up the emblazoned quar-
terings of the shields containing the coats of arms of the
Langdales, and of families with whom they had intermarried,
which were set in the dark stone above the fire-place.

When the maid-servant had arranged Florence's sitting
room for the evening, she came close to her young mistress,
and told her that there was some one below—two persons in
fact—who wanted to see her ; the soldier who used to lodge
in the Gateway Tower at Noel Hall, and his daughter.

Florence looked up joyfully. Her eyes sparkled with unwonted animation. She desired Sibella to show her visitors
at once upstairs ; and prepared, with revived spirits, for their
reception.

A strange sort of shy wonder overcame Florence's sensa-
tions of pleasure, when the door opened, and a tall man
entered the boudoir appropriated to the young Lady of
Langdale, with a slender, beautiful, dark-eyed girl leaning
on his arm. She looked at him fixedly, and recognised,
with difficulty, her old friend the General. He was the same,
yet different,—and, on his part, Florence's changed aspect
made him gaze at her with wonder.

" What is the matter with you, little one ?" he said, reproachfully, taking in his own her thin, trembling hand. "I heard that you had been to look for me at Noel Hall, and that you were vexed to find that the old owl had flown off his perch. But, tell me, what makes you look so pale and ill ?"

Florence burst into tears. "It is all so changed," she said, at intervals. "Home is not home. Langdale is not Langdale. Even you are altered, and who is that grand young lady ? I never heard you had a daughter."

"I have one who is not ashamed of her old father," said the General. "Come nearer, Bertina, and kiss the little one. She looks as if she sorely needed affection."

The two girls looked at each other for a moment. Then Florence's reserve gave way, and, with a sob, she embraced Bertina.

"That's right," said the General. "Marina Langdale's child, and Bertie Noel's, should be friends. Florence, I am that spendthrift, that vagrant,—or, rather, I was the man who squandered his inheritance and then returned to the old Hall, glad to sit by the old crone's hearth whom Maud Langdale had thought fit to place under the roof-tree of the Noels,—thankful for food which, in my reckless profusion, I once thought fit only for swine to eat.—I am Bertie Noel and this is my dear child, Bertina."

Florence pressed the young girl to her heart. They were friends at once. She did not exactly understand the drift of the General's harangue, but she was rejoiced that he was about to assume, *or resume*, a more befitting station. The ruined Noels had always excited her romantic imagination.

"You are Bertie Noel," she exclaimed, "and we have fitted up the Hall for you,—that is just as it should be,—and your daughter will keep house for you, and take care that you do not spend too much money. For, *remember*, you must *never* leave Noel Hall again."

" Nay, nay, I have left it now. My home is in the little stone house in Calder Dale, with Bertina," said the General. " That home has never ceased to be ours, and I have learnt to be thankful for honest independence."

" I tell you Noel Hall is just as much yours as ever it was," said Florence, doggedly. " I heard Mr. Haywarden tell Miss Langdale, while the old place was under repair, that it was so much money thrown away if Cuthbert Noel was alive ; and that, as I was to be her heiress, I should be the sufferer ; and we both agreed, when he walked away in a passion, that we only hoped Cuthbert Noel might come back and enjoy his own again."

At that moment the door softly opened, and Miss Langdale came in. She did not look at Florence's visitors, but went straight up to her sofa.

" What has changed you, my darling ?" she said, astonished at her flushed cheek and excited manner. " I have not seen a smile like that upon your face, for months."

" Cousin Maud,—look at him. It is Bertie Noel !" exclaimed Florence. " And he wants to go away again, and spend all his money, and be a vagrant and an outcast. Only he has got one tie to respectability. This dear girl,—whom I love, who is going to be a sister to me since I have lost my own,—is his child, his only daughter, Bertina Noel. Must they not live at the Hall, now that we have fitted it up for them ? She is just like the picture of her grandmother, Lady Barbara."

Maud looked full at the young girl, who had risen and stood confronting her with modest dignity. The tall, graceful figure, the dark eyes, and stately bearing, indeed resembled, though in a softened manner, those of Cuthbert's beautiful, haughty mother.

" The child is right," Miss Langdale said, holding out her hand. " You are a Noel, every inch of you ! Cuthbert,

I knew you when we stood on the knoll, looking at the white buildings on the cliff; Noel Hall is ready for you. I looked to find you there last week. And now Flo," she continued in an altered softer tone, " are you able to bear a yet greater, pleasanter surprise? Your father is below. He is waiting to forgive, and embrace you."

Florence threw herself on her neck. " Has he forgiven *you ?*" she said. " Nothing can part us now."

Miss Langdale kissed her fondly. " Yes," she said; "For your dear sake, even I, sinner as I have been, am pardoned. Let me bring him to you ?"

Mr. Langdale gravely and tenderly returned his weeping daughter's caresses. The change in Florence's appearance since he last saw her in the churchyard, alarmed him seriously. He controlled his own emotion in order to sub-due her agitation, which was each moment increasing. Cuthbert Noel's disguise had been penetrated by him long ago, and Bertina had for some months been like one of his own children.

" Listen to me," said Miss Langdale, to her cousin, while a flood of blushes overspread her aristocratic lineaments. " Noel Hall is no longer mine. It belongs to Cuthbert; but he may, if he likes, repay the sum I have laid out on the place, by instalments, to Florence; who will inherit my savings and private fortune. This night, I burnt, with my own hands, before I ventured to enter Godley Grange, the iniquitous will, which has given us all such heartburn-ings. You and Fritz are heirs of Langdale, but you must not take the little one away from me. She is all I have left to live for. You both have other treasures."

Florence let go her father's hand, without opposition on his part, and came and knelt at Miss Langdale's feet. " I will never, never, leave you," she said. " You have won me to your side now, for ever.

CONCLUSION.

The times are changed, and o'er the land
　　New men and measures move ;
Labour and wealth go hand in hand,
　　With God's bright skies above.
The grass lies soft before thy door,
　　The sunshine gilds the dale,
The swallows dart across the moor,
　　Though man's proud boasts may fail.
And still there are Halls in the old West Riding,
Where warm hearts, high hopes, and Christ's love are abiding.

MAUD LANGDALE'S straightforward proposition was at once accepted, and, without any suit-at-law, Cuthbert Noel, and his beautiful daughter, took quiet possession of the old Hall. The sale of the larger portion of the family property had long since satisfied his clamorous creditors ; and the last of the Noels was free from debt and difficulty, while the fortune which the General had jestingly promised Mr. Langdale should one day be the portion of the little one, was accumulating year by year.

There was no pomp and show when Bertina and her father came to dwell in the home of their ancestors. Meg and her mistress, and curly-haired Ned, continued to occupy the sunny rooms near the portal, although a suitable establishment was set on foot. Florence's advice, that Bertina

should regulate the household was adopted, and the virtues
learnt in adversity were practised on a larger scale. When
Christmas came the mansion glowed with warmth and
comfort—the poor were relieved at the gate, and hospitality
was the rule of the hour; but the reckless extravagance
of the Noels, under Bertina's gentle sway, ceased to be a
common saying. After all, the wilful woman at the Hall
carried her point. Florence remained with the Mistress of
Langdale; but, no longer estranged from her family, the
young girl speedily recovered her health, and was gayer than
she had ever been before. She and Bertina were intimate
friends, and constant intercourse was kept up between the
Halls at the upper and lower ends of the valley, and the
Grange. It was even reported that Cuthbert Noel renewed
his suit to the Mistress of Langdale Hall; but, if so, his
wooing was unsuccessful, Maud remained unmarried.

Dr. Forsyth and Mr. Haywarden rejoiced in the reconciliation between the two families, as well as in the return of
Cuthbert Noel to his own home and station. Both were
in the habit of declaring that they had all along recognised
him; and neither of them would ever admit that he had
been deceived longer than the other.

Meredith, now that all her young mistresses were quite
grown up, and her long, faithful term of nursing was over,
expressed a wish to leave her situation, at the Grange, and
to live with Miss Langdale and Florence, at the Hall. The
little one had always been her favourite, and she had a great
respect for the head of the family. Affection for Florence
was a sure passport to Maud's favour; and Meredith was
warmly welcomed, and enjoyed a comfortable, easy existence,
with charge of the linen and charitable distributions at the
Hall. Florence's pretty young handmaiden was not dis-
possessed, but her old nurse had the privilege of seeing her

constantly, and of superintending her wardrobe. The little one never forgot that Meredith had been her mother's devoted attendant; nor that she had striven, though ineffectually, to save her from the bitter pang of being absent at her last hour.

The time of singing birds had come round, and showers of white blossoms decked the hawthorn trees in Calder Dale. From the Dower-House of the Noels a column of white smoke ascended; the garden was gay with flowers, and the pigeons cooed and strutted on the walks, and on the walls and roof. The casements were set open, and the streaming tassels of laburnum gleamed golden in sunshine, alternating with lilacs, and sweet-scented syringa and sweet-briar.

Bertina came frequently to her mother's old home, where the old servant took care of the pigeons and poultry. Especially in the spring, the girl loved this secluded place, and this week, which included the anniversary of the death of her mother, she chose to spend in solitude. Now she was preparing to return to Noel Hall, but she lingered reluctantly. Nowhere were the spring flowers, the gleaming waters, so lovely as in Calder Dale.

Mechanically, the young girl had thrown over her head and shoulders, for the wind was still keen, the Rob-Roy plaid which hung in the passage; and pinned it under her chin with the Cairn-Gorm brooch which had been Bertie Noel's gift to her mother. Her dress was black, and her features wore an expression of deep sadness, when, having finished feeding her pets, she sat down on the stone bench in the courtyard, where the old soldier had rested on the day of Mrs. Noel's funeral.

Since that time many changes had occurred. Cuthbert

Noel's fortunes had brightened, and his daughter was no longer required to pursue an industrious calling,—yet there were moments like the present, when, oppressed by the gladness of rejoicing nature, while "the voice of the turtle is heard in the land," Bertina wished herself back into the past, when, with a girl's blithe spirit and light footstep, she came back, after the hours of labour were over, through the flowery thickets that filled the Eagle's Gorge, to the sunny homestead.

Past the banks where the primroses had faded, and the fragrant spring violets were succeeded by the scentless ones of early summer, a man, bronzed and bearded, a traveller to all appearance, came towards the old house. Young and of fair complexion, but somewhat weather-beaten of aspect, as though much exposure to the rough play of the elements had been the custom of the hour, with one whom nature had cast in her fairest mould. And, yet, that manly growth of beard and moustache—the shadow thrown by southern suns on the boyish complexion—the breadth of chest and shoulders—the firm tread—well replaced the slenderness and bloom of earlier youth.

Bertina started, as footsteps approached the gate. Her face flushed, but she did not move even when the latch was lifted softly. Had she forgotten that she had given directions to the attendant that no visitor should be admitted?

The traveller came straight up to the bench where the young girl was sitting.

"Bertina, are you still true to your motto—'Patience and perseverance?'" said Fritz, stopping in front of her. "I *have* struggled, I *have* persevered, I have at last conquered in the strife: not through fear or favour, but by honest industry, I have earned a position. I am looked up to in my profession; I can offer you a home, even if Miss Langdale chooses to shut the gates of the Hall against us for our mortal life. May I claim my reward?"

Bertina did not reply. It is to be supposed that in similar cases, silence lends encouragement. At all events, Fritz felt sufficiently emboldened to take the vacant place beside her. "What made you dress yourself like a Mill-girl, to-day?" he said laughing, as he took her hand, "it is as though I had followed you, but an' hour ago, through the Eagle's Gorge."

Bertina blushed excessively. "There are times," she said, "when old customs exercise a sort of tyranny over us. I have been fancying all the morning that I was coming home through the hawthorn bushes, from my post at the Mills."

She stopped in confusion. "Did you recall one particular afternoon, when a boy was bold enough to follow you? a boy who has a man's heart now, Bertina, which beats for you alone. Must I spend manhood, as well as youth, in pursuit of the slight form, which ever since has been before me on my path? or will you generously wait for me, and tread the world's high road, be it rough or smooth, by my side?"

The girl unfastened tremulously the Scottish brooch, and let the shawl drop away from her flushed face. "Are you sure," she said archly, "that it is really the Mill-girl you have been pursuing all this time, in imagination. The last time we fell in with each other, you were playing the knight errant to a lady of high degree?"

It was Fritz's turn to blush now; which he did very visibly, in spite of his bronzed complexion. Man though he was, and very much in earnest, his conscience gave him a sharp pang, as memory recalled some passages of his career.

"Oh, that was nothing, mere idle nonsense," he said,

after a momentary pause, "Miss Ellinor Langdale and I are cousins, nothing more. The moment I saw you on the North-Riding Moors, veiled, hooded, disguised as you were, I followed you. I tracked you to the cavern under Filey Brig, I discovered your retreat, and I fancied—do not punish me too severely, Bertina, if it was a folly—that you gave me to understand that, in time, patience and perseverance conquer all obstacles. Was I right, and if so, may I draw my own conclusions?"

"At all events, you shall not perish of starvation," said the girl, starting up, and avoiding his embrace, though she did not withdraw the hand he had taken. "The old house in Calder Dale has not lost its claim to be considered a hospitable shelter, because I am its mistress. You see," she added, tenderly turning towards her lover, "I, too, have a home, Fritz, my father says this house belongs to the women of our family. He has made it over in perpetuity to me: so, even if Noel Hall as well as Langdale Park are too grand for us, we shall still have a home in the old Dower House in the Eagle's Gorge."

Ellinor Langdale did not hear without a pang, of the happiness of her rival; but she strove, with all the might which was consistent with her gentle nature, to surmount the jealousy which also was a part of her constitution. She did not revisit Langdale until so many changes had occurred there, that the romance of her girlhood assumed a lighter form; but even then, she was never entirely cordial with Bertina.

Though she had resisted her sister's will, Ellinor did not marry. Moriscombe continued to be her home, and there Miss Langdale and Florence frequently visited her. The new Watering Place continued to flourish, and the white-walled town on the cliff assumed larger dimensions ; but, as the trees, planted where its first foundations were laid, grew in proportion with the buildings : Marina was no eye-sore from the Knoll.

Ellinor and Florence Langdale often went there together, and Maud was sometimes found sitting there alone, contemplating the surging sea and the indented headland. Florence's last wish, in which, as usual, her adopted mother indulged her to the utmost, has been, to give a life boat to that dangerous sea-board. Under the black reef on which her mother was shipwrecked, the boat, which is to preserve many a human life when the heavens are black with tempest, is housed. A hardy crew are kept in readiness to go out into that tempestuous ocean in moments of peril ; and they are true to their duty.

When the minute-gun flashes out in darkness, and the storm-wind sobs and sighs through the rent sails and cordage of a ship tossed about by the mountainous waves—when hope dies out in the bravest bosoms, and the lightning's jagged ribands tear along the foaming crests of the black waters,—a bold, manly cheer rings out, and Marina's name peals over the billows.

The life-boat named after Frank Langdale's beloved wife, in memory of her rescue from shipwreck on that terrible reef, is launched. Her bold and practised crew know well how to handle her in the storm ; and, through the troughs of the waves of the North Sea, which Cuthbert Noel breasted to save the drowning child, the life-boat named after the infant, dashes to the rescue of many a perishing mariner.

May God be with her and her gallant crew, bearing them unscathed through the raging waters to the sinking ship ; and encouraging to endure to the last, those whose hearts, in that dread darkness and conflict of the elements, were sinking with affright.

Hurrah! The cry rings out faintly over the waters. The life-boat has reached the point where aid can be afforded, and on shore, in the white house under the Moor, is comfort, warmth, and shelter, for those whom "Marina," has rescued.

Often and often, during autumn and winter tempests are such scenes enacted; when the dark ocean and the gloomy sky are black with rain and wind, and, save the distant light-tower near Flamborough Head, there is no guide past those dread rocks, over the heaving deep, for the brave mariners.

At such moments, over land and water, Marina's name gives cheering hope; and those who tremble, and think themselves about to perish, hearing the glad sound, rise up as though they were her children, and call her blessed.

Florence has never ceased to love the coast of the North Riding, and her gentle cousin Ellinor Langdale; but still the little one's heart remains true to its early instincts, and no after affection will ever displace from her throne, the mother of her adoption—Maud Langdale, the Mistress of the Hall.

THE END.

BILLING, PRINTER, GUILDFORD, SURREY.